IMAGINATION AND POWER
A Study of Poetry on Public Themes

Imagination and Power

A STUDY OF
POETRY ON PUBLIC THEMES

By

THOMAS R. EDWARDS

1971
CHATTO & WINDUS
LONDON

Published by
Chatto and Windus Ltd
42 William IV Street
London W.C.2

ISBN 0 7011 1698 6

Printed in Great Britain by
R. and R. Clark Ltd
Edinburgh

For Nancy, and Sarah,
and (of course)
John Morgan

Contents

Acknowledgments

I cannot hope to name all the people—teachers, colleagues, students, friends—who in some way helped make this book possible. But it pleases me to thank Paul Bertram, Reuben Brower, Maurice Charney, Daniel Howard, Nancy Kuriloff, C. F. Main, Anita Van Vactor, David Van Vactor, and William Youngren, for various kinds of interest, encouragement and advice.

The Rutgers University Research Council generously provided me with a year's respite from teaching, without which there could have been no book, as well as grants-in-aid for preparing the manuscript.

I am especially grateful to Frank Bidart and Herbert Lindenberger for readings of the manuscript that gave me more confidence in it and helped me improve it. Richard Poirier did that and so much more that mere gratitude seems beside the point.

Quotations from copyright material are reprinted by kind permission of the following: W. H. Auden, Faber & Faber Ltd. (*Collected Shorter Poems 1930-1944* and *Collected Longer Poems*), and Random House, Inc., New York (*Collected Poetry*, Copyright © 1945 by W. H. Auden); Faber & Faber Ltd. and Harcourt Brace Jovanovich, Inc., New York (*Collected Poems 1909-1962* by T. S. Eliot); Robert Lowell, Faber & Faber Ltd. (*Life Studies*, *For The Union Dead* and *Notebook*), and Farrar, Straus & Giroux, Inc., New York (*Life Studies*, Copyright © 1953 by Robert Lowell, *For The Union Dead*, Copyright © 1964 by Robert Lowell, and *Notebook 1967-68*, Copyright © 1967, 1968, 1969 by Robert Lowell); M. B. Yeats and Macmillan & Co., London and The Macmillan Company, New York (*Collected Poems of W.B. Yeats*, Copyright © 1928 by the Macmillan Company, renewed 1956 by Georgie Yeats).

Part of Chapter III is a revised version of an essay which appeared in *In Defense of Reading* (ed. Reuben Brower and Richard Poirier) published by E. P. Dutton & Co., Inc., 1962.

Introduction

This, in effect, is a book about a dramatic situation that occurs frequently enough in the poetry of the last 400 years, a situation that can be described rather simply. A man who is a poet finds himself writing (for whatever reason) a poem about men who are not poets but 'public men'—kings, soldiers, politicians—or about the 'public conditions' that seem the consequence of what such men do. But there is also an implicit third party to this situation, the reader of the poem, who has to serve as representative of 'ordinary men' in general, that great majority of people who are neither poets nor public figures. Presumably a poet commonly thinks of himself as being in some way different from ordinary men, with their famous incapacity for or indifference to the disciplined reflectiveness of art; yet in imagining public events and public men the poet may be led to something like a provisional and partial identification with ordinary men and their outlook.

This is to say that in contemplating public events the poetic imagination, a proud and essentially private capacity of mind, may in some way be 'socialized', made aware of its connections with a state of awareness that is much more extensive, if less coherent and subtle, than the imaginative awareness that creates art. The undertaking of a 'public poem' can lead the poet to a fuller consciousness of what he, as artist, has in common with the general condition of men in his society; in this sense the socializing of imagination is also a humanizing. But at the same time, as my readings try to show, the successful public poem criticizes and chastens the public awareness of ordinary men by seeing through the habits of rhetoric and feeling that conceal from us the full complexity of our relation to politics and power.

Obviously the terms in which this altered sense of things is formulated will vary greatly, according to the poet's temperament and mood, the conditions of the style and genre he has to work with, and the nature of the public circumstance to be expressed. The poems I consider range in time from the late sixteenth century to the late 1960's, and I hope that they fairly represent the very different forms that public poetry can take on—it is not the general dramatic situation but its possible variations that most interest me. I have not pursued any firm theoretical or historical thesis, on the assumption that extensive critical conceptualization would be tactless in a book that is so sceptical about other people's system-building. Though I do venture some hypotheses about the relation of poems to political or social history, these are meant to sound hesitant, as befits an obvious lack of expertise. But it is more than diffidence that makes me want to avoid a systematic and exhaustive treatment; the 'objective' bearing of public events on poems is much too mysterious for me to fathom, and it seems more sensible to limit myself to speculating about the ways in which poets have *imagined* the 'public world' they write about, ways which tell us more about the poets, and about poetry generally, than about public events themselves.

Though the poems are discussed in a roughly chronological order and I venture some 'developmental' hypotheses from time to time, my readings aim less at historical fullness than at suggesting the persistence of imaginative concerns despite the transformations and discontinuities of history. Marvell's *Horatian Ode*, for example, is a seventeenth-century poem; it draws upon the age's assumptions about 'heroic' and 'panegyric' poetry, and it deals with a particular and extraordinary seventeenth-century man, Oliver Cromwell. In discussing the poem (Chapter II) I try to take account of these historical conditions, by juxtaposing the *Ode* with an earlier and very different poem in praise of a ruler, Spenser's *Colin Clouts Come Home Againe*, and by remembering that Cromwell was an actual public man, about whom controversy clustered. But as I read it, the poem has to do with a problem that is not exclusively a seventeenth-century problem, however Marvell's formulation of it may depend upon contemporary terms and ideas. To be brief about it, the *Ode* asks how a poet, a 'private' man accustomed to thinking that wisdom and virtue flourish and are best recognized in the meditative privacy for which 'art' is the familiar symbol, can imagine and publicly express a kind of wisdom and virtue that is not private but instead is based on a ruthless, illegal violence. Marvell didn't have to write this poem, obviously; what was there about Cromwell that drew his imagination to such a perilous subject, to a 'praise' that seemingly must destroy the values upon which imagination ordinarily subsists? How can a poet praise a man whose public nature seems to make poetry itself irrelevant?

I try to answer these questions by suggesting that the *Ode* plays off such difficulty against an enlarged sense of what 'art' may mean, the possibility that political and military power is itself a mode of art; my point here is simply that the poem can't profitably be thought of as imprisoned in the seventeenth century, or in someone's critical system, as may appear when one thinks of it in connection with (for example) Robert Lowell's poem 'R.F.K.', in memory of Robert Kennedy, which ends thus:

> Doom was woven in your nerves, your shirt,
> woven in the great clan; they too were loyal,
> and you too more than loyal to them, to death.
> For them like a prince, you daily left your tower
> to walk through dirt in your best cloth. Untouched,
> alone in my Plutarchian bubble, I miss
> you, you out of Plutarch, made by hand—
> forever approaching our maturity.[1]

One supposes that this poem came hard for Lowell—the praise is for qualities in the man that are teasingly close to defects, in another way of thinking about men, and we know (if we need to) that Lowell's own loyalties were to one of Kennedy's rivals in that very Plutarchian tragedy. My point depends on just this sense of difficulty, the way the poet in his 'Plutarchian bubble', securely remote from the politician and his dreadful end, is made aware of a significance that threatens to make irrelevant his own role as contemplative man and the values that support that role. A heroic myth threatens to re-establish itself in an unheroic time, through the agency of a man the poet had grave reservations about while he was alive. And although the final line keeps the alternatives under some control—we see Kennedy from the viewpoint of a 'maturity' his own life never achieved even as we recognize that 'our maturity' is in a way feeble and pitiful compared to the princely potentiality he will now eternally represent—it is clear that the public event, and the act of writing a poem about it, has importantly modified the poet's idea of himself and his relation to his world.

This is not to say that Lowell's poem is as good as Marvell's, or that they are poems of the same 'kind'. That sort of score-keeping is for those who enjoy it. I mean only that in addressing themselves to a particular and difficult public case, both poems dramatize an imaginative process that is instructively similar to yet soberingly more subtle and complete and generous than our own ways of imagining the figures and events of public life. That our own relation to 'politics' *is* essentially imaginative should need no proof. We do not know the people who control a good part of our lives, we seldom if ever see first-hand the great or small events that radically or almost imperceptibly alter our own reality in such important ways. We may smile at Hemingway's Harold Krebs, home from the war and 'really learning' about it from books and maps, but our own information, despite the liveliness of the television image or the judicious styles of 'serious' journalism, may not bring us much closer to the thing itself.

Indeed in some moods imagining politics is not only necessary but decidedly helpful. As a schoolboy Joyce's Stephen Dedalus discovered something important: 'It pained him that he did not know well what politics meant and that he did not know where the universe ended. He felt small and weak.' And well he might have —politics is not the universe but it is just about as hard to understand unless imagination intervenes. We see that part of our life is more or less under our own control, in our 'personal' dealings with objects, people, ideas, or money, and that part of it is so far beyond any human control that it can only be entrusted to God or Fate or Natural Determinism—but between these areas lies another ground, in which *we* may have no role but which does look like human territory. The hopeful imagination *populates* this middle ground. We like our politics personified, so that leaders may have private lives to speculate about and large movements of power (The Industrial Revolution, The First World War, The New Deal) may be ascribed some of the traits of living creatures. Emerson's remark that there is no history, only biography, states our disposition—our need—to make history consist of the decisions of individual men and the personal causes of those decisions. Evidently we must believe that power is subject to human influence, that politics at its best can serve our human needs.

Thus the ordinary citizen's relation to politics is an imaginative act. Out of whatever information is available, we invent 'men'

4

with the same names as our leaders and argue happily or angrily about their behaviour. We imagine the happy home life of Caesar and are comforted; we imagine a paranoid in the White House or the Kremlin and are terrified; mostly we terrorize and comfort ourselves at the same time, as in the pleasure of supposing that the masters are at least as stupid and weak and self-serving as we would be in their place. And as we know, imagined things are not therefore always false.

To the extent that Marvell and Lowell are doing what all private men do when they think about public matters, they are doing the same thing in their poems. Of course they are doing it in different ways, since both politics and poetry change with time; but while I have tried to take account of such change, my main concern is with politics as imagined, the style and tone of poetic versions of great men and great events rather than the men and events themselves. It will become evident that I find the flawed public poem to be marked by a static attitude, by the indifference to development and redefinition that is so disastrous in actual politics. Conversely, the successful public poem shows susceptibility to experience and learning; it is the record of a journey taken, a conflict met and faced. To put it more pretentiously, such a poem negotiates between public, 'official' terminologies of political fact and some other set of terms that may be able to humanize the blank face of power.

This negotiation can be less cosy than it sounds—the face of power can be pretty dreadful in human form. Nor will it do to seek humanization in the vulgar hunger for the 'exposé'; poet and reader alike must suspect the motive Sir Lewis Namier memorably found in Lord Hervey's *Memoirs* of the court of George II:

> He takes [his readers] to the places of their snobbish dreams, to the seats of splendour and power, where they enter with a reverential awe, an avid curiosity, and an unconscious readiness to befoul: and there he has arranged for them a monkey-show.[2]

But if simple mediations between power and humanity will not do, even complex ones can at best be only tentative. If no new perception of the public case is achieved, the poem is dead; yet complete transformation makes the poem only a glibber version of the politician's own magical rhetoric, which smoothes all conflict into the glassy calm of easy solutions. But if the poet ends by being unsure about the value of opposing positions, this is only to say that he has reached the centre of politics and accepted its painfulness and its necessity. And he has come closer to the centre of his and our 'private' predicament, by learning that the struggle between political demands and our yearning for peace and order mirrors the larger strain between reality and justice Yeats saw as the human condition. The poet who can only approach politics from outside, in some distant moralistic rejection, had better not write about it at all, for he is as simplistic as the propagandist whose verse is merely a catchier version of his employers' self-interested cant. It is the note of uncertainty or even dismay that I am looking for, the imagination's troubled recognition of its own involvement in the spectacle of power.

NOTES

[1] Robert Lowell, *Notebook 1967-68* (New York, Farrar, Straus & Giroux, and London, Faber & Faber, 1970), p. 118.

[2] L. B. Namier, *Crossroads of Power* (London, Hamish Hamilton, and New York, Macmillan, 1962), p. 164.

CHAPTER ONE

The Disappearance of Heroic Man

It will surprise no one to hear that for some three centuries our literature has been haunted by a figure the imagination seems unable to be rid of, that of the hero, the great public man who in older literatures epitomizes the human lust for action and raises grave questions about its moral status. Ordinary men, well aware of their weakness, find strength and self-assurance compelling objects of thought. We may venerate them as ideas and yet fear or despise them when embodied in actual men, or we may yield admiringly to them in reality yet privately question their value; in any case, the idea of a man possessing more power than most men can even imagine themselves possessing teaches what it is like to accept and reject something simultaneously. A common way of escape is to suppose that a hero doesn't in fact 'possess' his powers but is possessed by them, which lets you respect the powers but remember the reassuring human limitations of the man.

The rediscovery of classical epic as a serious literary fact, rather than a set of legends and vague pieties, gave the late Middle Ages and the Renaissance a subject that obsessed critics and moralists for centuries. Here it is enough to say that this obsession, for all its elaboration in debates about the Rules, epic style, and the relation of strength to virtue, seems at root to have concerned a more general question. How are ordinary men, aware of their weakness and persuaded by Christianity that weakness enhances one's salvational prospects, to conceive of their place in an idea of the world that includes creatures who seem to be men also and yet are superhumanly forceful in deed and word? (That the question should have shifted from epic heroes to epic *writers*, the Ancients to whom modern poets and critics found it so hard to relate themselves, is amiable sign of the power of self-concern over literary minds.)

It is a problem of political as well as literary judgment, since in their imagined, mythic existence great men remind the reader of his own world, where greatness—or its semblance—has obvious effects on how power is distributed and how mere citizens or subjects figure in the existing order. The *Iliad* is in part a political poem; it deals, for example, with the struggle between Agamemnon and Achilles, the man who derives power from agreement and custom and the man whose power is physical and personal. For the Homeric singer and his listeners this confrontation of powers gave a perspective on history, the legendary war of wars that perhaps said what it meant to be 'Greek' more powerfully than any particular geographical, cultural, or political circumstance. The *Iliad* domesticated history by imagining it in terms that were intelligible in any village. There, as anywhere, one needed to know how the political life of debate, consultation, and the pursuit of conflicting ends reflects upon that possession of the self and its experience which every man thinks his right even when it conflicts with other men's claim to the same right.

Some such 'political' motive is I think implicit in Aristotle's comments on epic. Mimesis finds its best object in 'men in action', and the epic poet deals with action and men in their highest form: 'Homer, for example, makes men better than they are.' Not 'better' ethically or morally, I take it, but in their fuller representation of capacities that in other men remain undeveloped, unexpressed—in short, more *potent*. Aristotle can talk about the 'higher' types of character, 'noble actions', 'the actions of good men', as though these all referred to a common idea, some combination of personal nature and social role that makes the epic or tragic character seem a more vivid embodiment of power, whatever its ethical bearing, than the men in the audience can hope to be. Such a notion colours his remark that 'poetry . . . is a more philosophical and a higher thing than history: for poetry tends to express the universal, history the particular'. The universality of poetry is presumably less abstractness or generality than the created sense of a richer and larger 'symbolic' potency in the poetic event. In the audience's knowledge that epic characters are higher or better or more expressively potent than themselves epic becomes politically relevant. To an audience of heroes Achilles' existence would seem natural enough, and they would at once see that *competition* was what he required; but mere men have to invent a relation to him, and this is a perplexing job.

Now of course 'the ordinary man' is, like 'the hero', a fiction. I am not ordinary, nor you, nor (unfortunately for us) all those others. The normal has meaning only in reference to the abnormal, the unexpected phenomenon that creates an opposing sense of mutality where none was apparent before. Epic formulates such mutuality by depicting men who are different enough from us to make us herd together in a feeling of ordinariness. And this is something like the effect of politics, which also makes us recognize the existence of men who differ from us, if only in their possession of superior power, their ability to enforce upon us the claims they make. And the mixture of veneration and hostility in our view of the epic hero resembles our feelings about being subordinate to the state and its leaders, who 'represent' us in their great doings but require us to become the Common People, the Electorate, the Crowd, the Mob. In life as in art, the ordinary man, by being made to *feel* ordinary, comes to observe and imaginatively participate in movements of force that aren't of his own making but seem—exhilaratingly or frighteningly—to include and affect him, serve his purposes or, by denying them, serve those of his enemies, who are ordinary men too.

But there are consolations in this doubleness. If epic is a celebration of national or racial history and destiny, it is also a reminder of how remote history and destiny can seem from the substance of ordinary life. Reuben Brower's comment on the Homeric simile comparing the fight over Sarpedon's body to the swarming of flies about a milk-pail is pertinent:

> Read this simile without some allowance for the context of oral poetry, and it becomes comic. . . . But if read properly, in relation to the poem rather than the passage, this simile like many others in Homer has the important and beautiful effect of removing us from the immediate scene of gore and battle to a world of peace, the pastoral world familiar to the singer and his listeners. We look out from 'tearful war' to a life of tending cattle and sheep, of woodcutting and building, to all sorts of activities of a peaceful and productive sort. So Homer assures us that he and his audience recognize values other than courage and glory.[1]

It may follow that such a simile, besides reminding us of peace and productivity, points back to the epic world with quiet political irony. So *that* is what it means to be powerful, *these* are the men to whom we entrust our purposes and lives! There would of course be wonder in such exclamations, but also some whisper of sceptical asperity and self-congratulation.

1. Epic and the Modern Reader: A Note on Simone Weil

Before getting on to the question of what happened to heroic literature and what kinds of poem replaced it, I want to venture some propositions about epic to prepare the ground:

(1) Epic poetry is an oral art or, as 'literary' epic, a written art that aspires to some of the directness and impersonality of traditional oral style.

(2) Epic thus implies the dramatic situation in which a bard sings to men who may be strangers but who share with him a general cultural identity, a common language (with all this implies) and some prior awareness of the matter of his song. Or, if he is not a wandering rhapsode but an *aoidos* or kept bard, he sings to men whose faces and names he knows but in whose practical life he doesn't directly share—he doesn't hunt or farm or trade or fight as they do, even though he is in some sense a member of their community.

(3) The bard is not one of those he sings about; he is no hero, not a prince or warrior, he was never at Troy. Nor are his listeners heroes; while there may be princes or warriors among them, even these feel a distance between their own deeds and those of Achilles or Hector, the sense that time has diminished the possibilities of action. It is not now as it was then.

(4) The dramatic situation of epic is thus a complicated one. It is in essence a provincial event remote from the great world of heroic action, often in space and always in time. It is a peaceful event, since men cannot sing or listen while fighting; it is, though communal, a private event, in that men cannot debate or conduct public business while singing or listening. In this sense epic allows a potentially critical or ironic perspective on action.[2]

(5) Thus, while the purpose of epic is to record and praise the deeds of men who are better or more potent than we, it does not exclude another response, of reservation or even self-congratulation. It is not now as it was then, and thank goodness!

(6) But the temptation to relax in the comforts of being un-heroic is challenged by the complicating presence of the bard himself. If we share his remoteness from the events he sings, we uneasily sense that there's something about him we don't share in. He takes his song very seriously, and while we know he didn't compose it himself—he wasn't *there* as he pretends to have been —still his *possession* of the song somehow does relate him more closely to the matter than we are related to it. What we under-stand may not be all there is to understand; something enigmatic and teasing about his art, something mysterious, even magical, about his ability to perform it, forbids us to think him ordinary like ourselves.

(7) One of the virtues of epic may thus be the exercise in complicated self-awareness it provides. It associates us gratifyingly with past greatness, with heroes who are *our* heroes; yet it also reminds us soberingly that it all *is* past, that we are less than our heritage. It allows us an imaginative association with greatness even as it makes us recognize that we are ordinary men—and it allows us some comfort in this rueful understanding. And it gives a perspective on our mixed relation to our own public world and its powerful creatures, our dependence on them, our suspicion of their 'superior' purposes, our pleasure and horror at what they do in our name.

The substance of epic action is of course war. But I suppose that war is less the subject of epic than a metaphor for a larger subject, which is power itself, the ways in which men impose their will on other men. Battle, in this light, is only a concentrated image of the conflict of purposes that must (we assume) always characterize human relations if life is to be more than solitary and self-centred; it is no original observation to say that war, like business and games and family quarrels, is a form of politics and a mirror of its nature. But war is more than this. Though in many ways it shares the annoying but useful indecisiveness of other political modes, it yet is utterly decisive in another way—it makes men die who would prefer to live. War is both an image of politics and a destroyer of men, a dreadful literalizing of the aggressions politics keeps in discreet disguise. Here the complexity of epic becomes most evident and crucial, and hardest for modern men to respond to as men once did.

Simone Weil's brilliant essay, 'The *Iliad* or the Poem of Force', is a compelling expression of this difficulty.[3] It is not a difficulty that in any way questions the value of epic; indeed, for Simone Weil the *Iliad* is 'the purest and loveliest of mirrors' reflecting the pervasive and dreadful effect of force on men's lives. The essay deserves attentive reading in its entirety, but for convenience I will summarize its argument briefly.

Force, according to Simone Weil, is 'that x that turns anybody who is subjected to it into a *thing*'; its denial of the individual life of its object leads to turning that object into a corpse, literally a thing, to be dragged around Troy behind a chariot. More subtly, force can turn a man into a thing, a 'stone', while he is still alive, by stripping him of his weapons and armour to leave his life hanging on his conqueror's whim, or by making him an irrelevant object like Priam in Achilles' tent or a slave who has lost all memory of freedom. But force is not simply what the strong possess and the weak succumb to. In the *Iliad* 'there is not a single man who does not at one time or another have to bow his neck to force' or who is 'spared the shameful experience of fear'. Winning hinges on destiny, not strength or valour, and this creates a kind of ironic justice, though neither the strong nor the weak perceive it until too late. War is in fact a shifting balance, which no one is moderate or virtuous enough to stabilize while he still can. By making men face every day the imminence of their own death, war 'effaces all conceptions of purpose or goal, including even its own "war aims". It effaces the very notion of war's being brought to an end.' The mind simply cannot accept 'the idea that an unlimited effort should bring in only a limited profit or no profit at all'; having become a thing, the warrior is unresponsive not only to the life in other people but to the operation of reason itself. There are moments of insight in the *Iliad*, recognitions of love and mutual respect, but they serve mainly to sharpen regret for the pervasive violence and helplessness. And this regret is endorsed by the poet's bitterness about the action he sings of, his pity for victims, his painful recollections of the world of peace, his amazing sense of 'equity'.

Thus for Simone Weil the greatness of the *Iliad*, as of Attic tragedy and the Gospels, is that it reveals the relation of human suffering to its cause, 'the subjections of the human spirit to force, that is, in the last analysis, to matter'. Justice and love can grow only from a recognition that all men are fellow creatures, not members of distinct species, none of them 'exempt from the misery that is the common lot'. And such recognition is not to be found in western literature, except flickeringly in a few great writers:

> Nothing the peoples of Europe have produced is worth the first known poem that appeared among them. Perhaps they will yet rediscover the epic genius, when they learn that there is no refuge from fate, learn not to admire force, not to hate the enemy, nor to scorn the unfortunate. How soon this will happen is another question.

I have paraphrased Simone Weil at such length because I think her view of force is morally almost inescapable in our time and yet also imaginatively limiting. It would be foolish to pretend that she has simply misread Homer, and self-deceiving to insist too hopefully on the special circumstances of the essay—how the *Iliad* looked in 1940, in a conquered and occupied country, to a woman whose cultural heritage was Jewish, political views leftist, religion Catholic and increasingly mystical. It is hard not to feel that we all live in occupied countries, conquered (as she helps us to see) by the appalling force of a history whose consequences we are just beginning to understand. And her moral resistance predicts our efforts to resist, whether through politics or insurrection or inward withdrawal from public concern. It looks as if her experience of force and its meaning will for a long time remain our conception of our case, beset by forces that threaten our humanity by creating in us—in our very resistance to them, perhaps— something like their own indifference to everything that makes a man more than a manipulable object. As for Homer, one can see the risks of contemporizing the past (the idea of an 'absurdist' Shakespeare and the like) without wanting to deny that unless art has meaning for living people it has no meaning, and that our life, our sense of our own condition, is what reaches out to the work and measures its relevance.

I have no doubt that 'Homer' knew what Simone Weil knew about force. The trouble is that he knew other things too, as Shakespeare knew things that Beckett and Ionesco and Professor

Kott don't. And the dominant moods of an age—what we mean when we say that Simone Weil speaks for 'our' sense of things—have more than diagrammatic value only when they can be qualified and expanded into some further perception. For Simone Weil, war is only the ultimate literalization of the tendency of any life that is 'materially' rather than 'spiritually' oriented. War, when looked at steadily and whole, as Homer does, makes us see what we risk by permitting ourselves to be unmoved by suffering:

> He who does not realize to what extent shifting fortune and necessity hold in subjection every human spirit, cannot regard as fellow-creatures nor love as he loves himself those whom chance separated from him by an abyss. The variety of constraints pressing upon man give rise to the illusion of several distinct species that cannot communicate. Only he who has measured the dominion of force, and knows how not to respect it, is capable of love and justice.

War, this seems to say, is ethically necessary. It is the concentrated image of our subjection to necessity and constraint, and only by enduring and learning to abhor it can we appreciate our bonds of suffering with other men and so come to brotherhood with them. If there is a scent of Manichaeanism in this, it is nonetheless persuasive and moving. But by implication it cancels out a great deal that the *Iliad* also expresses in its thorny complexity; though one participates in Simone Weil's feelings, hers is not the only conceivable view.

Her idea of force cancels out all but the minatory value of the 'material' world, the world that includes not only war but politics, business, legislation, litigation, all secular exercises of power to any end at all. (She of course means to do just this.) But for Homer and his audience, the war at Troy was a public event that summed up, without denying the dangers, the ability of individual glory to confirm one's national and cultural identity. One must agree with Simone Weil that it is well that Homer saw the cost of glory. But her formula—that the moments of glory and grace measure the bitterness of the vision of force—could as well be turned around: does not the bitterness also measure and enhance the glory, by suggesting that great suffering may be needed to achieve great enterprises? However unpalatable this is to an age that has known

suffering of a magnitude that threatens to make *any* great enterprise, any idea of public greatness at all, seem hollow and fake,
it's hard to believe that such scepticism adequately comprehends
the literary reality of the *Iliad* and its effect on the European
imagination. It is not surprising that Aristotle and Virgil, Chapman and Pope and Fénelon, Keats and Arnold and Andrew Lang,
saw Homer differently; but it may be important to remember that
they did.

Epic literature grows out of the belief—or the desire to believe
—that heroism is a possible and valuable image of man. It assumes
that collective exercise of power may encourage great individual
achievement, and that great individual achievement may confirm
the worth of group enterprises. Rachel Bespaloff, without denying
the grim perception of Simone Weil, adds what may be a salutary
qualification of the idea of force:

> Force revels only in an abuse that is also self-abuse, in an
> excess that expends its store. It reveals itself in a kind of
> supreme leap, a murderous lightning stroke, in which cal-
> culation, chance, and power seem to fuse in a single element
> to defy man's fate. Herein lies the beauty of force. . . . In
> the *Iliad*, force appears as both the supreme reality and the
> supreme illusion of life. Force, for Homer, is divine insofar
> as it represents a superabundance of life that flashes out in
> the contempt for death and the ecstacy of self-sacrifice; it is
> detestable insofar as it contains a fatality that transforms it
> into inertia, a blind drive that is always pushing it on to the
> very end of its course, on to its own abolition and the
> obliteration of the very values it engendered.[4]

There is an alternative to the picture of a man turned to a stone
by exercising or submitting to force, and that is a picture of a man
possessed (briefly) by a strength and purpose that seem super-
human and imaginatively liberating to men who are only human.
This picture is I hope no more comforting to me than to Simone
Weil; in literature it is a short step to mindless patriotic hagiology,
in life an even shorter step to the posturings of an American
political convention or the Nuremberg Rallies. It is easy to agree
with her that the *Iliad* is the greatest epic poem because it is the
most suspicious in its scrutiny of how 'great men' behave and its

computation of the human cost of great achievements. But the poem and the tradition it governs are troublingly less easy to understand than that. To suppose that it or any authentic epic writing exists only to assess the ironies, to show the world of power only so that we may save our own souls by despising and rejecting it, does some damage to history and—much more important—to our capacity for a literary experience (to say nothing of life) that may for all its difficulty be uniquely valuable.

2. The Absolute Hero: *Tamburlaine*

Simone Weil can conveniently represent what is best and most serious in modern views of public greatness. Her anti-heroic view, which like the best mock-epic practice of the English Augustans can exist only if the epic is venerated and thoroughly known, challenges the idea that there can be glory in war and, implicitly, the idea of positive value in any mode of public, secular life. Her own gradual withdrawal into the keen, cold air of her kind of mysticism is significant. The particular aspects of contemporary experience that feed our mistrust of power and public greatness are well enough known; here it is enough to say that one can come to something like Simone Weil's view without recapitulating her personal history. Disillusionment with politics, at least in its traditional forms, is a condition of the times, even among those who continue to practice it or talk about doing so. The naive yearn for apocalyptic resolutions, the moderate fear them, the bitter expect them. We can amuse ourselves by reversing Yeats' dark formula—the worst lack all conviction, maybe, while the best are full of passionate intensity, but in any case some second coming looks imminent.

It is hard for anyone of a certain age not to share some of Frank Kermode's suspicion that the future has looked this way before;[5] intimations of apocalypse are recurrent and perhaps necessary phenomena of an imaginative history that may be less linear and progressive (or regressive) than one wants to suppose. We are always at the end of something. But it may be that real, literal endings can be thought into being; perhaps apocalyptic yearnings and anxieties can create apocalypse if they become general and intense. At any rate, the present mood colours our view of the past, and in reading the poems of other, possibly less nervous, ages we should try not to see only ourselves writ small and quaint. The Renaissance, in its more exuberant moods, was such an age. Or at least it was an age when one could celebrate power and glory as well as question claims to greatness in war and politics. There does seem to be some historical connection between heroic writing and periods of national growth and vigour. Great deeds are done in great times, in the adolescence or early maturity of cultures, or least great deeds find responsive literary audiences at such times. No significant epics were written in Rome during the decline, although there were stirrings of the epic impulse in the barbarian languages; and the 'rediscovery' of Homer and Virgil and the concerted effort to imitate them in vernacular tongues coincide pretty well with the growth of national identities in the early Renaissance. (This is admittedly somewhat tautological, since the vernaculars had first to exist in some potentially literary form.) The popularity of a genre has something to do with the reader's circumstance—the best audience for epic is one that knows enough of actual greatness to be stirred by its actions and aware of its ironies.

Certainly, when one postulates something called 'the Renaissance mind', one at once attributes to it a primary, intense fascination with the possibilities of secular power. If the fascination often implied appreciation of the moral dangers of power, such ironic linkage was not automatic—perhaps one was prepared for irony, but without precisely *expecting* it. From *The Faerie Queene* and *Tamburlaine* to *Gondibert* and the 'heroick' charades of the Restoration stage the air was full of open, even simple-minded glorifications of strong men, some of them also concerned about their virtue but others not. Such presentation worked best on the stage, where the need to keep up with the speeches and sort out the plot interferes with the reflective pause that generates irony. And a hero on a stage is different from one in a book, in the privacy of one's closet. The *Iliad* is more than the story of Achilles, the *Odyssey* and the *Aeneid* involve their main figures in a much vaster arena of issues and relevances than they themselves can grasp or embody—something like the 'totality of objects' Hegel admired in epic. *The Faerie Queene* needed a virtual horde of heroes (and heroines—a sign of decadence there?) to fill up its limitless landscape, and even *Paradise Lost* required several quasi-heroic male leads. But in the theatre a hero tends to expand, filling up the available space and bullying the ear and eye of the spectator; it is through him, *in* him, that the treatment of greatness unfolds. This concentration of heroic significance in a single human figure, resembling as it does the concentration of our affections and hostilities upon the single figure of the military or political leader, with his aspirations to charisma, is what I want to consider here. Marlowe's *Tamburlaine*, surely the most unabashed exploitation in literature of the glamour of power, is the obvious place to begin a few test-borings into English heroic literature.

Tamburlaine is the Renaissance dream of epic man at its most absolute pitch. Like Shakespeare and modern undergraduates, Marlowe paid lip-service to the critical dualism that makes all serious plays 'tragedies'; the two parts of *Tamburlaine* are labelled 'Tragical Discourses' in the 1590 edition, and the Prologue speaks of 'this tragic glass', but it soon becomes clear that Marlowe's purpose is less general and philosophical than high tragedy:

> We'll lead you to the stately tent of war,
> Where you shall hear the Scythian Tamburlaine
> Threatening the world with high astounding terms,
> And scourging kingdoms with his conquering sword.

Though Tamburlaine threatens kingdoms and civil orders, 'stately' may associate him with a potentiality for rule, combining ideas of personal spendour and high social estate into a hint that this tent of war is like a state, that from it emerge powers that subdue kingdoms and nations into a possible new political order. Military energy may be an image of the disciplined exertion of force that sustains civil equilibrium in peace. This is of course not a meaning the play will explore overtly—Tamburlaine the Governor is an inconceivable role—but it does suggest that excitement about his military potency may bear upon the hopeful idea of a strong national state under a strong monarch, a matter of considerable interest in the late 1580's.

Tamburlaine himself is anything but a politician or statesman. But by dramatizing his personal power as a capacity for a mighty kind of *speech*, Marlowe provides a continuing thread of relevance between force and government. The first words in the play are *about* words, as King Mycetes exposes his own incapacity for good, kingly talk:

> Brother Cosroe, I find myself agriev'd,
> Yet insufficient to express the same,
> For it requires a great and thundering speech:
> Good brother, tell the cause unto my lords;
> I know you have a better wit than I.

The audience, to whom politics and government are known only through words, the speeches and proclamations and rumours they hear from time to time, would get this quickly enough; a king who can't tell his own cause really has none. His mincing inarticulateness is dramatically equivalent to the breakdown of authority (as other failures of kingly speech would be in *Richard II* and *Lear*), for words and the power to make them *known* in forms of action define kingship. Mycetes' envious respect for men who talk well—

> Full true thou speak'st, and like thyself, my lord . . .

> Go, stout Theridamas; thy words are swords,
> And with thy looks thou conquerest all thy foes . . .

> He tells you true, my masters; so he does.—
> Drums, why sound ye not when Meander speaks?

—must make room for the overwhelming verbal presence of Tamburlaine, as suggested in their droll encounter on the battlefield:

> Tamb. Are you the witty king of Persia?
> Myc. Aye, marry, am I: have you any suit to me?
> Tamb. I would entreat you to speak but three wise words.
> Myc. So I can when I see my time. (II, iv)

And the usual reaction to Tamburlaine begins in awe at his strength of language, his high astounding terms:

> Not Hermes, prolocutor to the gods,
> Could use persuasions more pathetical. (I, ii)

> Won with thy words, and conquer'd with thy looks,
> I yield myself, my men, and horse to thee. (I, ii)

> You see, my lord, what working words he hath. (II, iii)

> Thy words assure me of kind success. (II, iii)

Thus far it may seem only a matter of Elizabethan stage-rant, the bombast we rather condescendingly assume the Elizabethan audience, with its famous greed for any new and strong linguistic fare, ate up whenever offered. But *Tamburlaine* has more point than that. The shepherd-king quite literally has 'working words', his engagement with the established civil world stresses his verbal command over reality, his power to say things into being.[6] (In this he resembles the shepherds of pastoral, whose innocent belief that their feelings affect weather and landscape similarly postulates a direct interaction of nature and mind.) 'Thou shalt find my vaunts substantial' (I, ii) is not, coming from him, a threat or a prediction but a statement of fact, and his greatest contempt is for those whose vaunts aren't so: 'tush, Turks are full of brags,/And menace more than they can well perform' (III, iii). He is full of brags he *can* perform—it's not simply that he eventually does perform them but that his way of saying them wrenches the future into the present, like his favourite verb tense: 'For *will* and *shall* best fitteth Tamburlaine' (III, iii). Time can get curiously mixed up in the Tamburlaine grammar:

> Then fight courageously: their crowns are yours,
> This hand shall set them on your conquering heads,
> That made me Emperor of Asia. (III, iii)

The crowns are at the moment still on the heads of the enemy kings, but he doesn't need to say 'they will be yours if you fight courageously'—courage and possession of the crowns are determined by his statements, after which the 'future' itself remains a mere formality of time. The spectacle of rhetoric creating the condition it names reaches its wonderful, zany climax at the end of the Second Part:

> Farewell, my boys! my dearest friends, farewell!
> My body feels, my soul doth weep to see
> Your sweet desires depriv'd my company,
> For Tamburlaine, the scourge of God, must die.
> [*Dies.*

This has been thought a moment of tragic reckoning, as the conquerer faces the bitter fact of his human vulnerability, but it won't wash; he dies when he says he does, and only then, which is the ultimate triumph of language as power.

Now *Tamburlaine* will strike even the moderately sophisticated as a thoroughly incredible play; lovers of 'camp' will know just where they are with it. There is no consistent ironic dimension to Tamburlaine's career, no way of respecting the conditions of the play while questioning his own sense of what he is and what his life means. To readers trained on Shakespeare, it seems inconceivably crude of Marlowe to provide no counter-movement of action or image that challenges the hero's absolute belief in his own primacy. Yet if the play is to exist as anything more than cartoon-fantasy or curious relic of our ancestors' crude tastes, we need a way of approaching it without expecting to find the concern with moral justice we ordinarily (if rather gullibly) associate with representations of great men and their deeds. *Tamburlaine* resists the desire—which may feel like a *need*—to punish greatness by imagining secret suffering and weakness at its heart. Tamburlaine can act out unhappiness, as he does when Zenocrate dies, but such moments seem more like cynical concessions of Marlowe's to the piety of sentiment than significant stages of developing moral awareness in the hero. And Tamburlaine's grief is rhetorically indistinguishable from his vaunts of power.

It is no secret that Marlowe's imagination inclined toward subversion and mockery. *Tamburlaine* shows him in a particularly challenging mood, posing a quintessential figure of power against our moral resistance to power, which he fully understands but has no intention of pandering to. The drama is psychologically 'open', to adopt a fine concept of Robert Martin Adams'—it deliberately courts imaginative and formal suicide to avoid being falsified or enervated by any concession to prior conventions of order.[7] Marlowe has us dancing on a razor: to condemn Tamburlaine's absolute victory over the world is to invent ironies that aren't in the play, but to accept it is to embrace an adolescent fantasy no one would care to be seen with in public. Either way one feels the dupe of the hard, illusionless intelligence one senses behind any of Marlowe's works. The play is more than the silly charade it can be reduced to in summary, and yet no one in his right mind 'believes' in it enough to find its sensational brutality shocking. (Shock, as in Dr. Johnson's reaction to the death of Cordelia, is a recognition of intensity in the dramatic illusion; I suppose Johnson would have thought *Tamburlaine* too absurd to be bothered by.)

No doubt the original audience had less trouble; for them absolute power was a magnificent enough idea to hold the attention for several hours, and it was for the Gossons and Sidneys to worry out the morality of the thing. But they were Christians, and they must have had *some* trouble. *Tamburlaine* demands a suspension of ordinary categories of dramatic credibility and moral judgment; our inability to meet the demand is thus Marlowe's mocking proof that we are prisoners to our aesthetic and moral preconceptions, which are no more fit to cope with the operations of actual power than with mere images of power like Tamburlaine. Deploring something is not the same thing as taking it seriously—the first step in coming to terms with force is surely not to locate it in some existing moral scale but to confront and believe in the reality of its consequences. Our accumulated theatrical sophistication makes the 'reality' of Tamburlaine and his violent acts hard to swallow, admittedly; but this may be part of the joke too, since it is just such sophistication, such reliance on 'experienced' scepticisms, that allows us to gloss over actual horrors as they occur. Once you admit that Tamburlaine's acts might have some relation to real human violence, Marlowe begins to make you squirm.

Tamburlaine, to repeat, faces us with a hero who is both incredibly absolute and maddeningly invulnerable to irony. He claims divine sanction for his secular triumphs, and the play takes the claim at least half seriously. He is 'the scourge of God' in that his triumphs are over heathens, and within his classical, mythological idiom—itself humanistic and 'western' by contrast to the oriental paganism of his victims—there are stirrings of at least a vague monotheism, in his nominal adherence to Islam and his final testimony to a more Hebraic God when he burns the Koran (II, V, i). Here the surface excitement about secular power and magnificence makes contact with ideas about power as a sacred possession deifying its human vessel. Tamburlaine himself has no doubt about his divine attributes, and Marlowe never really gives you much leverage against it, despite moments of uncertainty (as in the Prologue to Part II: 'Where death cuts off the progress of his pomp,/And murderous Fate throws all his triumphs down,' which quite misrepresents the mood of the conclusion). This treatment of the hero faces both ways: towards the new Renaissance excitement (and anxiety) about the secularization of power, the liberation of energy and will from traditionally religious sanctions, and also backwards toward the medieval congruence of civil and divine orders that governs the ironies of *Dr. Faustus*. Tamburlaine destroys old orders and their custodians, leaders who profess to manifest the will of the gods, and yet his rhetoric aims at re-sacramentalizing the force he exerts, by making even destruction and cruelty acts of divinity.

I suspect that Tamburlaine was most interesting to Marlowe in his ability to *invent* the deity he serves, by working backwards from his own glory to the idea of some god adequate to have inspired it. His 'conversion' from Mahomet to what can only be Jahweh—'a God, full of revenging wrath,/From whom the thunder and the lightning breaks,/Whose scourge I am'—is, one imagines, a moment of secret authorial glee. It cuts several ways at once: it mocks the cosy Christian who wants to condemn Tamburlaine's brutality by invoking his own sentimentalized God; it mocks Tamburlaine, whose egoistic need to be in constant control of everything compels him to create deity after his own image; it mocks the pseudo-Machiavels who suppose that power can comfortably be its own sanction, without need of divine reference; it mocks the religious chauvinist by cynically giving Tamburlaine 'our' God, seemingly reconciling a naughty delight in his prowess with the official religious pretensions (it's not *really* bad to be cruel to wogs and Paynims). And I suppose it mocks the solemn critic who badly wants a moral handle to the play, a stable point of ironic reference or whatever; we in fact get no such thing, since after his conversion Tamburlaine, though a little peevish about his medical ailments, is quite as loud and violent and self-congratulating and successful as ever.

The play does say that power creates its own moral justification and that it *needs* to feel justified—it's a short step from Tamburlaine to the politician who talks himself into thinking his cause right and just because he can't function while he feels guilty. But mockery is not sustained moral irony. Marlowe knew the shady side of greatness, as *Dr. Faustus* and *Edward the Second* make clear; but apart from teasing hints like Tamburlaine's conversion, he excludes such matters from this play. If *Tamburlaine* is in one of its aspects a crude, sensational charade, it is also an uncompromising exercise in the de-moralization of politics and violence, a challenge to the imagination to face the painful fact that 'greatness' may be based solely on force and may be invulnerable to any judgment except the measuring of its magnitude. Like Homeric epic. *Tamburlaine* is a 'poem of force', but without any of Homer's mitigating concern for the equities of pity and compassion. At the icy centre of Marlowe's imagination is a ruined landscape, where Bajazeth rages in his cage, the Virgins hang slaughtered on the broken walls of Damascus, Tamburlaine's timorous son lies dead by his father's hand, the Governor of Babylon's bullet-riddled body slumps in its chains, and harnessed kings draw their gloating conqueror to and fro in his chariot. Power, divorced from the illusions of its moral purpose, has a bleak appearance; we cannot *like* such a vision, but the effort to believe in it, without the evasive comforts of condemning it as 'wrong', may be a useful exercise in moral endurance.

3. The Hero in Politics: *Coriolanus*

In *Coriolanus* Shakespeare places the absolute hero, the Tamburlaine-man, in a dramatic context that grimly resists the idea of freedom he so arrogantly insists on. Coriolanus is of course much the more 'present' figure; unlike Tamburlaine he has an everyday self, based on the idea that he's only a simple soldier, a servant of the state without personal ends in mind. But he lacks psychological depth—Shakespeare denies him even one serious soliloquy— and he is not much given to the insistent self-dramatization that so strongly marks Hamlet, Othello, and Lear, or the anxiety about failure of self-dramatization that haunts Antony and Macbeth and in his depressive phases Hamlet too. (I'm of course thinking of 'the attitude of self-dramatization assumed by some of Shakespeare's heroes at moments of tragic intensity' that T. S. Eliot long ago pointed out, and of Lionel Abel's recent elaboration of the insight into a general theory of Shakespeare's tragic method, which Abel is rightly reluctant to call 'tragic' at all.)[8] Coriolanus seems the least consciously theatrical of Shakespeare's heroes, the least given to inventing and manipulating personal roles; but the play is concerned nevertheless with conflicts between roles, ones

24

that are not so much chosen as imposed by education, social class, and public circumstances. The simple soldier is also a man who, when his will is challenged, intensely asserts his own absolute power and rightness. The expedient duplicities of policy outrage his sense of honour, and at his greatest moments his 'natural' voice is something like the voice of Tamburlaine, insisting on his difference from ordinary human nature in images of god-like destructive energy.

Coriolanus, however, is usually on the defensive, fighting against heavy odds, *driven* by some offence to his nature into self-assertion or self-justification. It will be enough here to consider only the ending of the play as it relates to the hero's whole 'action' and its meaning. His last big speech, confronted by hostile Volsces who think he has betrayed them, achieves Tamburlainean assurance only gradually:

> Cut me to pieces, Volsces; men and lads,
> Stain all your edges on me. Boy! False hound!
> If you have writ your annals true, 'tis there,
> That, like an eagle in a dove-cote, I
> Flutter'd your Volscians in Corioli:
> Alone I did it. Boy! (V, vi)

The mood is first defensive; like a hunted animal at bay, he turns on his attackers and defies their collective force. But a 'false hound' (beyond the simple insolence of 'treacherous dog') is one 'at fault', checked and foiled by having lost the scent; and Coriolanus' passion works into a reversal whereby the hunted becomes the hunter, an eagle in a dove-cote, and the lonely victim is transformed into the solitary hero, the man who 'did it' alone and unaided. We think back to earlier images of his solitude, such as 'he is himself alone,/To answer all the city' (I, iv), with its hint that he is 'himself' *only when* alone, that for a 'lonely dragon' any companionship is a threat to his very identity.

Now obviously Coriolanus never earns high marks for diplomacy. This absurdly tactless speech, in the teeth of old enemies who can hardly be blamed for thinking he's sold them out, is only the last of a series of impolitic lapses that began with his first entrance, where he ruined the efforts of Menenius to pacify the mob. It's not at all clear that Aufidius' plot will succeed—both the First and Second Lords try to interpose in the name of restraint and legal process—until Coriolanus' reckless rage inflames the crowd to a pitch that makes assassination seem justified. It is something close to suicide, and it painfully cancels out the stirrings of self-knowledge and recognition of other views in Coriolanus' great confrontation with his mother:

> Behold! the heavens do ope,
> The gods look down, and this unnatural scene
> They laugh at. O my mother! mother! O!
> You have won a happy victory to Rome;
> But for your son, believe it, O! believe it,
> Most dangerously you have with him prevail'd,
> If not most mortal to him. But let it come.   (V, iii)

To see yourself as a figure of comedy is a usefully humbling variation from the ordinary heroic perspective, and it is moving to find him for once able to look beyond his immediate place and mood toward an awareness of ends and consequences. 'But let it come' shows his Stoic Roman training fulfilling itself in human dignity and potential wisdom; like Hamlet's 'The readiness is all', Macbeth's 'Yet I will try the last', Edgar's 'Men must endure/Their going hence', it acknowledges a fatal future even as it summons up a noble posture in which to confront death. But it is just this learned acceptance of what one's career has led to that Coriolanus negates in his final fury—if he is not a 'boy of tears' as Aufidius claims, there still is something childish in his susceptibility to rage, as his hostile critics always point out happily.

But it would be heartless to find in Coriolanus only a case of arrested development, as it takes a depressing political Puritanism to denounce him as just some sort of proto-Fascist. The ending of the play poses a conflict of views that seems to me instructively unresolvable. Against the awful buffoonery of Coriolanus' last and biggest gaffe must be set those qualities of his dramatic presence that *make* the effect awful, the magnificence of his commitment to a heroic self as the whole play has rendered it. 'Alone I did it' is not false bravado, it's a statement of fact (however disturbing the tone) and a surrender of one's life without a trace of regret for its shape and aims. In *Coriolanus* Shakespeare may, as L. C. Knights argues,[9] present a disapproving account of how 'disruption in the state—the body politic—is related to individual disharmony' by showing in Coriolanus (and Volumnia) 'an abrogation of those qualities of mutuality and trust on which *any* society must be founded'; but I doubt that this takes adequate notice of the range of political awareness the play reflects. It's hard to see that any society *must* be founded on mutuality and trust; it ought to be, of course, but one needn't be a hard-line Hobbesian to suspect that real societies seldom *are* founded on such a condition, whether 'founded' means originally established or functionally sustained. (Shakespeare was no political idealist, as the history plays and Prospero's government of Caliban and Ariel can remind us.) Nor does it seem fair to locate the 'individual disharmony' solely within the patrician's aloofness from inferiors; the play takes some pains to show equal mistrust and malice in the Citizens and their Tribunes, and it would be fruitless to argue about which side first started the trouble. Indeed, a clear alternative to the cynical manipulative politicizing Professor Knights finds 'monstrous' in the patricians is just the absolute contempt for compromise and deceit that Coriolanus asserts.

At the end of *Coriolanus* two views of heroic individualism come into difficult, impossible juxtaposition. Coriolanus' violent rejection of his own near-achievement of wisdom proves that he has imperfectly understood his human stake in other people and their needs. His death is an act of folly and desperate waste, to which we respond with both sorrow and grim amusement. Like all of Shakespeare's 'tragic' personages he falls short of the full redemptive illumination *we* can imagine and hope for him. But such illumination would nullify much of his potency as heroic figure and moral object. Hegel points out that one virtue of heroes is in demonstrating an admirable early stage in the history of ethical awareness:

> The self-consciousness of heroes (like that of Oedipus and others in Greek tragedy) had not advanced out of its primitive simplicity either to reflection on the distinction between act and action, between the external event and the purpose and knowledge of the circumstances, or to the subdivision of the consequences. On the contrary, they accepted responsibility for the whole compass of the deed.[10]

Some such acceptance of whole responsibility is what makes Coriolanus so impressive and maddeningly mysterious to our more sophisticated, ethically devious minds. It's his struggle to preserve his heroic identity, to remain *himself* in all his relations to life and fate, that makes him 'Coriolanus', the fiction that compels our attention as few living people can ever do. Shakespeare works at a lower level of mimetic generality than Greek tragedy: where we value Oedipus for his 'representative' capacity for suffering (we preserve the imaginative and moral distance the theory of *katharsis* seems to imply), we value Hamlet and Lear and Coriolanus because their need to be themselves through all adverse circumstances, the need upon which their action is founded, abolishes 'distance' and involves the spectator in a moral situation that is less potently representative as myth but humanly closer to home.

In Coriolanus' struggle to remain himself—a struggle Tamburlaine could never be put to—come to focus the conflicting views of 'public' life with which I am concerned. Shakespeare's kind of equity forbids us either to value political and social necessities over the claims of personal identity or to endorse self-commitment at the expense of peace and public order. To ignore Coriolanus' claims to greatness would be obtuse—he is simply more alive and compelling than anyone else in the play, including those excellent politicians Menenius and Aufidius, who come close to showing that able public men sort out into Fools and Knaves. Yet Shakespeare knows well enough that the cost of greatness is for ordinary men intolerably high. In a civilized society, where tensions and animosities have to be stylized into the impersonal, collective play of power and interest, there probably is nothing to do with a Coriolanus except kill him. But, as in *Julius Caesar*, the killing humiliates those who perform or endorse it; Aufidius does 'a deed whereat valour will weep', and he himself is 'struck with sorrow' and prophesies 'a noble memory' for his victim, now 'the most noble corse that ever herald/Did follow to his urn'. Nobility is acceptable in death, when it no longer can trouble the delicate balances of public life, and a 'noble memory' seems to say both that he should be remembered for being noble and that his nobility will ennoble those who do remember him so. With the life safely gone out of him, it does us good to have him, like a heroic statue, posed in a permanent mental abstraction.

28

This solution isn't adequate either. It is obviously too easy to be generous to the dead. But there is an implied understanding that noble memories aren't achieved by men whose lives are routine, comfortable, accommodating. If to be yourself is to be alone, then death, the perfection of loneliness, is also the perfection of the heroic condition. Only someone whose life is forceful enough to be intolerable *needs* to be murdered into monumentality, and it may require such violent transformation to make force memorable and morally significant.

'Those who restrain desire, do so because theirs is weak enough to be restrained; and the restrainer or reason usurps its place & governs the unwilling'—Blake's terms implicitly comment on Coriolanus or any heroic man. In his failure to restrain desire, his passion to exist solely according to his own nature, he deeply offends ordinary, weak men who find his energy a rebuke to their placid acceptance of external restraints. Their literal or symbolic murder of the hero aims at reducing him to their measure, imposing on him the restraint they practice so unprotestingly, supposing it to be right and natural. And in Blake's terms this practice of reason refers to politics as ordinary men know it, the imposition of 'government' upon an otherwise perilous anarchy of desire. That they may *need* to do this, or think they do, is no concern of Blake's—radical innocence seeks literal Paradise, not secular artifacts that palely imitate its nature. *Tamburlaine* would probably have seemed to him more like it, remembering his belief that 'the grandest poetry is Immoral the Grandest characters Wicked'.[11]

From any established social point of view, of course, Blake's comment postulates chaos, and Knights is right to say that Shakespeare perceives in the symbiosis of personal will and social intolerance a dreadful threat to the order of the state. Like *King Lear*, however, *Coriolanus* shows the nature of passion and will being so thoroughly intuited and expressed as almost to give them a kind of endorsement. The play's greatness is not that it shows that unrestrained heroic desire subverts public order and thus is to be discouraged in real life— what Good Citizen could think otherwise?—but that it takes imaginative possession of such desire, making it known and felt as a living possibility and not just an easily rejectable moral bogey.[12] And by knowing and feeling

Coriolanus's desire one may discover unexpected value in his role. He is indeed a menace to politics as practised in the 'Rome' of the play; he, far more than the Citizens, disrupts the organic order urged by Menenius's fable of the body-politic. But that order is not an absolute good. Would Shakespeare's audience have been much more enthusiastic than we would be about living in a state that prohibited individual or collective political expression, where status was hereditary and unalterable, where complaints about famine were met with bland reminders that the belly mustn't rule the body? The metaphor of organism, a medieval legacy of obvious use to the Anglican establishment, faced ominous challenge in Shakespeare's day, as Puritan theorists worked to replace it with figures (such as the state as ship) that could accommodate attempts at active reform.[13] Although Coriolanus doesn't mean to do so, his resistance to the politics of accommodation, as practised by organicists like Menenius, oddly parallels the Citizen's refusal to stay in place any longer. If politics means the perpetuation of fixed hierarchy, then Coriolanus, though he means to defend 'degree', is really subverting it; if it means the pursuit of public ends without regard for traditional definition of roles and appropriate powers, then Coriolanus is an unwitting agent of political freedom, a prediction of how 'heroic' attributes would later be imaginatively attached to a figure like Cromwell.

Coriolanus in effect makes you pay for the dream of political order by discovering how it contradicts the dream of greatness, the achievement of a better self through the exertion of will and energy. To be sure, Coriolanus himself only imperfectly represents this latter dream, but in him at least stirs a possible union of traditional heroism with the pursuit of a new political life that is more than the haggling of selfish interests, routine compromises that give everyone a scrap but no one what he most wants or thinks right, the dreary stratagems of dreary men. It should be possible to believe this of the play without forgetting its ironies or making Coriolanus seem more noble than he is; if Shakespeare values energy and will, he also values the older idea of order and wholeness that energy and will threaten to destroy, and he knows that the peaceful domesticity we take to be our private right depends more than we like to admit on the very hagglings and compromises and stratagems his hero so contemptuously rejects.

4. The Hero as Subversive: Satan

Coriolanus thus complexly represents the strain between individual will and collective social expectations and hopes that exists whenever power is held and exercised by a single man. Behind the play stand Tamburlaine and the sensational heroes of Kyd, Greene, and Chapman, as well as Shakespeare's own early soldier-politicians in the history plays; ahead lies the greatest work of heroic literature in the language, and the most difficult and controversial figure of heroic man.

Whether or not one wants to read *Paradise Lost* as Blake did, it is clear that Satan would be even harder to understand if the poem had never been read in that way by someone of supreme honesty and genius. Blake's interpretation, as we reconstruct it from *The Marriage of Heaven and Hell, Milton*, and scattered remarks elsewhere, makes defiantly overt an attitude already implicit in the idea of epic. There is always compelling force in the spectacle of greatness opposing circumstance and fate, massive energies sustaining magnificent images of self even at the expense of moral law and civil order. It takes a narrow piety to deny some admiration in Milton's rendering of Satan and his career; a logic that argues 'Milton was a Christian, Satan's "magnificence" is flatly subversive of Christian doctrine, therefore the magnificence is only a delusion of Satan's and must be rejected by the fit audience', is hardly the best route to an understanding of the poem, though its premises need to be remembered and dealt with.

A lay reader may hope to be forgiven for beginning with the familiar idea that Milton's combining of epic methods with Christian matter threatens to make Satan unmanageable from the start. Only with grave risk can he be allowed even the general contours of a heroic role—the idea of Evil collides with even the mixed capacities for virtue and magnificence of the traditional epic man. Schematically there would seem to be only the large choice between Blake's belief that Satanic magnificence reveals unconscious and welcome heresy in Milton himself—his inability to dissociate energy from virtue—and the pietistic idea that every sign of Satan's magnificence is ironic proof of his apostasy from a sober Christian virtue that Milton thoroughly and properly endorses.

But responsive readers of Milton may not want to make so clear and exclusive a choice. The poem has other dimensions than the polarity between Christian submission and 'heroic' self-assertion; among others, it raises questions about authority and individual will that were in the seventeenth-century political questions as well as religious ones. Revolution was obviously much on Milton's mind during the 1640's and '50's and in the years after the Restoration when *Paradise Lost* was at last fully conceived and written out. It must have given him some trouble, to say the least, to write a poem in which rebellion against a monarch is the proof of ultimate evil. If he was not exactly a tender-minded, self-doubting man, still he must sometimes have felt enough anxiety about the success of the Puritan cause, if not about its justness, to have been capable of sympathetic insight into Satan's spiritual agony. I am not the first to observe that Milton, like most people, *knew* the Devil better than he knew God or His Son.

Knowledge is of course not approval, exactly, any more than Milton's famous passion for freedom of conscience and intellect is the same as Satan's passion for freedom of will, or Milton's pride in his own powers the same as Satan's in his. (Even Empson, in *Milton's God*, interrupts his defence of Satan's earlier states of mind with the concession that 'I am not denying that Milton felt a *personal dislike* for Satan', a distinction that seems very helpful.)[14] But the fact that Satan seems to have a knowable mind, to which passions and sufferings can be ascribed, is a mark of the distance between *Paradise Lost* and older versions of epic literature. The Homeric heroes behave more like stable mythic figures, and less like conscious, introspective, variable personalities, than Satan. While they are at times visited by illumination and deep under-standing, these moments—such as Sarpedon's great meditation on the motives of warriors, or Achilles and Priam mourning together for different reasons—seem to reflect the singer's own pondered wisdom at least as much as the character's grasp of his condition. Erich Auerbach notes that the 'multilayeredness' of individual character in Biblical stories

> is hardly to be met with in Homer, or at most in the form of
> a conscious hesitation between two possible courses of
> action; otherwise, in Homer, the complexity of the psycho-

logical life is shown only in the succession and alternation of emotions; whereas the Jewish writers are able to express the simultaneous existence of various layers of consciousness and the conflict between them.[15]

I suspect that Simone Weil may have been responding to this quality of style when she saw the *Iliad* as a poem in which men blindly and ignorantly achieve the status of unreflective things, 'stones', by subjecting one another to force; and although Auerbach's point is that the Homeric style renders 'an independent and exclusive present' that resists allegorization by leaving nothing unsaid, still the Homeric indifference to psychological depth might have seemed to Spenser to offer 'heroic' sanction for peopling *The Faerie Queene* with representative emblems in representative action. And a freedom from complex self-consciousness governs the 'heroic play' of the Renaissance, which assumes that the man of force is best represented by his public actions and speech; his significance would be diluted if he took on the burden of some reflective inner life that was less than perfectly consonant with the self he presents to others. The distance between Tamburlaine and Faustus, Coriolanus and Hamlet, owes something to an understanding of what 'heroic character' traditionally requires, as does Thomas Rymer's horrendous confusion about *Othello*.

Now Satan has a consciousness of self, an inner life often profoundly at odds with his public postures, although its revelations are intermittent and increasingly infrequent in the later Books. This concession of Milton's has important consequences, which may be represented by considering the soliloquy on Mt. Niphates, where Satan comes to his great choice of an inflexible self by way of some impressive waverings and agonies. Milton starts with some jokes—Satan is losing his nerve, 'not rejoicing', as the Temptation draws near, his evil intent will recoil upon him like some 'devilish engine' of moral farce betraying its inventor—but this framing mood of scorn yields to a much less hostile tone that allows Satan's moral reality to grow as we watch, in keeping with the virtually telescopic method of these earlier Books, which show him expanding and shrinking as Milton changes the focus:[16]

> . . . horror and doubt distract
> His troubled thoughts, and from the bottom stir

The Hell within him; for within him Hell
He brings, and round about him, nor from Hell
One step, no more than from himself, can fly
By change of place. Now Conscience wakes Despair
That slumbered, wakes the bitter memory
Of what he was, what is, and what must be
Worse; of worse deeds worse sufferings must ensue.

(IV, 18-26)

The last line avoids the bullying tone Satan is so often subjected
to by making the grim statement of necessity seem as much his
own thought as the poet's moralizing comment. And to modern
ears, at least, it doesn't sound entirely diabolical for someone to
have hell within him; it sounds human and rather grand, just
what an interesting literary hero ought to have in the way of a
complex awareness of the self and its history. Doubt, troubled
thoughts, a deep nature ('from the bottom stir'), conscience,
bitter memory, even despair—these seem to mark him as a
fellow-spirit one wants to get to know better, even at the risk of
finding him just another Romantic poseur. If Milton's first
readers can hardly have seen him in quite this light, still they
might have found something oddly affecting about a 'memory' that
contains not only past suffering but present and future as well,
as if his awareness of consequences had abolished time as a
sequential process. To remember the present and the future is to
have time and fate collapse on you in an eternity of failed desire,
the doom reserved for any hyper-imaginative mind, and the
repetitions of 'Hell' and 'worse' and the non-progressive, circular
syntax (condensed to chiasmus in the third line) enforce the effect
of inescapable entrapment.

Satan, that is, here occupies the attention as a figure in whom
are combined a massive, inflexibly negative will and a distinct and
affecting awareness of the limitations of his moral role. Milton's
nephew Edward Phillips said that part of the soliloquy was
written around 1642 as a speech for a tragic play about the Fall,
and certainly it has considerable dramatic fullness:

Farewell remorse! All good to me is lost;
Evil, be thou my Good: by thee at least
Divided Empire with Heaven's King I hold
By thee, and more than half perhaps will reign. (109-112)

34

The taste of melodrama in this great choice may be sharper when one knows what comes later—Byronism, for example, and its tragi-comic synthesis in Stephen Dedalus ('Non serviam'), or the sanctified Satanism of naifs like Huck Finn ('All right, then I'll *go* to hell!') and various modern epigoni—although something of the sort would have been perceptible to an audience who had Barabbas and Iago and Edmund to show that the choice of evil could be theatrical as well as shocking. But Satan, with his pitiful dream of divided empire, is more than a stage-villain. His mind reaches out to an imagined power that can best be figured in political terms, and he reminds us how thoroughly Milton's age conceived of spiritual issues as matters of polity, analogues of civil concerns even as these were analogues of divine ones.

Insofar as his role has political substance, Satan obviously signifies disorder; it then becomes a matter of how one values order, and what order one values. From the Christian point of view, the energy Blake and Shelley so admired is really bent upon the blasphemous *waste* of energy; Satan searches for power, but the search can only spend and dissipate power in abortive parody-creations that deny Logos even in the act of imitating it.[17] Even in his most private and honest attempt at introspection Satan is unable to see what Milton and the Christian reader see, that his ambitions are hopeless, his quest for empire as destructive as Tamburlaine's and as thoroughly impelled by a need for self-display through acts of conspicuous waste.[18] (This aspect made him especially useful to Dryden and Pope as an analogical model for Shaftesbury, Sporus, and Cibber.) But theological waste is not literary waste; it seems hard to condemn Satan for possessing imaginative power that exceeds the acts available to it, and we do not automatically despise literary characters who don't know everything the author and reader know, since that is the necessary condition of *any* fictive creature. By the measure of religious order Satan is evil; by the measure of artistic order he is only what he has to be, and Blake was right to say that it was Milton's being 'a true Poet' that made him 'of the Devils party without knowing it'.

If Satan's guilt is theologically certain, then, the case may yet remain humanly moot. Helen Gardner nicely says of him that 'there remains always, untouched by the argument, the image of enormous pain and eternal loss',[19] and Empson's crankish-sounding complaints about Milton's God are finally hard to dismiss. While Satan's sorrows mustn't be sentimentalized, or his fallacious explanations of them ignored, still his experience can strike close to home:

> Oh, had his powerful destiny ordained
> Me some inferior Angel, I had stood
> Then happy; no unbounded hope had raised
> Ambition. (IV, 58-61)

To be sure, it seems childish to blame it all on God, and the implied theory of organizational psychology looks dubious—why, in sound hierarchies, should there be no temptation in the lower ranks but irresistible temptations in the top echelons? Where exactly in the scale does proper desire to serve become evil desire to serve oneself? For all its logical shakiness, however, the complaint is hard to resist. Men generally do get more ambitious as they approach the source of power, and this quite as surely in the theoretically stable scale of medieval polity as in the more fluid ambiance of modern politics—there were self-made kings and popes before Machiavelli. Though the economy of Heaven is hierarchical, Milton took a dim view of fixed hierarchy at the earthly level, in church or state, and Satan is not just a theological token but also an admonitory yet moving individual case, whose error here mirrors a human weakness that is easy to deplore yet hard to disclaim entirely. While his programme is evil—a large qualification, to be sure—his attempt to remake the existing system is not entirely remote from the revolutionary cause Milton gave his best years to. And anyone who has ever felt confused or frightened by proximity to power and its temptations will understand Satan's yearning for mediocrity, his confession that his career has made him miserable, his poor baffled wish to be just a simple NCO.

The ramifications of Milton's politics are not my concern here, but any reader of the prose tracts notes his passion for liberty and his secular iconoclasm, as they mix with a curiously *ad hoc* view of the forms of temporal power and with his significant reservations about Cromwell's regime. (Northrop Frye soberingly remarks that Milton shows 'the plight of the liberal intellectual who sees in every revolution an apocalyptic struggle of tyranny and freedom and finds it so hard to understand that revolution is a technique of transferring power from one class to another'.)[20] But Satan's discovery that rebellion leads to personal desolation, a tragic scepticism about both power and the security of being powerless, would touch the confusions of a time when power had taken off political costumes and shown itself as naked violence. If the soliloquy on Mt. Niphates was conceived in 1642, it shows Milton's accurate prophecy of what rebellion would seem to have led to twenty years later.

To postulate some systematic parallel between *Paradise Lost* and Milton's own political experience would reduce a difficult and 'open' masterpiece to a wind-up poetical toy. But it may be that the poem assumes and draws upon a fund of political experience that was troublingly alive for the poet and his readers; one can, I think, see in Satan, shifting and blurring from moment to moment, the outlines of both the typological tyrant-monarch and the typological rebel-hero, and the audience, fit or otherwise, would have had contemporary public analogues for both outlines ready to mind. Certainly the Debate in Hell has more point if taken not just as a joke about devils but also as a serious comment on political process and its uncertain relation to divine truth. To see only hollowness in the rhetoric of Moloch, Belial, Mammon, and Beelzebub, and mere fraudulence in Satan's management, is to miss something. The experience of Parliaments implied in the passage includes satiric hostility but also a measured assessment of what parliamentary process is capable of doing. Fake or not, the proceedings accomplish something: the constituencies are heard from, the representative body defines itself and confirms its complex nature, and the decision, however rigged, takes account of that nature. It is not the least dignified idea of politics that sees it as the art of doing what *should* be done (Satan's plan, diabolically speaking, promises most accomplishment at least public expense) in a way that will displease fewest people.

In a fallen world this may be all that can be expected. The paradox of Calvinism, that one sought to serve God's purposes in this world without hope of knowing certainly what they really were, led to a hard and illusionless political realism, emphasizing discipline and pragmatic policy.[21] The state is an order of power and repression, not an order of love, and to this extent Pandemonium is nearer Westminster than most maps show. Milton's irony stares not only at devilish perversions of reason and public spirit but also beyond, toward the cruel distance between *any* politics and true equity, between human dialectics and Heaven (presumably the only place where the wills of the ruler and the ruled coincide more spontaneously than at producers' conferences at MGM). It can hardly be an accident that Belial, seemingly the sanest and most humane of the debaters, is the one for whom Milton reserves his most suspicious scorn: 'Thus Belial, with words clothed in reason's garb,/Counselled ignoble ease and peaceful sloth,/Not peace.' This could be only the poet's special irritation at a character who could keep the rest of the poem from happening, but it sounds like the anger one feels toward someone who *almost* sees it one's own way, compared with whom the Enemy is almost lovable in his clear-cut, stationary antagonism. Belial is hateful because he's so nearly reasonable, a caricature of truth rather than a downright lie; the Council in Hell is hateful because it's so close to being an authentic parliamentary occasion, because (I speculate) it may represent something like Milton's own nostalgic disillusionment about what the Long Parliament and the Commonwealth once had seemed to promise.

This is about as close as one can get to any idea of particular political content in *Paradise Lost*; perhaps it is too close. I mean only to suggest that in a political situation like Milton's, moral and religious subjects could not well be insulated from political subjects, and that the political subjects, once they entered the picture even peripherally, added to the complexity of a true poet's view of a creature like Satan. Questions about Satan's role are also, inversely, questions about the Law that condemns and punishes him and about the status of the poetic imagination that does the questioning. The neoclassical decorum that pleased Dr. Johnson by moralizing Satan ('There is in Satan's speeches little that can give pain to a pious ear') works to lessen the doctrinal distance between the Evil Hero and the Christian Reader. That reader, I think, can see in Satan's introspective moral consciousness, without embracing it, a significant image of intensity of will modulating into a painful *assertion* of will after it has in fact faltered, an idea of freedom being sustained even as one almost sees through it to discern one's true passivity and helplessness.

To find expressed in Satan's role a complex, reluctant scepticism about the aims and means of secular effort (even if 'sanctified' in theory), a deep suspicion of the agreement of worldly order with the nature of divine love—a nature that *will* be falsified if figured in terms of polity alone—should not finally damage the status of *Paradise Lost* as a Christian poem not distort Milton's sense of the ultimate discontinuity of temporal power and Grace.

5. The Hero Emasculated: *Hudibras* and Mock-Epic

This has been rather like looking at the Alps through a keyhole; but my present concern is only with what *Paradise Lost* implies about the fate of the heroic idea. In Satan the possibility of a great man, or spirit, who is not God gets put to such ironic pressure that it seemingly could never spring back to its former shape and size. Once you know about Satan, Tamburlaine will seem in some danger of being a loud-mouth, Aeneas a fuddy-duddy, Odysseus a garrulous bore, even Achilles a sullen bully. (Shakespeare's *Troilus* is the needed reminder that such devaluation is possible at any time, but also that before the Restoration it seems exceptional and rather puzzling.) Heroic man begins to seem an object of pious nostalgia more than of imaginative imitation in the later seventeenth century, when of course the literary future was in comedy, or at worst in earnest triviality. 'Serious' drama would deal with public greatness either by abstracting it entirely from credible human worlds, as in the Heroick Play of Dryden's theatre, or by banishing it from the stage altogether in favor of 'domestic' tragic actions, as in Lillo or Rowe, who adapted *Tamburlaine* but then, in the Prologue to *The Fair Penitant* (1703), significantly renounced 'the fate of kings and empires' in favour of 'a melancholy tale of private woe'; can the best eighteenth-century English play be anything but *Tom Thumb*? The new genre, the novel, would base itself on ironic, critical moods, the anti-heroic sense (learned largely from stage comedy) that great men and common men are equally pretentious, insincere, self-deluded, and the great master who set the major tone for fiction for almost two centuries would think he was writing 'comic epic in prose'.

The first canto of *Hudibras* was published four years before *Paradise Lost*, and in poetry too it was the travesty-burlesque rather than the serious Christian epic (soon to collapse into Sir Richard Blackmore) that was to preside over the new age. *Hudibras* is still reasonably funny in small doses, as Butler's mind is still attractive for being so entranced by the cant and hypocrisy it sought to ridicule; but for most people the poem remains one of those landmarks of literary history—like *Gorboduc*, *The Orphan*, *Shamela*, the sonnets of Bowles, Swinburne's *Poems and Ballads*—that one can safely avoid actually *reading*. But if *Hudibras* needs no extensive revaluation, still its attitude toward public enterprise is worth glancing at, as a way of seeing how the Renaissance concern with heroism finally foundered and sank.

From the beginning Butler distances the world of political controversy by describing it in an idiom of plain sense and homely scepticism that is lethal to its pretensions:

> When civil dudgeon first grew high,
> And men fell out, they knew not why,
> When hard words, jealousies, and fears
> Set folks together by the ears,
> And made them fight, like mad or drunk,
> For Dame Religion as for punk,
> Whose honesty they all durst swear for,
> Though not a man of them knew wherefore.... (I, 1-8)

This folksy talk builds up a fairly complex joke. Only such a voice can keep the epic potentialities of the subject under control, as we first of all imagine the 'singer' to be a simple-minded soul who really is trying to tell a heroic tale but fails because his style is hopelessly low, too close to Hudibras' own level of taste and wit. In this sense Butler relates to his fiction as a condescending ironist who invites you to see through the Hudibras-style to his own cultivated, mocking intelligence. And of course we do this—no one fails to divine a sophisticated mind in there somewhere, making the machine go. But another effect blurs into this simple ventriloquism. The blunt, direct voice is also the right voice, the one that most accurately locates one's objections to sectarian hurly-burly, which after all is most objectionable not because it violates good literary and social taste (as the epic jokes are going to suggest) but because it upsets the relatively sane stability of normal human behaviour, however high or low its level of style.

While mock-epic seizes upon fighting for a punk as a gross betrayal of high imaginative possibilities, common sense can accept it as an understandable mood of honest passion, not wholly different in kind from fighting over Helen of Troy, say; common sense will really boggle only when Dame Religion is dragged into the ale-house to be brawled over. The Honest Man (so to label Butler's plain speaker) is presumably upset because 'For Dame Religion as for punk' shockingly degrades sacred devotion to the level of profane lust. There is no reason to ascribe the shock to Butler himself, whose point must rather be that you can't be any surer of the chasteness of your religion than of your whore, so that neither is worth fighting about; but in either case, whether you take its judgments to be reassuringly sensible or hopelessly vulgar, the every-day world measures and annihilates heroic ideals and hope for dignity in public causes.

Hudibras draws its satiric force from a myth of normative peace and quiet. There was a time *before* 'civil dudgeon first grew high', before 'men fell out', before imagined differences 'set folks together by the ears'; and the incidents of the poem figure as annoying little obstructions to that prospect of agreement and decent quiet. (Butler's aversion to sectarianism and its endlessly multipliable vocabularies seems to reflect not only the Restoration suspicion of eloquence but also a personal distaste for loud noises as strong as his scorn for curious, ungainly costumes.) This allusion to innocence seems simple and clear in its intentions: the late unpleasantness stirred up by fanatical clowns like Hudibras and Ralpho violated the ante-bellum state of repose, as if history had been continuously peaceful until the 1630's, but now that sanity has been restored, we can afford to look back with marvelling amusement on that momentary nightmare. But Butler's amusement is too vehement and caustic to express the *secure* contempt of a mind in full possession of a resolved present and future, and the jokes often seem miniature portraits of mixed impulses, uncertainties about what one's aggressive intentions really are:

> This said, as once the Phrygian knight,
> So ours with rusty steel did smite
> His Trojan horse, and just as much

He mended pace upon the touch;
But from his empty stomach groaned
Just as that hollow beast did sound.
And angry, answered from behind,
With brandished tail and blast of wind.
So I have seen, with armèd heel,
A wight bestride a Commonweal,
While still the more he kicked and spurred,
The less the sullen jade has stirred.   (I, 917-928)

The main point is to end the canto with an image of absurd inertia,
Hudibras' martial will thwarted by his starveling nag's stubborn
exhaustion—or rather to merge horse and rider in a single image
of empty impotence, so that you see not Zeal Confounded by
Animal Nature (as in Swift's favourite jokes) but the unmanly
pretensions of Zeal itself. But the whole effect seems a little
blurred: Hudibras exactly *lacks* the prudent suspicion of Laocoön,
and the sneer at Richard Cromwell in his father's saddle is over-
prepared and lame. While Hudibras is the kind of bumpkin who
would have a bad horse, it still looks as though not just Hudibras
the aberrant knight but the whole possibility of significant
energy itself is being mocked here. The political animus of the
poem requires us to take Hudibras and the Cromwells as imposters,
men who choose a role they can't fill because of their disabling
commitment to false premises and bad principles; but the implied
alternative isn't real heroism, some opposing mode of significant
action, but a modest and domestic *inaction* that would keep you
from getting on a horse at all except to make journeys or perhaps
hunt a fox. Butler's assault on Hudibras seems to me less political
than sexual in aim, a gelding of heroic potency, if you like.

Mock epic is not just a contrived, arbitrary kind of literary
irony. It's quite simply what happens to epic when it gets too close
to real life, the reader's sense of what his world is like and what its
values are worth. For all their sober intentions, *Annus Mirabilis*,
Hobbes's translations of Homer, and Blackmore's *Arthur* are
cases—or contain cases—of mock heroic quite as certainly as
Hudibras, *MacFlecknoe*, or *The Rape of the Lock;* and mock epic,
as in the Fourth Book of the *Dunciad*, can reconvert itself into epic
despite the persistence of comic intentions. The chief determinant

is style, the writer's ability to sustain a consistency of diction and rhetoric that can hold the reader's attention within the frame of the work, not allowing it to wander outside and stumble over some trivial object he recognizes as part of his own existence. (The *Peri Bathous* shows Pope's serious awareness of how terribly hard it is to keep things straight, to distinguish what it involves to write an English *Iliad* from what it involves to write the *Dunciad*.) Inside every epic poem there is a mock epic struggling to get out; inside every reader of epic a reader of mock epic reminding himself not to snicker.

As I began by saying, this is a complexity inherent in the idea of greatness; it is not simply a consequence of history. But the later seventeenth century seems to have been a time—the mid-twentieth century is another—when images of human grandeur were particularly vulnerable to ironic devaluation. *Paradise Lost* preserves the venerable properties of heroism by to some extent disguising them or at least allowing their relation to public realities to remain tentative and unsystematic. Above all it preserves them by encapsulating them in a style whose marvellous eccentricity draws a high degree of attention to its own beauty and thus forbids too literal inquisition of the subject.[22] But if Milton gives us a bee in amber, *Hudibras* solemnly presents us with a dead, shrivelled insect. Hudibras's rusty spur (Butler allows him only one) and wind-swollen horse monumentalize not only the frustration of Puritan militarism by an age of internal agreement but also, with more accurate prophecy, the emasculation of the image of heroic man in action. Such a man, shaping public reality through physical and rhetorical acts of will, would never again get a fully convincing embodiment in English literature. Butler's speaker, the honest man, defeats the hero by opposing to him the curious power of common sense and the common forms of life, the reduction of noble public roles to what are presented as their deflating domestic equivalents. The heroic idea, once the property of kings and princely warriors, had in effect passed to the Puritan side and attached itself to the zealous yet businesslike Cromwellian type who pursued politics and war as methods of subverting the old monarchic state. It is a nice irony of history that Butler the Royalist, seeing rightly that 'action' now meant politics and that modern politics made nonsense of the self-regulating, organic body-politic of Establishmentarian theory, should have been the one to lampoon heroism out of even imaginative existence.

Future poets would face the task of assessing politics and power without serious appeal to heroic images. But if this was a loss of a useful standard of judgment, it brought a compensatingly closer and more demanding involvement of imagination in the contingent, unformulaic nature of modern politics, itself a way of making do with a fragmented public order in which traditional 'authority', once conveniently located in a monarch, blurs into the parody-form of authoritarian mock-heroes or the indeterminacies of legislative government. The poet himself would increasingly be the dominant presence in public poems, as the citizen would be in Lockeian political theory. In either case, the prime concern shifts from the moral nature of power, and its relation to the existing sources of authority, to the question of how private men can participate in or resist power as it touches on their lives and property. The new relations of imagination with public actuality would take many forms, with a corresponding diversity of poetic moods and methods; it is this diversity I try to illustrate and explore in the pages that follow.

NOTES

[1] Reuben A. Brower, *Alexander Pope: The Poetry of Allusion* (Oxford, Clarendon Press, 1959), pp. 98-99.

[2] The heterogeneous nature of the Homeric dialect suggests that the poems achieved their final state in some enclave, such as Athens, secure from the Dorian invasion for a period long enough to allow 'mingling and concentration of ethnic traditions'; see Cedric Whitman, *Homer and the Heroic Tradition* (Cambridge, Mass., Harvard University Press, and Oxford, Clarendon Press, 1958), pp. 58-61. If so, the Homeric poems as we know them would represent the view of a relatively advanced culture upon a simpler, lost world.

[3] Simone Weil, 'The *Iliad* or the Poem of Force', tr. Mary McCarthy, *Politics*, November 1945. (Reprinted in *The Proper Study*, ed. Quentin Anderson and Joseph A. Mazzeo [New York, St. Martin's 1962], pp. 3-29.)

[4] Rachel Bespaloff, *On the Iliad*, tr. Mary McCarthy (New York, Pantheon, 1947, and London, Oxford University Press, 1968), pp. 44-45.

[5] Frank Kermode, *The Sense of an Ending* (New York, Oxford University Press, 1967); for the history of apocalyptic ideas and their bearing on political

theory, see Ernest L. Tuveson, *Millennium and Utopia* (Berkeley, University of California Press, 1949, and London, Harper and Row, 1964).

[6] See Harry Levin, *The Overreacher* (Cambridge, Mass., Harvard University Press, 1952, and London, Faber & Faber, 1954), pp. 43-47, for an account of how *Tamburlaine* uses rhetoric to express physical power; for Levin, however, the pattern leads to a moral reckoning for the hero (pp. 52-54).

[7] See Robert Martin Adams, *Strains of Discord: Studies in Literary Openness* (Ithaca, Cornell University Press, 1958, and London, Oxford University Press, 1959).

[8] T.S. Eliot, 'Shakespeare and the Stoicism of Seneca', *Selected Essays 1917-1932* (London, Faber & Faber, and New York, Harcourt, Brace, 1932); Lionel Abel, *Metatheatre* (New York, Hill & Wang, and London, MacGibbon & Kee, 1963).

[9] L. C. Knights, *Poetry, Politics and the English Tradition* (London, Chatto & Windus, 1954), pp. 13-15.

[10] Hegel, *The Philosophy of Right* (1821), tr. T. M. Knox (Oxford, Clarendon Press, 1952), p. 81.

[11] Blake, annotation to Boyd's *Historical Notes* on Dante.

[12] In *The Herculean Hero* (New York, Columbia University Press, and London, Chatto & Windus, 1962), Eugene M. Waith argues that 'admiration' rather than any 'strict moral accounting' is what such heroes in Marlowe, Chapman, Shakespeare, and Dryden are meant to evoke; Waith's reading of *Tamburlaine* is a useful corrective to over-moralistic views of the play.

[13] For these figures, see Michael Walzer, *The Revolution of the Saints* (Cambridge, Mass., Harvard University Press, 1965, and London, Weidenfeld & Nicholson, 1966), pp. 171-183.

[14] William Empson, *Milton's God* (London, Chatto & Windus, 1961), p. 44. (My italics.)

[15] Erich Auerbach, *Mimesis*, tr. W. R. Trask (Princeton, Princeton University Press, and London, Oxford University Press, 1953); quoted from the Anchor Books edition (New York, Doubleday, 1957), p. 10.

[16] Geoffrey Hartman notes this effect, as Milton's way of keeping our sense of the reality of Hell from becoming too secure: 'Milton's Counterplot', *ELH* [*English Literary History*], XXV (1958), 1-12.

[17] This point is extensively explored by Michael Lieb, *The Dialectics of Creation* (Amherst, University of Massachusetts Press, 1970).

[18] For Satan's lack of full self-awareness here, see Anne Davidson Ferry, *Milton and the Miltonic Dryden* (Cambridge, Mass., Harvard University Press, and London, Oxford University Press, 1968), pp. 52-53.

[19] Helen Gardner, 'Milton's Satan and the Theme of Damnation in Elizabethan Tragedy', in *Milton: Modern Essays in Criticism*, ed. A. E. Barker (New York, Oxford University Press, 1965), p. 206.

[20] Northrop Frye (ed.), *Paradise Lost and Selected Poetry and Prose* (New York, Rinehart, 1951), p. xiii.

[21] See Walzer, *Revolution of the Saints*, pp. 22-65 for an extensive account of Calvinist politics, upon which I have freely drawn.

[22] For a good discussion of this aspect of Milton's style, see Donald R. Pearce, 'The Style of Milton's Epic', *Yale Review*, LII (1963), 440-441.

CHAPTER TWO

The Shepherd and the Commissar

The simplest difference between heroic poetry and drama and the 'public' poems now to be considered is in size. The epic writer needs plenty of room and time for working out a large-scale action that can accommodate a variety of perspectives upon individual greatness. The hero must perform a number of representative deeds, and these must be placed in contexts of sufficient magnitude to show the vast consequences of his existence as it affects the fate of other men. The alternative is to present great men as *men*, circumscribed by their individual acts, important not for any predefined mythic potency but because they did a given thing at a given time and place. You can perhaps work back from the particular event to 'heroic' meanings it seems to express, but the relation will seem tentative at best—the event itself comes first and is important even if no mythic force can be securely ascribed to it.

This latter assumption will govern a poem that deals with the operations of political power in the poet's own world, rather than with the indirect, slanting relevance to that world of some remote heroic image like Tamburlaine or Coriolanus or Satan. Michael Walzer speaks of 'the new political spirit, the new sense of activity and its possibilities, the more radical imagination that mark the sixteenth and seventeenth centuries' in England, as the essentially static theory of medieval society begins to give before the pressure of a new idea of 'politics' as organised collective action aimed at altering the existing order—politics as work, or even as war.[1] I begin with two very unlike but at least comparably difficult poems of this period, Spenser's *Colin Clouts Come Home Againe* and Marvell's *Horatian Ode Upon Cromwell's Return from Ireland*, which may fairly represent alternative ways for poets to express their relation to political power. The poems are not exclusive alternatives, of course, and I mean to imply no categorical generic polarity. But in a rough way they show the difference between talking about power from a potentially 'inside' position and talking about it from a position that is understood to be separate from the public world. For Colin Clout, the Court is where everything is and where one wants to go and be a poet; for the voice that speaks the *Horatian Ode*, the place of power is *another* place, which one may need to stay away from, imaginatively, if one is to get things right. These distinctions, it will emerge, are less clear and distinct than formulation makes them seem, but that is part of the story too. The public poet has first to decide where he is; the difficulty of doing so becomes the main subject of his poem.

1. *Colin Clout*: The Power of Art

Colin Clouts Come Home Againe is anything but a tightly-knit, 'organic' poem after the modern taste. Its pleasures are partly those of leisurely narrative meandering, action without dramatic pressure or urgency, suiting the ideality of its pastoral frame and its interweaving of the present, in which Colin tells the shepherds his story, and the narrative past, in which he visited the Court and found it lacking. But the poem's tolerance of interruption and digression doesn't exclude question about its design; if the design is finally more cumulative than sequential, still a relation of parts may be sought out and described, at whatever risk of over-schematizing.

One could begin almost anywhere, but my mind pauses first at lines 88-155, where Colin interrupts his tale of visiting Cynthia's Court, which the shepherds have been eager to hear and he to tell, to explain at unexpected length the 'tenor' of the song he sang when he first met the Shepherd of the Ocean (Raleigh). This song concerned the ill-fated romance of the rivers Mulla and Bregog, crossed in their love by the insistence of Mulla's father, the mountain Mole, that she marry the more respectable River Allo, or Broadwater. It seems a straightforward and conventional tale of metamorphosis, a 'mery lay' as Thestylis calls it, which presumably pleases the shepherds by using the local landscape in its innocent domestication of Ovid. But it has some odd features.

Bregog, to begin with, is no pathetic thwarted lover of sentimental romance. His name means 'deceitful'—'So hight because of this deceitful traine,/Which he with *Mulla* wrought to win delight' (118-119)—and Colin never questions Mole's belief that

48

his daughter deserved better. The nymph herself preferred Bregog, but on less than reasoned grounds:

> Nath'lesse the Nymph her former liking held;
> For loue will not be drawne, but must be ledde,
> And *Bregog* did so well her fancie weld,
> That her good will he got her first to wedde.   (128-131)

Deceit ('leading') has more power over feeling than straight compulsion, and it is in the 'fancie' that romance flourishes. The connection between passion and cunning is confirmed by the description of Bregog's stratagem:

> The wily louer did deuise this slight:
> First into many parts his streame he shar'd,
> That whilest the one was watcht, the other might
> Passe vnespide to meete her by the way;
> And then besides, those little streames so broken
> He vnder ground so closely did conuay,
> That of their passage doth appeare no token,
> Till they into the *Mullaes* water slide.
> So secretly did he his loue enjoy.   (137-145)

This underground coition of waters is, for all its Ovidian precedent, oddly explicit in its sexuality considering the innocence of Colin's rustic society. Bregog's 'slight' leads the romance to an unexpectedly overt consummation, even while his cunning self-division foreshadows his final punishment, when Mole rolls down 'huge mighty stones' into his course and obliterates him:

> So of a Riuer, which he was of old,
> He none was made, but scattered all to nought,
> And lost emong those rocks into him rold,
> Did lose his name: so deare his loue he bought. (152-155)

Apart from its obvious use as decorative interlude, delaying the main story to whet the shepherds' and the reader's appetites, what does the tale contribute to the poem? The apparent moral, that deceit even in love is criminal and finds just punishment, is somewhat complicated by Colin's earlier remark that 'my riuer

Bregogs loue' is not just a past emotion but a continuing one:

> Which to the shiny *Mulla* he did beare,
> And yet doth beare, and euer will, so long
> As water doth within his bancks appeare.   (93-95)

The apparent contradiction—if it was destroyed, lost its name, then it can't very well be Colin's river *now*, still flowing (loving) now and forever—begins to resolve itself when one learns that the Bregog, which flowed through Spenser's estate at Kilcolman, in dry weather 'sinks underground through the limestone and re-appears . . . only some two miles lower down'.[2] The basis in native topography is important; it was 'under the foote of Mole', 'by the Mullaes shore', that Colin first met and exchanged songs with the Shepherd of the Ocean, and evidently he tried to impress the visitor by showing him that even so primitive and provincial a scene was dignified by mythological presences. But the Ovidian paradox, that in metamorphosis living creatures exchange a transitory humanity for the permanent but only figurative 'life' of natural objects, doesn't quite apply. Bregog was a river *before* his punishment by Mole; no miracle occurs, but only simple natural events—a river-bed fills up with rocks, a stream sinks underground. Whatever Colin means by the song, Spenser may have something more in mind.

The song says most simply that cunning and guile cannot permanently secure a love that is opposed by wise authority, and that deviousness (*de-via*, straying from one's proper course) may cause irreparable division of self. (Compare the good, dull wholeness of 'Broadwater'.) But this simple moral conflicts with Colin's assertion that Bregog has *not* lost its name and identity but still flows and loves Mulla in its own person. The truth of song doesn't equal the truth of fact—no novel idea in the age of Sidney's *Defense* and the troubled Platonism historically behind it. Colin has pointedly denied that he sang any 'hymne' or 'morall laie' or 'carol made to praise [his] loued lasse', as Cuddy, who knows how shepherds usually sing, has naturally assumed. Indeed Colin rather insistently excludes any connection between the song and his own emotions:

> Nor of my loue, nor of my losse (quoth he)
> I then did sing, as then occasion fell:

> For loue had me forlorne, forlorne of me,
> That made me in that desart chose to dwell.   (88-91)

The defensiveness is touching—like any poet, he resents people who try to take his songs as personal revelations. But he did sing about love and loss, and since Bregog is for him 'my riuer', some association of loves seems hard to escape. Although Colin didn't know it at the time, the song has point for the Shepherd of the Ocean too, as his own song about his cruel banishment from Cynthia, his 'loue's queene', soon was to make clear (164-171). What is love, that it can be lost and yet kept? How can love both destroy the lover and leave him intact to love forever and describe every painful detail? Or, if these are pretty easy questions for readers of Elizabethan sonnets, then what has the whole business to do with a shepherd-poet going to court and then coming home again disappointed?

Both Colin and the Shepherd of the Ocean sang as banished men, one exiled by disappointed love, one by royal disfavour. Poetry serves each as a consolation for loss, 'each making other mery,/Neither enuying other nor enuied' (77-78). In singing they make up a relation immune to envy and grief in its shared concern with 'love' as subject for art. The old pun on 'feign' and 'fain' is relevant here: to desire someone or something leads to pretending, inventing qualities in the other before they can be determined in fact, inventing a self who cherishes those qualities even though other people see through them, and finally inventing substitutes for the object—false memories, impossible futures—when it is absent or lost. (William Empson's discussion of this pun assumes that Spenser took it for granted.)[3] The point is that for both Spenser and Raleigh, the poet as reluctant recluse and the poet as unemployed soldier-politician, art is a response to banishment and a way, through the 'feigned' re-creation of distant objects of desire, to make banishment endurable or even 'mery'.

But such feigning art remains in tension with the prospect of the Court, the place where art exists not to compensate for loss but to celebrate present gratifications, where the Queen herself is a 'maker':

> Whose grace was great, and bounty most rewardfull.
> Besides her peerless skill in making well

And all the ornaments of wondrous wit,
Such as all womankynd did far excell:
Such as the world admyr'd and praised it:
So what with hope of good, and hate of ill,
He me perswaded forth with him to fare.   (187-193)

Colin's guileless terms, however, recognize that Cynthia is a
maker not only of poems but of *men*; her grace is manifested in
bounty, she rewards good men, good poets, by giving them more
than the pleasure of her wit. In a significant reversal of the pastoral
formula, England, the court world, seems to Colin the seat of
peace and natural delight:

No wayling there nor wretchednesse is heard,
No bloodie issues nor no leprosies,
No griesly famine, nor no raging sweard,
No nightly bodrags, nor no hue and cries;
The shepherds there abroad may safely lie,
On hills and downes, withouten dread or daunger:
No rauenous wolues the good man's hope destroy,
No outlawes fell affray the forest raunger.
There learned arts do florish in great honor,
And Poets wits are had in peerless price.   (312-321)

The enthusiasm is tempered by his discovery that such graces are
more potential than actual, since 'graceless men them greatly do
abuse'; but for him the great good place is the civilized world
thinly disguised as a safer pastoral scene than the rustic, savage
Ireland of his retirement. And Cynthia's qualities are no disappointment. Indeed her perfection is not to be expressed—it is
'vaine' to 'thinke by paragone/Of earthly things, to iudge of
things diuine' (344-345). The poet's feigning art of paragon, or
analogy, treads close to blasphemy when it seeks to manifest her
greatness, and Colin must retire into reverent silence, knowing
that 'More fit it is t'adore with humble mind' such heavenly perfection. It seems impossible for poetry to represent the emotion
such an object evokes.

But the object, Cynthia, is absent when Colin tells his story,
and his renunciation of poetic paragon is itself part of the story,
having the force of any effective rhetorical device, as Alexis says:

> By wondring at thy *Cynthiaes* praise,
> *Colin*, thy selfe thou mak'st vs more to wonder,
> And her vpraising, doest thy selfe vpraise.   (353-355)

That is, he *does* succeed in telling at least something about what
it is like to meet perfection. Although the richness of her presence
made art impossible and pointless, in absence he can say something about it. But there is grave risk in such art, as he remembers
after praising the court-ladies:

> Therefore in closure of a thankfull mynd,
> I deeme it best to hold eternally,
> Their bounteous deeds and noble fauors shrynd,
> Then by discourse them to indignifie.   (580-583)

When he goes on to describe Cynthia beholding 'with high aspiring thought, / The cradle of her owne creation' (612), Cuddy
quickly points out the breach of decorum in moving too easily
and directly from low and homely matter (honey, grapes, sun-
dappled flocks) to ideas of angels and deity itself; this offends not
just technically but morally, profaning images of ultimate virtue.
(Cuddy is rather like Johnson on *Lycidas*.) But Colin is in a hard
situation for a poet:

> True (answered he) but her great excellence,
> Lifts me aboue the measure of my might:
> That being fild with furious insolence,
> I feele my selfe like one yrapt in spright.
> For when I thinke of her, as oft I ought,
> Then want I words to speake it fitly forth:
> And when I speake of her what I haue thought,
> I cannot thinke according to her worth.
> Yet will I thinke of her, yet will I speake,
> So long as life my limbs doth hold together,
> And when as death these vitall bands shall breake,
> Her name recorded I will leaue for euer.
> Her name in euery tree I will endosse,
> That as the trees do grow, her name may grow:
> And in the ground each where it will engrosse,
> And fill with stones, that all men may it know.

The speaking woods and murmuring waters fall,
Her name Ile teach in knowen termes to frame:
And eke my lambs when for their dams they call,
Ile teach to call for *Cynthia* by name.
And long while after I am dead and rotten:
Amongst the shepheards daughters dancing rownd,
My layes made of her shall not be forgotten,
But sung by them with flowry gyrlonds crownd. (620-643)

This magnificent outburst of emotional bravado brings together
most of the ideas that shape the poem. The poet's art is feigning
but his exercise of it is more like literal inspiration, a filling of the
spirit with another spirit; 'insolence' here has its special Spenser-
ian sense of 'exultation' as well as its general Elizabethan sense
of 'pride'—in public, social terms the poet's rapt enthusiasm
looks like disrespect for its object, but such 'insolence' is really
love, an overflowing of feeling that no social or literary decorum
should presume to measure or condemn. His rapture *works*, too,
as the other shepherds—'moov'd at his speech, so feelingly he
spake'—show by their astonished silence. But even in his enthusiasm the poet is doomed to a consciousness of failure; when he
thinks of her he lacks words, and when he speaks his words distort his thought. Thus his determination to go on thinking and
speaking of her anyway—to make Nature itself be the language
of praise his own words can't become—has some heroic force,
and we are persuaded of the strength of his Platonic devotion by
seeing it survive a fully grasped image of physical corruption—
'after I am dead and rotten'. Words like 'leisurely' and 'decorative' leave something unsaid about Spenser's art, after all.

The natural and difficult question follows. If Cynthia and her
court were so unspeakably magnificent, Thestylis asks,

Why didst thou euer leaue that happie place,
In which such wealth might vnto thee accrew? (654-655)

Though Colin first replies that he didn't *dare* put his country
mind to 'such vnknowen wayes' as he found usual at court, it is
clear that much moral distaste was involved. Court life is selfishly
competitive; success there depends on guile and slander, a kind of
artfulness that makes mockery of true art and knowledge; men

are judged by their clothes and conversational skill, their styles of
outward show and not their inner qualities and talents. But Colin
saves his strongest scorn for a somewhat less stereotyped court
failing; when Corylas asks if love is known at court—he had supposed it only a country diversion—Colin replies ferociously:

> Not so (quoth he) loue most aboundeth there,
> For all the walls and windows there are writ,
> All full of loue, and loue, and loue my deare,
> And all their talke and study is of it.
> Ne any there doth braue or valiant seeme,
> Vnlesse that some gay Mistresse badge he beares:
> Ne any one himselfe doth ought esteeme,
> Vnlesse he swim in loue vp to the eares.   (775-782)

This would be just a little puritanical for the author of *Amoretti*,
and I can only imagine that Spenser found Colin's sternness
almost as amusing as the amatory pageantry that so outrages him.
The courtiers offend by 'prophaning' Cupid's 'mightie mysteries'
(788), treating love as a social form instead of private devotion,
and Colin doesn't disclaim the role of love's 'priest' which Cuddy
half-teasingly ascribes to him. Indeed, as the poem ends he rather
pontifically rebukes the shepherds for their light talk about his
own mysterious love, the scornful Rosalind, and his final praise
of her, like his earlier praise of Cynthia, dwells on her 'sacred'
remoteness from ordinary people and their ordinary feelings:

> For she is not like as the other crew
> Of Shepheards daughters which emongst you bee,
> But of diuine regard and heauenly hew,
> Excelling all that euer ye did see.
> Not then to her that scorned thing so base,
> But to my selfe the blame that lookt so hie:
> So hie her thoughts as she her selfe haue place,
> And loath each lowly thing with loftie eie.
> Yet so much grace let her vouchsafe to grant
> To simple swaine, sith her I may not loue:
> Yet that I may her honour paravant,
> And praise her worth, though far my wit aboue.
> Such grace shall be some guerdon for the griefe,

And long affliction which I haue endured:
Such grace sometimes shall giue me some reliefe,
And ease of paine which cannot be recured.
And ye my fellow shepheards which do see
And heare the languours of my too long dying,
Vnto the world for euer witnesse bee,
That hers I die, nought to the world denying,
This simple trophe of her great conquest.   (931-951)

Her resemblance to Cynthia is no accident. Colin has the same
sense that she's above him and beyond his poetic powers, that his
devotion nevertheless compels him to praise her perfection even
at the risk of profaning it and with the certain consequence of in-
tensifying his own misery, and that by permitting his praise she
confers on him a 'grace' that makes his hopeless pain somehow
worthwhile. His final words thus define a structure of parallels
in the poem. The poet at court learns his own inadequacy, the
unbridgeable gap between the capacities of his art and the supra-
verbal perfection of its royal object; and this inadequacy is mirrored by his hopeless devotion to Rosalind, whose indifference to
his love, like the Queen's indifference to his poetry, signifies not
blamable human neglect but the necessary disjunction between
'low' talents and 'high' existences that characterizes the state of
things, from the divine through the political and social down to
the amatory. Colin finds what you would expect Spenser to want
him to find, that a world governed by hierarchy and 'degree'—
for all one's determination to believe it a good world—is a hard one
for humble, low-born talent to make its way in.

The Bregog-Mulla story foreshadows this meaning. Like Colin
(and Spenser) Bregog conceived a desire that sought gratification
in possessing its object. The 'hope of good' which Colin took to
court included the hope of substantial profit from the Queen's
'bounty most rewardfull', and Thestylis' association of 'that happy
place' with 'wealth' confirms the hope as natural and reasonable.
For Spenser being a poet is not essentially different from being
anyone else at court. Poetry is an accepted and common mode of
'service'—Colin names twelve poets now or recently in Cynthia's
train. The poet aimed frankly at reward and self-advancement;
his craft, like soldiering or administration or personal body-service,

was understood to involve political calculation and to have political consequences. His 'feigning' art is thus not easily distinguished from the 'deceitful wit' and 'fained forgerie' Colin so scornfully condemns in courtly style (693 ff.), nor is it wholly unlike the 'deceitful traine' by which Bregog had his way with Mulla. Desire begins as an imagined relation with an object you haven't yet possessed, and imagined, invented relations are the currency of practical fraud as well as of disinterested art.

Bregog shows the impropriety of deceitfully pursuing what's above your worth, and it is hard not to connect his punishment, loss of 'name', with Colin's failure to make a name for himself at court, not to mention Spenser's bitter fascination with the idea of the anonymous poet, the Immeritó of *The Shepheardes Calender* whose fame even in the early 1590's was less than satisfying, as the first line of *Colin Clouts Come Home Againe* hints: 'The shepheards boy (best knowen by that name)', the name he *gave himself* some twelve years before. Even the introductory letter, with its imposing salutation—'To the Right worthy and noble Knight Sir *Walter Raleigh*, Captaine of her Maiesties Guard, Lord Wardein of the Stanneries, *and Lieutenant of the County of Cornwall*' —dwindling down to the signature 'Yours euer humbly. *Ed. Sp.*', makes its wry point about names.

But if the underground resemblances between Colin and Bregog hint at the presumption and necessary failure of the poet's attempt at service, the inadequacy of his arts to compete with the arts of seasoned courtiers, they also identify an opposing mood in the poem. The pastoral frame brings with it the idea of an art of moral innocence, a skilled simplicity that can look at sophistication without being caught by its ironies and evasions. Colin has a troublesome task, to be sure. He must tell difficult, strange things in simple terms, if the other shepherds are to understand him, and his occasional impatience and condescension show his awareness that he can't hope to tell all he knows. But mostly the issues seem clearer simplified, as when something 'makes better sense' when fancy narrative subtleties are dispensed with. Colin speaks of initially pleasing Cynthia but no more is said of it, and although Elizabeth accepted the dedication of *The Faerie Queene* Spenser's hopes of new preferment came to nothing; but the art that failed at court succeeds at home, in expressing and evaluating the experience of failure. All the conventions in fact *require* failure; we can be sure that Colin would immediately be sceptical about the virtue and talent of a poet who made a big success at court, and such a poet would probably have to invent some failures and disappointments to keep the poems coming out right. The defeat of art is the great subject for the art of a poet with Spenser's scrupulosity about the moral seriousness of his calling. Even Bregog's defeat, with its apparent moral lesson, seems more than a defeat when you reflect that he didn't lose his name, wholly, but still flows as a river and lives in Colin's 'mery lay' and Spenser's poem. Just so, Colin's failures with Cynthia and Rosalind become, in his telling, something more than failures; they become perhaps the most powerful moments in a strong and moving poem, the occasions which demonstrate the fullest resources of feeling in Colin and of poetic art in Spenser.

This suggests a different idea of the poet's relation to public life, one more familiar to us than the idea of him as just another sort of politician. In failure and exile the poet assumes the role of the detached ironist, the satiric mind that mocks the impersonations and insincerities of politics. (Any suspicion that Spenser only needed to get back 'in' for such ironies to dissolve is beside the point; Colin himself clearly has had enough and would not go back, even if he has had to talk himself into this position.) In this view—the normal satiric one, as in Wyatt's 'Mine Own John Poins' and Raleigh's 'The Lie'—the poet stands against the Court, asserting in his deliberately simplistic moral clarity and vigorous plain speech the values that shame the deviousness and obfuscation of public practice.

But *Colin Clout* resists strict generic classifying. The satiric motive is certainly present in Colin's pungent complaints about the Court and its amatory mystique—without them his country simplicity and occasional Puritan intonations would seem wildly out of tune with the eloquent discourses on Platonic love. But for Spenser satire is an inadequate vehicle for the whole of Colin's experience. For all its normal insincerity of style, the Court remains a focus of positive commitments, an expressive synthesis of what was valuable in the national life. It would be naive as well as ungenerous to suppose that only hope of personal gain led Spenser to want to criticize the Court without implicating the

Queen herself. A loyal subject could deplore particular abuses without questioning the great idea of a national order with enlightened monarchy and reformed religion consorting together. Spenser's satire makes no fundamental challenge to the prevailing political actualities; his 'Puritanism' is a tentative dramatic colouring, not revisionary zeal.

The poem pursues an idea of service that depends neither upon personal feeling ('love' or its satiric alternatives) nor upon formalistic routines of 'duty'. Colin's story develops an attitude of 'devotion' that mediates between personality and duty, and here again the tale of Bregog and Mulla has emblematic value. For all his reservations about Bregog's tricky selfishness, Colin feels considerable admiration and affection for him:

> But of my riuer *Bregogs* loue I soong,
> Which to the shiny *Mulla* he did beare,
> And yet doth beare, and euer will, so long
> As water doth within his bancks appeare.   (92-95)

This almost boastful assertion of love's power over time echoes in his later vows of loyalty to Cynthia and Rosalind. What he admires in Bregog is a persistence that transforms personal love into devotion, which differs from love in renouncing all hope of possessing the object in any literal way. Bregog loves forever even though his punishment prevents further enjoyment of Mulla; for him, as for Colin and the Shepherd of the Ocean, disappointment and exile don't disturb steadfastness of faith. Bregog's moral flaws point toward the ironic shadings in Colin's devotion: he praises Cynthia (620 ff.) knowing that he risks the gravest impropriety, and his final pledge of devotion to Rosalind leads him to a confession of unworthiness from which it is only a short step to death, transformation into 'this simple trophe of her great conquest'.

Colin Clouts Come Home Againe is thus a poem about suffering a loss that can be dignified and partly repaired by maintaining devotion to the lost object of desire. Clearly such devotion can be sustained only in the form of art. It is only in Colin's song, and the continuing interest and admiration it expresses, that Bregog's imperfect love for Mulla has serious meaning; it is only Colin's determination, even at the risk of blasphemy, to transform the landscape itself, low as it is, into a song about Cynthia that provides the attitude of devotion that makes his loss of her grace meaningful and bearable; it is his resolve to make his own life a work of art by converting it into emblematic death, becoming a 'trophe' and not a living creature, that measures the completeness of his devotion to the unattainable Rosalind. In each case the irony is clear: devotion requires loss, and perfect devotion is death, as the other shepherds are asked to 'see/And heare the languors of my too long dying'—witness his transformation into an object that in its lack of autonomous life and will perfectly expresses his subservience to Rosalind.

This set of parallel analogies makes an interesting adjustment between politics and art. The artist, the man who can't get along at court in the court's own terms, proves the limitations of those terms by demonstrating the more intense devotion of exiled imagination. But the *objects* of his devotion exist not in the pastoral world of his exile but at court or in some world of romance that other shepherds find puzzling and a little dangerous, as they find Colin's devotion to Rosalind. As the case of Bregog hints, love, like going to court, is venturing beyond your familiar, socially proper sphere; and 'grace', the word for what Colin seeks from Cynthia, is used three times in seven lines (939-945) to name Rosalind's favour to her lover. To abandon hope of finding a role in the operations of power is as painful as abandoning hope in love; and the imagination's triumph over practical desire is, as Colin finally admits, hard to dissociate from a feeling that life itself is gone. The other shepherds may return to their routine, with its saving indifference to what lies beyond the familiar and domestic; but to Colin, the shepherd who knows the cost of domesticity, there seems to be nothing to do but die, if he is to be true to his idea of how art and its public objects are related.

Now the very considerable difficulty of *Colin Clout* is not to be solved by postulating any consistent 'structure' of theme or analogy in the poem. Generically it is a mélange of satire, love-complaint, panegyric, and autobiographical allegory, and I see no way to establish the 'primary' impulse behind it. The notion of a single main subject was less inevitable for the Renaissance poet than it became in the more rationalizing age that followed, and the author of *The Shepheardes Calender* and *The Faerie*

Queene was pretty indifferent to the charms of categorical system.[4] *Colin Clout* is the poetic equivalent of a mind occupied by a variety of matters to which it can't confidently assign priorities. Private love and public ambition are both serious concerns; in *Colin Clout*, to be sure, ambition and its defeat is a particular, recent experience, while love is a generalized recollection of Spenser's passion for the mysterious 'Rosalind' fifteen years in his past, but the point is not that one takes precedence over the other but that each has its independent existence in his mind and that the poem brings them together in almost an experimental way, to see what affinity they may have. Nor does the poem resolve into neat metaphorical order. You can't comfortably say either that the subject is Colin's or Spenser's experience at court and that all matters of 'love' are merely vehicles for ambition and its disappointments, or that personal love is the subject and public experience the metaphorical medium. It's a question not of 'thinking about A in terms of B' but of thinking about both A and B in whatever terms their momentary conjunction may generate.

For Spenser, I think, the conjunction of love and ambition shows that both prove the value of devotion. One learns to understand the Court, the world of power and policy, by investing its central figure of authority with some of the properties of a love-object (it's of course convenient, but not essential, that this figure should be a woman), and one learns to cope with failure at court by associating it with failure in love. Each kind of failure makes available a role of devotion-despite-rejection that feels dignified and imaginatively fruitful. Colin's anticipation of death is symbolically right—devotion is a kind of monumental pose, a rejection of the active pursuit of gratifying ends that life reputedly consists of, a self-justifying passivity that rebukes the aggressions of both politicians and lovers. But Colin Clout, like Tiny Tim, does *not* die. Spenser's choice of a pastoral identity for his poet-self allows a pleasant final touch of back-spin:

> . . . That hers I die, nought to the world denying,
> This simple trophe of her great conquest,
> > So having ended, he from ground did rise,
> And after him vprose eke all the rest:

All loth to part, but that the glooming skies
Warnd them to draw their bleating flocks to rest.

There's no question of literal dying—achieved devotion is enough
like death to make the real thing superfluous. (Even the pseudo-
rhyme *rest-rest* is somehow a little deflating.) Like Bregog, Colin
can go on doing the usual things even while his continuing existence proves the miraculous persistence of the affection that fact
has made hopeless. Having learned about politics from love, one
returns to love with a better grasp of its own paradoxical nature.

It was of course Love that theoretically validated the old metaphor of the state as ordered hierarchy, held together by reciprocal
affections (and consequent duties) between degrees. Calvin and
Hobbes were to preside over the formulation of new metaphors,
ones that assumed not Love but Power as the basis of political
order, and Spenser represents a tradition that, although it remained a pious ideal much longer, was effectively dead as a
practical possibility even as he wrote. But for him it still seemed
natural to locate 'public' experience in a continuum of feeling that
included divine worship and amatory passion as well. England is
very different from Ireland, the Court from the country, and yet
one's response to the Court resembles country experiences like
love, and vice versa. By taking the role of shepherd the poet seeks
a stable identity—responsively 'simple' and yet naturally shrewd
—that can cope with both worlds without ironically cheapening
either.[5] There is a lot of foolishness at court, but Colin can hope
to impress this on the shepherds only if they know folly as a
possibility in their world too. The method unites simple and
sophisticated moods in a pure Empsonian case: courtly imperson-
ation and intrigue are part of the whole human world, knowable
in other terms, and the Court's positive value is personified in
Cynthia-Elizabeth, herself the receptive object of personal love
that has purified itself of acquisitive sensuality. The poem represents such purification, in the miniature-pictorial form of Bregog's transformation and, corresponding to that miniature, the
larger conversion of Colin's frustrated desire for actual service
and reward into a devotion for Cynthia—and for sanctified authority generally—that is endorsed by the 'history' of his love for
Rosalind and *its* purification. And one could enlarge ever further,

so that Spenser's own sense of public failure would seem to be transformed and purified by writing *Colin Clouts Come Home Againe*—so that he too, 'so having ended', could rise and continue the devotion of his great epic task even though it had failed to achieve its practical, acquisitive purpose.

2. The Decline of the Court

For Spenser and most of his contemporaries, the Court was not just the symbolic source and focus of political power, which in any society will seem remote and mysterious to poets and other lay citizens, but also a possible avenue, through service, by which ordinary men might approach the source and take part in its rewarding business. One could *go* to court, supposing some modest advantages of birth, education, and talent; it was a place, occupied by people, and many of those people had reached that place by presenting themselves for use. No doubt you needed some introduction—friendship with a Leicester or a Raleigh was no disadvantage—but a poor boy who made his way on sheer ability through the Merchant Taylors' School and Cambridge could hope for notice in such quarters, and a poet's work would usually recommend him even if he couldn't dedicate his first book to Sir Philip Sidney, as Spenser did *The Shepheardes Calender*. One of the paradoxes of modern popular government is that it has increased the psychological distance between citizens and governors; between the ambitious young public servant and the seats of majesty in Washington or Moscow or Paris stands the intimidatingly impersonal process of competitive examinations and efficiency ratings, the mountainous hierarchy of the civil service, or the fierce initiation and depressing discipline of local politics. (With larger populations, of course, there is also more competition.) But the Court of Tudor and Stuart England seemed, at least from a distance, to present fewer barriers; you could hope to attach yourself to an established patron, share in his ups and downs, in time even move (with talent and energy) toward his own status, as did commoners like Raleigh and the great Burghley himself. And for those whose interest was more disinterested and theoretical, the Court provided a by no means empty symbol of a national order whose basis was still felt to lie in personal relations and loyalties of a quasi-feudal kind. Even the lowly players were nominally Lord Strange's or the Lord Chamberlain's or the Admiral's Men, and practitioners of more gentlemanly arts could anticipate more significant identification with powerful names.

To be sure, the usual mode of relation between poet and Court was satire, the expression of *failed* attempts at service, in effect. But satire implies experience of what it rejects. The poet has been there, teasingly close to success; he has moved through the corridors of power and known the strength of its temptations. Even his satiric scorn claims a knowledgeable relation with its objects, for him not curious and remote human types but hateful reminders of a weakness he has felt in himself and overcome only with difficulty. The satiric object embodies the freedom and licence the satirist's claim to virtue debars him from, and his dealings with the object show him justifying his painful aloofness by inflicting pain upon their enviable moral recklessness. His pride is the sign of his attraction to licence, and his only sure defence against it. But if the satirist most readily finds his relation to the public world in ambivalence about glamour and power, this suggests that communication remains open, that he himself sees his irony as a special case and suspects (shamefully) that he *might* change his tune if things were to work out better for him at court. *Colin Clout* expresses the acceptance of imaginative exile and the discovery that exile may be artistically and morally bracing; it does not, I think, indicate any essential disjunction of poetic imagination, and the 'common life' it speaks for, from the public business of politics and power.

In the seventeenth century this potentially close relation between poet and Court dissolved, as the monarchy itself lost much of its potency as the literal and symbolic centre of national life and power. C. V. Wedgwood's *Poetry and Politics under the Stuarts*[6] instructively outlines the decay of morality and morale in the later reign of Elizabeth and under James I: the corrupt grants of monopolies to courtiers, the sale and resale of the reversion of court offices, James's much resented largesse to his avid fellow Scots, his withdrawal from the Protestant alliances against Spain (especially unpopular because of the national outrage over the Gunpowder Plot), the frustration of popular dreams of glory with the death of the martial Prince Henry, James's failure to support the Protestant revolt in Bohemia led by his own son-in-law, the disastrous failure of the projected marriage of Prince Charles to the Infanta of Spain, the false dawn of popular hopes at the accession of Charles I—these are some of the landmarks in the progressive estrangement of monarchy from the national will that fed the hopes of the dissenting Saints and led to the Civil Wars. Poetic celebrations of English glory found better symbolic matter elsewhere, in the civil perfection of great private families and their domestic styles ('To Penshurst', *Upon Appleton-House*) or the value of native landscapes as political emblems (*Cooper's Hill, Upon St. James's Park*). The monarchy itself lost the capacity to imaginatively appease the antagonism between satire and panegyric as it was appeased in *Colin Clout*, this symbolic potency decreasing in rough proportion to the degree to which James and Charles avoided active roles in the troubled affairs of the continent. Thomas Carew, declining Aurelian Townshend's invitation to write an elegy for the slain Protestant hero Gustavus Adolphus of Sweden, found terms that appreciate peaceful delights even as they raise questions about the dignity of what Miss Wedgwood calls 'the artificially induced legend of the calm and happy 1630's':

> Tourneyes, Masques, Theatres, better become
> Our *Halcyon* dayes; what though the German Drum
> Bellow for freedome and revenge, the noyse
> Concernes not us, nor should divert our joyes;
> Nor ought the thunder of their Carabins
> Drowne the sweet Ayres of our tun'd Violins;
> Beleeve me friend, if their prevailing powers
> Gaine them a calme securitie like ours,
> They'le hang their Armes up on the Olive bough,
> And dance, and revell then, as we doe now.[1]

For Carew, the delights of such a peace are both grounds for self-congratulation and the source of a certain shameful uneasiness—the poem begins with a rueful confession that he *can't* strike the heroic note in such an easy time; we next will consider how a stronger poetic mind assessed the conflicting claims of peaceful order and heroic public action a few years later, when the vacancy at the national centre had been filled by a figure with all the attributes of proper kingship except legitimacy.

3. An Horotian Ode: The Art of Power

The *Horatian Ode* studies the difficult relations between the lawless world of action and the world of imagination in which justice can operate; but Marvell complicates the relation by adding a third term, in the person of the martyred King Charles:

> That thence the Royal Actor born
> The Tragic Scaffold might adorn:
> > While round the armed Bands
> > Did clap their bloody hands.
> He nothing common did or mean
> Upon that memorable Scene:
> > But with his keener Eye
> > The Axes edge did try:
> Nor call'd the Gods with vulgar spight
> To vindicate his helpless Right,
> > But bow'd his comely Head,
> > Down as upon a Bed. (53-64)

The theatricality of it all is the essential thing—treating regicide as a show both intensifies and distances its horrors. Cromwell's soldiers, hatefully oblivious to the tragic meaning, are yet part of the occasion: like any audience, they are complicit in the dramatic event yet not exactly responsible for its happening. The saintly grace and decorum of Charles are not 'personal' qualities so much as signs of successful dramatic performance; his suffering calls neither for mourning nor for vengeance, for his identity as human victim and political sacrifice is framed by dramatic ceremony and estimated by terms (common, mean, vulgar, comely) that judge life as though it were art. For once in his life, Marvell may even be saying, he found an occasion that allowed even so unlikely a talent as his to play King successfully!

But if we know that the stage is only a stage and the actors only actors, still Marvell's tableau, like any tragic art, makes complex demands upon our feelings. Helpless right is still *right*, evidently, and if horror aesthetically distanced becomes a mode of pleasure, it does not do so by losing all relation to horror. (Is 'bow'd' just Charles's gentlemanly acquiescence, or does it—since the applauding hands are already bloody—blur into the slump of the severed head toward the basket?) Every reader sees this moment as a moral crux, a teasing challenge to find out just where Marvell's sympathies lay. How can a poem so ready to admire a public man's qualities dwell so intently on their dreadful source?

I think it best to begin by considering Cromwell not as historical personage but as literary agent, a figure Marvell invents out of traditional heroic materials and whose relation to the real Lord Protector may for a time be left undetermined. Like any epic figure, Cromwell is seen as a man in whom natural force is vividly concentrated:

> So restless Cromwel could not cease
> In the inglorious Arts of Peace,
>> But through adventrous War
>> Urged his active Star.
> And, like the three-fork'd Lightning, first
> Breaking the Clouds where it was nurst,
>> Did thorough his own Side
>> His fiery way divide.
> For 'tis all one to Courage high
> The Emulous or Enemy;
>> And with such to enclose
>> Is more than to oppose.
> Then burning through the Air he went,
> And Pallaces and Temples rent:
>> And Caesars head at last
>> Did through his Laurels blast.
> 'Tis Madness to resist or blame
> The force of angry Heavens flame. . . .   (9-26)

This is a notable withholding of judgment. As hero, Cromwell seems as mysteriously irrelevant to ordinary values as Achilles or Tamburlaine. The repeated action is going 'through' something, and Cromwell is quite indifferent to the medium he operates in. He makes no distinction between friends and foes: his fire scorches his own companions, to be on his side is not to feel an ennobling intimacy with greatness but to risk getting trampled. His action is pure impulse, so pure that it may not even be his own impulse—Marvell allows the possibility that he may really embody a force whose origin is supernatural, and the simile of lightning is felt as something like *identity* by the time the climatic 'blast' strikes.

Here, that is to say, Marvell can't quite sanction a view of the forceful public man which would subject him to the ironies that so clearly govern his victims and his audience, a process whose workings have the shape and feel of moral justice, as Simone Weil argues:

> They do not see that the force in their possession is only a limited quantity; nor do they see their relations with other human beings as a kind of balance between unequal amounts of force. Since other people do not impose on their movements that halt, that interval of hesitation, wherein lies all our consideration for our brothers in humanity, they conclude that destiny has given complete licence to them, and none at all to their inferiors. And at this point they exceed the measure of the force that is actually at their disposal. . . . And now we see them committed irretrievably to chance; suddenly things cease to obey them. . . . Gone is the armor of power that formerly protected their naked souls; nothing, no shield, stands between them and tears.

Simone Weil here states the issues a man like Cromwell poses, but in terms that measure the resistance to irony of Marvell's 'Lightning' figure. To speak of Cromwell's 'relations with other human beings' would concede him a fellowship in humanity Marvell for the moment refuses to assume: he may *not* be just a man. To say that forceful men 'do not see' the limits of their force implies that someone else does see them, and it's just this assumption of the superior vision of inactive philosophical detachment that Marvell here finds hard to make (though he will see Cromwell 'committed irretrievably to chance' at the end of the poem). Even to think for a moment that Cromwell had a 'naked soul' or that he could weep tears would hopelessly sentimentalize the case. The arts of peace *are* 'inglorious' if 'glory' bears its traditional epic meanings. Only the superstitious suppose that lightning strikes temples and palaces deliberately, and even they would think such devastation meant the institutions were corrupt and needed purging. The inclination to call secular insurrection 'unnatural', and thus to resist or blame Cromwell, *is* madness—even if it were right to think Caesar equal in value to 'angry heaven', would it be *possible* to support his cause? One's awe at the lightning blasting Caesar through his laurels is morally neutral: not the lightning itself, but what (if anything) aimed it, invites speculation.

Marvell, in short, uses heroic perspectives upon Cromwell—perspectives that weren't mere poetic fancies but established commonplaces of the popular imagination—to make it harder to subject him to the moral irony that seeks out human limitations inside the impressive public performance. But of course the ironic impulse remains active in the *Ode*, in the questioning reservations that keep intruding upon the poet's panegyric performance. That it *is* a poet speaking is made clear at the start:

> The forward Youth that would appear
> Must now forsake his Muses dear,
> > Nor in the Shadows sing
> > His Numbers languishing.
> 'Tis time to leave the Books in dust,
> And oyl th'unused Armours rust:
> > Removing from the Wall
> > The Corslet of the Hall.
> So restless Cromwel could not cease
> In the inglorious Arts of Peace. . . .   (1-10)

A conventional alternative to action is poetry, emblem of retirement, contemplation, the arts of peace. But if Marvell's tone is rueful, his view of creative retirement is less than simple. In peacetime, poetry is a medium for ambition (as Spenser knew) just as soldiering is in time of war; to Marvell's contemporaries 'forward' would have suggested aggressive, immodest presumption as well as eager readiness, and the youth who seeks to 'appear' by means of his writing may be no more disinterested than the ambitious public man. Cromwell, indeed, in 'his private Gardens, where/He liv'd reserved and austere,/As if his highest plot/To plant the Bergamot', could fairly claim greater dignity for his kind of retirement, which at least doesn't *seem* self-serving. The poet is not exactly a perfect contrast to the man of force, though he might like to think he is. His armour, after all, is close at hand, ready to be oiled and worn, and war may serve his forwardness as readily as peace.

Marvell both associates himself with the youthful poet and distances himself from him in a way that resembles his treatment of Cromwell. He often speaks in the *Ode* as if he were not a poet but a practical public man, whose vocabulary can't tolerate the terms of high ethical detachment:

> Though Justice against Fate complain,
> And plead the ancient Rights in vain:
>> But those do hold or break
>> As men are strong or weak. (37–40)

An element of parody has to be allowed for here—'this is how we talk now, and alas we're right to do so'—but the degree of irony is hard to estimate. Can the poet, the contemplative moralist, authoritatively plead the cause of Justice when he recognizes his own fascination with forceful action, the fascination that led him to write the poem in the first place? Cromwell, confusingly enough, is not just Simone Weil's man of force without reason or reflection but a man in whom action and rational awareness support one another:

> What Field of all the Civil Wars,
> Where his were not the deepest Scars?
>> And Hampton shows what part
>> He had of wiser Art.
> Where, twining subtile fears with hope,
> He wove a Net of such a scope,
>> That Charles himself might chase
>> To Caresbrooks narrow case. (45–52)

'Art' is the term that links Cromwell's force to its apparent contrast in the poet's world, those 'Arts of peace' that war has seemingly rejected. Cromwell, who 'does both act and know' (76), brings to war and politics some of the creative intelligence that directs poetry and gardening. If he is a heroic figure, to be celebrated in images of lightning, falcons, and huntsmen, the marvellous concentration and efficiency of his destructive power is not to be neutralized by any of the easy jokes intellectuals like to make about athletes or soldiers.

The poet, then, finds the conventional idea of his own role an inadequate basis for coming to terms with Cromwell. As the alternate rhythms of the 'Horatian' form suggest in miniature, the poem incorporates opposing views in a way that suggests both judiciousness and the inner hesitancies that a judicious manner sometimes masks. Cromwell's freedom from weakness and self-doubt may be disturbing, but there is no invitation to hug ourselves in our happy 'human' preference for our own disorderly, inept lives. If Cromwell ruins the great work of time, we can't just condemn him—he's creating a new and 'happy Fate' (72), exercising curative powers as 'clymacterick' to unhealthy 'States not free' (104). To oppose him is to ally yourself with the old, the primitive, the outworn, to 'shrink underneath the Plad' with the poor bewildered Pict (105-108). Cromwell brings creative order, and if that is always the cry of the Commissar, he does live up to it as he casts 'the Kingdome old/Into another Mold' (35-36), tames the wild Irish (74), and hunts down the 'Caledonian Deer' (112) like any anointed King. If he has murdered Caesar, he himself will become 'A Caesar . . . ere long to Gaul' (111), as Nature (and Law) 'make[s] room/Where greater Spirits come' (43-44).

This is to say about as much as one can for a totalitarian hero. But if Cromwell's creative force rather shames the 'Numbers languishing' of the effete young poet in his shadowy retirement, still the poet of the *Ode* is far from indifferent to the dignity of old orders or unaware of the ironies of power. Caesar and Hannibal (101-102) recall frustration and inglorious death even as they remind us of public triumphs, and the anticipation of Cromwell's future victories (97-112), with its dazzling comic wit, poises patriotic fervour on the brink of absurdity. The drama of Charles on the scaffold lingers in the mind—Marvell twice calls it 'memorable'—and from its place in the precise middle of the poem pulls everything else toward its sobering timelessness. If the execution is theatrical art, then Cromwell is the playwright: 'And Hampton shows what part/He had of wiser Art.' Charles is the Royal Actor because Cromwell has cast him in that part; his comely dignity is his own interpretation of the role, but his human freedom has been forced into the confinement of being a fictional figure, one whose function is to die, nothing more. The quality that makes Cromwell more than the unknowing creature of our ironic sense—the conscious 'artistry' he interposes between himself and the world his power affects—is also the quality that most sharply focusses our uneasiness about him. He reminds us, I think, of a radical impurity in art itself, the possibility that even the most disinterested exercise of imagination may reflect a desire to impose one's mind on a world that (for all one can know) might have got along very well as it was in the first place. It is obviously wrong to decapitate a king for the sake of an effective denouement; once you discern an analogy between politics and art, you may learn something troublesome about art itself.

At any rate, the affinity between art and political power provides a curious tone for the poem's conclusion:

> But thou the Wars and Fortunes Son
> March indefatigably on;
> > And for the last effect
> > Still keep thy Sword erect:
> Besides the force it has to fright
> The Spirits of the shady Night,
> > The same Arts that did gain
> > A Pow'r must it maintain.

This seems both a loyal hurrah and an oddly menacing warning, centred on the ambiguity of 'Arts'. Cromwell, who gained power by artistic inventions like 'The Tragedy of Charles I', has involved his own fate in a Hawthornian artistry of the actual. He has become the leading character in his own life drama, and he must get his gestures right if he is to make a successful 'effect' as The Hero. It is the poet who, having captured him in his own art, now pipes the tune and runs the show. Art, having become public action, reverts to art of another, sterner sort; the pastoral shadows of the young poet's retirement darken into 'shady Night', and Cromwell will never get back to his own place of innocent repose, those private gardens whose 'plots' have nothing to do with either politics or dramaturgy.

But this concluding irony is less than a full resolution. The poet, after all, here does to Cromwell what he has shown Cromwell doing to Charles, fixing him in a role that denies him his

human freedom. The forward youth, though a poet, was singu-
larly ready for war—arms were at hand in his retirement, and he
is an analogue of Cromwell despite Cromwell's not having been
a literary sort. The poet himself is a kind of proto-Cromwell, and
the poet of the *Ode* is implicated in both their cases: his art is
action too. Indeed, art and action are something like variants of
the same impulse, with similar effects upon their objects. Each
turns life into literal or figurative death by depriving living beings
of their freedom. Cromwell's plot for Charles, Marvell's 'plot' for
Cromwell—both politics and art turn people into objects. But of
course they may differ radically in intentions and means, in the
qualities of mind and feeling required for their best practice. Here
the matter of 'style' must be considered.

Marvell's style is habitually equivocal; 'metaphysical' and
'Augustan' characteristics combine, as in Cleveland and Waller
though at a higher level, in modes of 'wit' that are moving from
intellectual analysis toward facetiousness and satiric looseness.[8]
The verse form and overall decorum of tone in the *Ode* substan-
tiate the invocation of Horace, but the Augustan manner is inter-
spersed with metaphysical moments, where the main effect comes
less from the movement of a poetic argument than from essentially stationary conceits that detain the mind momentarily while
a richer range of associations is drawn in. The portrait of Cromwell in retirement is such a moment of arrested progression:

> And, if we would speak true,
> Much to the Man is due.
> Who, from his private Gardens, where
> He liv'd reserved and austere,
> As if his highest plot
> To plant the Bergamot,
> Could by industrious Valour climbe
> To ruine the great Work of Time,
> And cast the Kingdome old
> Into another Mold. (27-36)

For all the elaborate subordination, with its air of careful and
circumstantial reasoning, the lines add little to the argumentative
movement of the poem once it is established that Cromwell is a
man as well as a heroic figure. The phrase 'reserved and austere'

forbids any very intense response to the humanity claimed for him; like the forward Youth, he has been called from arts of peace to arts of public action, and if he is not wholly an instrument of nature and fate, still his human independence from his public role has been severely limited by the analogy of 'Lightning' just before. The passage is a pause in the poem, indeed a reversal of its progress from present to future, and it draws considerably on the witty possibilities of relation between the idea of gardening and words like 'plot' and 'Mold'. To cast the kingdom into a new mould is not only to melt it down and give it another form but also to sow it, as seed, in a different soil, from which new and altered growth might spring.

It is even possible, if remotely so, that Marvell, whose other early poems show him to have known a lot about both words and horticulture, may have known that the 'Bergamot' of his day derived its name from a corruption of the Turkish *beg-armūdi* or 'prince's pear' (*OED* 1616), a derivation literally preserved in the German word for the fruit, *Fürstenbirne*. (The more familiar bergamot, *Citrus bergamia*, does not seem to have been mentioned in England until the 1690's.) If one imagines that he did know it, the wit expands—in his garden state, Cromwell seemed as if he were up to no serious plotting, but he was planting a royal fruit whose growth would parallel his own 'climbe' to what even in 1650 would have looked like becoming a new form of princeliness or kingship. At any rate, we see that something unlikely grows in that garden, where a country gentleman unrelated to royal seed turns into a kind of climbing plant that ruins great works of the past, like ivy destroying the stones it grows upon.

These witty interconnections bend the portrait of Cromwell as private man to serve Marvell's difficult, still tentative response to his present political arts. 'Industrious Valour' further complicates the effect. 'Industry' was a duplicitous word in the seventeenth century; both the approving sense of 'intelligent skill' and a more hostile sense of 'rich in crafty devices and expedients' come into play here, presumably with further complication by a third meaning, 'trade or manufacture',[9] not an assessment of mind but a measured social placement of a man whose 'climbe' is from the tradesman's humility to the level of his betters. If it is true that the manuscript of the *Ode* circulated among Royalists and not

Puritans,[10] then Marvell's first readers would happily have thought of the underground libels about Cromwell's petit-bourgeois antecedents:

> ... A Brewer may be a Parliament-man
> For so his knavery first began;
> And make the most cunning plots he can;
>> *Which nobody can deny.*
> A Brewer may be so bold a Hector
> That when he has drunk a cup of Nectar,
> He may become a Lord Protector;
>> *Which nobody can deny....*[11]

It would be absurd to suppose that Marvell's sense of Cromwell allowed more than a glance at such nervous snobbery or at any sense of 'industrious' that left him a figure of upper-class fun. But 'industrious Valour' is obviously not the impetuous, spontaneous valour of the epic hero—climbing is a slower, more deliberate motion than rushing into battle—and this passage points back to the 'lightning' figure with a qualifying force that is 'witty' in T. S. Eliot's sense, in that it involves 'a recognition, implicit in the expression of every experience, of other kinds of experience which are possible'.[12] Cromwell's industry is all the more impressive if you recognize—and then *reject*—the trivial joke that could be made about it by the wrong kind of mind, whose politics are so rigid and vulgarly intense as to make scurrility the only weapon against an enemy who has defeated you on every honest ground.

The *Horatian Ode*, it hardly needs saying, comes out of the *right* sort of mind, one whose decency and fairness will not tolerate even veiled partisan polemic. Modern commentaries seem to me to have often asked the wrong questions, as in the interesting controversy between Cleanth Brooks and Douglas Bush some years ago.[13] Brooks, while insisting that the *Ode* is a poem—it 'is diagnostic rather than remedial, and eventuates, not in a course of action, but in contemplation'—took some trouble to argue a Royalist bias in Marvell around 1650; it is hard not to smell partisanship here, and Bush tried to right the balance by claiming that the poem is if anything a defence of Cromwell and the Puritan side. But to try, however subtly, to locate the poem somewhere along a scale whose limits are acceptance or rejection of Cromwell's cause strikes me as confusing. This is the wrong question because, in accepting the problem about Cromwell as a public problem, it implies that Marvell's job was to adjudicate between adversary causes that are both essentially political, views that could be weighed in a law-court or a parliamentary debate or a history book. On the contrary, the problem is an imaginative one that can adequately be considered only in a poem. Nor is such a poem best described by a word like 'contemplation', which suggests more detachment and serenity than Marvell shows. The *Ode* is not a point of intellectual repose in the middle of conflicting demands; rather it expresses those demands in all their compelling urgency, in a poem that feels difficult and even unstable rather than secure and contemplative.

Expression transforms the thing expressed, and I should want to describe the drama of the *Ode* in other terms. A poet, a man whose *ordinary* role is contemplative judgment, becomes aware of a public figure whose powers seem mysteriously too large for such contemplation to assess. (The poet is also a political man, like most men, but his response to Cromwell is too intense for politics—Marvell's Royalist sympathies, such as they may have been, will get him nowhere with this problem.) It looks for a time as if poetry will have to give way, as if the only way to live in the same world with Cromwell is to abandon the imagination and join or oppose him in arms. But this the poet doesn't do; rather he goes ahead and writes a poem anyway. He finds, easily enough, that poetry has already established a way of talking about men of great power, the 'heroic' mode which holds in suspension our awe at greatness and our reluctance to accept it at face value. To speak of Cromwell as a bolt of lightning both dramatizes his force and underlines its mysteriousness; as he is unnatural and natural at the same time, our inclination to deplore destructive violence requires us to withhold full endorsement from someone we yet recognize to be greater and more venerable than ourselves. The issue is not whether Cromwell is admirable or horrible—he's of course both—but whether one can bear to think about his mixed value without either simplifying his nature or throwing up one's hands at the whole spectacle of power in action. The interesting strain is not between alternative political judgments but between politics (the whole works) and no politics at all. The poet must neither imitate and echo public voices nor refuse entirely to hear them; rather he must find an art, a 'language' that will both admit power into his own world and resist its tendency to transform his world into just another arena of power.

It is such a language that I find achieved by Marvell's play with kinds of 'art'. So long as Cromwell is a bolt of lightning he is no real threat to the poet, who has only a minimal concern for the objects and institutions it is shown destroying and who has the epic tradition to sustain his interested distance from the force he describes. He is The Poet, and Cromwell is The Hero, and action and contemplation can remain securely in their places. But for Marvell this solution is incomplete. 'And, if we would speak true,/Much to the Man is due' shifts attention from epic methods to 'personal' evaluation by admitting that it's hard to tell the whole truth about such a man with a mere epic simile. The truth or falsehood of metaphor was of course a complicated question in the seventeenth century; here it's enough to say that Marvell shows a suitable scepticism about the first terms he tries out on Cromwell. Another language, which tries to fit Cromwell's public effects to his private humanity, may work better; in fact it leads the poet to his key trope of 'art', as my reading of the 'industrious Valour' lines tries to show. But only in the scenic treatment of Charles's execution does the poem find the language it needs, one that can 'frame' the issues of politics and force without obscuring their human references. In the poet's imagination the scene remains 'memorable', not because the issues it represents remain alive, as issues, to the political passion but because it is the nature of the imagination to preserve images, to keep significant moments of human history symbolically present and available for the operations of justice. The 'drama' of the scene is finally not the clash of real political cases but the difficult, athletic effort of the poet to keep his mind attentive and sympathetic to *all* the possible significances of the public occasion.

If the mode of the poem is 'contemplative', it at least doesn't treat its subject from a moral distance but rather absorbs into its own poetic workings the troublesome sense of injustice that any public 'practice' imposes on private needs and desires. Marvell's art is an exercise of force like any art, but the style of the *Ode*, in its reliance on equivocation, incomplete definition, suspension of final judgments, seems an effort to withhold the full force of art by keeping it tentative and hovering, always open to further revision. Cromwell's art is *final*, as Charles fatally learned and as Cromwell himself may be about to find out at the end of the poem; it may not be possible to say that abolishing history and killing a king is either 'right' or 'wrong' in given circumstances, but it is certain that the regicide achieves perfect and unescapable self-definition, the achievement of a role he can never lay aside. By killing Charles, Cromwell invented his own fate, whatever it was finally to be; this may give disapproving onlookers some moral satisfaction, but it is also the perfection of the heroic role, the great man's desire to control his own life and create his own destiny rather than remain a pawn of events, as ordinary men must do.

At any rate, having in a sense mastered Cromwell by circumscribing his force within the imaginative force of the poem, the poet finds that as a result he can no longer presume to sit in judgment upon him. If Cromwell has invented his own heroic identity and fate, still the poem has co-operated with him by making this achievement known, clarifying and fixing it once and for all. Marvell's treatment of Cromwell's past and future conquests (73-120) seems almost jaunty in a way that can't quite be accounted for by thinking of the Englishman's amused contempt for Irishmen, Scots, and other foreigners; Cromwell has achieved heroic status, but this is oddly domesticated by images of him paying 'rents' to the nation like any mere tenant and hunting like an obedient falcon for the benefit of his masters. In part, I suppose, this tone makes practical concessions to the political realities —if you have a hero around the house, you can only pretend he's *your* hero and hope he'll go along with the game. But I think it also shows the poet's achievement of a more significant relation with Cromwell. If the soldier-politician's force and the poet's art resemble each other, the poet may safely approach his counterpart with a less cautious respect than one pays to greatness in the real world; if Cromwell has become a creature of the poet's imagination, it is the nature of imagination to treat its creatures with fanciful playfulness. The suggestion is of a curious intimacy, a sense almost of affectionate complicity which (as in Norman

Mailer's writings about John Kennedy) would be horrendously unsuitable for dealing with Cromwell the public man.

Thus the note of warning or threat in the concluding lines may need a final qualification. Marvell allows some rather dark ideas about the fate of force to hover about the heroic figure of Cromwell marching into an indeterminate future of violence and danger, but these ideas, in my reading, bear as much upon 'arts' as upon forceful public action. To initiate such art commits you to it forever—the man of force can never break his staff and drown his books. But if this is a grim joke on Cromwell, it also reflects upon the poet himself, who after all created the image and assigned Cromwell to it. The Cromwell who can never put down his sword is more a fiction of this poem than he is the real Oliver Cromwell, who in fact did stop fighting and died peacefully at home in Whitehall, as Marvell must have known he might do. To have its full force the image must stay inside the poem, keeping the *imagined* Cromwell subjected to the art that has led him to this 'last effect'. But of course the poet does have such power and will 'maintain' it—the poem ends here, it is finished in a way that Cromwell's art of power can never be, and nothing now can interfere with its achieved wholeness. What needed to be said about Cromwell has been said, the language has been found; the poet has imagined a mood which he and Cromwell can inhabit together, where their arts reflect and comment on one another not as antagonists but as (suspicious) accomplices. As the beginning of the *Horatian Ode* hinted, the poet copes with the man of power by in effect *becoming* him, or by making him become an artist himself but one whose medium is a more difficult one where last effects are harder to come by.

The case of Cromwell suggests that public authority is less available to private imagination when its claims to religious and legal sanction are withdrawn. For Spenser, the anointed monarch, with all her imposing difference from ordinary men and ordinary language, is yet approachable through terms drawn from the experience of human love, just as (even more paradoxically) God is. Cromwell was not long ago an ordinary man puttering in his garden, and it might seem that knowing this should help Marvell to come to terms with him, either by satirically remembering that there's still just an ordinary mortal body inside the heroic new clothes or by admiring him for having come so far from such a modest origin. Marvell actually does neither. Cromwell is a public fact, and his personal history is almost irrelevant to his present meaning. The *Ode* is remarkable for its refusal to speculate about motives—if anything, it treats such speculation as a kind of joke, since we will approve or disapprove of Cromwell largely according to how his actions bear on our own momentary interests and concerns. When we think of Charles and the virtues of tradition and political continuity, we will feel troubled and hostile; when we think of national glory and our own self-interest we will probably be enthusiastic about the new order and its leader. In neither case are we really thinking about *Cromwell*, and if we tried to do so we would face a profound mystery. For Marvell, I should say, politics seemed in a distinctly modern way remote indeed from common understanding and judgment. The *Ode* investigates the essence of power and reports back to us that it's humiliatingly unlike anything we're prepared to deal with. Where Spenser's static method of analogical parallels implies a public world you may (with luck) be able to find your place in, Marvell's dynamic method of unresolved alternatives implies a public world you must continually *create* through acts of political imagination or through literal force like Cromwell's own.

Marvell the man would live out the Commonwealth as a relatively minor functionary in the new regime, writing poems about gardens and other places of contemplative disengagement from politics, surviving eighteen years into the reign of Charles II as a conscientious M.P. and heavy-handed satirist. One can imagine that he thought the great poetry of the 1640's and '50's only an episode in his life, public service an adequate justification for existing. (We may find him a greater enigma than he found Cromwell.) But the *Horatian Ode*, his definitive statement about the relation of art and politics, expresses the strongest kind of belief that neither artistic detachment nor political engagement is for ordinary men an adequate response to a world in trouble. One must not turn away from Cromwell and what he represents, preferring some pastoral seclusion with the languishing numbers of idle, insulated art; nor should one 'take a stand' by enlisting with

Cromwell or his enemies in yet another war of half-truths. This seems to suggest impasse, stalemate, paralysis of will; but though the *Ode* has been read as a perfect achievement of non-committal poise, the quintessence of Trimming, I prefer to see its equities as signs of continuing imaginative action, the adjusting of conflicting motives and energies that politics endlessly requires, a dramatic miniature of the open mind with which anyone is well advised to approach the public world. The *Horatian Ode* is a poem about how public action resists final moral categorization; it represents a man trying to make up his mind and finding that the impossibility of doing so, conclusively, makes *having* a mind all the more imperative and exciting.

NOTES

[1] Walzer, *Revolution of the Saints*, p. 12.

[2] W. L. Renwick (ed.), *Daphnaïda and Other Poems* (London, Scholartis Press, 1929), p. 184.

[3] William Empson, *Some Versions of Pastoral*, 2nd ed. (London, Chatto & Windus, and Norfolk, Conn., New Directions, 1950), pp. 137-138.

[4] For a convincing denial that *The Faerie Queene* has 'fictional consistency of the sort usually ascribed to it, see Paul J. Alpers, *The Poetry of The Faerie Queene* (Princeton, Princeton University Press, 1967, and London, Oxford University Press, 1968).

[5] Like everyone else, I owe most of what I understand about the politics of 'simple' and 'sophisticated' to Empson's *Some Versions of Pastoral*, which more and more seems the great book of modern criticism.

[6] C. V. Wedgwood, *Poetry and Politics Under the Stuarts* (Cambridge, Cambridge University Press, 1960), pp. 1-33.

[7] Quoted by both Miss Wedgwood (*Poetry and Politics Under the Stuarts*, pp. 44-45) and Walzer (*Revolution of the Saints*, p. 240), neither of whom notes the irony that seems to me implicit.

[8] See George Williamson, *The Proper Wit of Poetry* (Chicago, University of Chicago Press, and London, Faber & Faber, 1961), pp. 97-107.

[9] Raymond Williams, *Culture and Society, 1780-1950* (London, Chatto & Windus, 1958), pp. xiii-xiv, says that 'industry' became a collective word for manufacturing and productive institutions only in the late eighteenth century; certainly the word 'industrial' emerged then to name what was not implied by the older 'industrious', and Williams is no doubt right about 'industry' acquiring new *collective* meanings, but the *OED* gives 'industry' as 'a trade or manufacture' as early as 1566.

[10] Cleanth Brooks suggests this in *English Institute Essays 1946* (New York, Columbia University Press, 1947), p. 129. For discussions of the political context of the *Ode*, see Harold E. Toliver, *Marvell's Ironic Vision* (New Haven, Yale University Press, 1965), pp. 178-203, and John M. Wallace, *Destiny His Choice: The Loyalism of Andrew Marvell* (Cambridge, Cambridge University Press, 1968), pp. 69-105.

[11] 'The Brewer', *Wit and Drollery, Jovial Poems*, 2nd ed. (London, 1661).

[12] T. S. Eliot, 'Andrew Marvell': *Selected Essays 1917-1932* (London, Faber & Faber, and New York, Harcourt, Brace, 1932), p. 262.

[13] See Brooks, *English Institute Essays 1946*, pp. 127-158; Douglas Bush, 'Marvell's "Horatian Ode"', *Sewanee Review*, LX (1952), 363-376; Cleanth Brooks, 'A Note on the Limits of "History" and the Limits of "Criticism"', *Sewanee Review*, LXI (1953), 129-135. My dissent to some of Brooks's terms should not conceal the fact that his essay established the critical issues I am concerned with.

CHAPTER THREE

From Satire to Solitude

Colin Clouts Come Home Againe and the *Horatian Ode* are poems in the panegyric mood. Their aim is to praise public virtues and accomplishments, and there is some generosity in such a motive. Even at its best, the public world may not seem to deserve the praise of contemplative mind, which may risk being compromised or contaminated by such praising. For all their honest humility, Colin Clout and Marvell's troubled political spectator speak from the assumption that thought is different from action and essentially more dignified, so that for it to concede some value to material action demonstrates its own superior powers of disinterested perception and analysis. The poet conceives of himself as the locus of thought or spirit that is disjunct from material extension, the realm of action where physical force and its political equivalents operate. But in these poems spirit can't wholly sustain the belief in its own purity, its essential distinction from matter; the Cartesian situation (if I may be allowed the whimsey) comes into conflict with what might be called the Hobbesian situation. Here spirit and extension, imagination and action, are not separate realms, as spirit wants to assume, but versions of a single universal state; thought is material motion, imagination 'decaying sense', and the private creative mind is indivisibly part of the public matter it is so prone to condemn. The drama of such poems could thus be schematized as a debate between a comforting dualism and a materialistic monism that would deny mind such a consoling idea of itself.

'Cartesian' and 'Hobbesian' are here of course idle fancies, without historical ambitions. But they may at least suggest that for Tudor and Stuart poets the vogue of panegyric verse was something less than a surrender of imagination to public force; men like Spenser and Marvell praised political power and its achievements not because they felt inferior to it but because they believed strongly enough in art to be able to afford praise. Their

83

poems could consort with men of action on something like equal grounds. But this situation did not persist for long. None of the poems I discuss hereafter originates in panegyric; rather than assuming that one's first response to the public world is a desire to praise it, the best any of them can do is to cultivate impartiality, and most of them frankly begin in hostility and contempt for politics and power, the impulse not to revere 'greatness' but to expose it as a sham. It's hard to think of a serious poet of the last 300 years who found much to admire in the political life of his day. Historical Hobbesianism, the cultivation of hard, practical *Realpolitik*, found its antagonistic counterpart in what I am calling the metaphorical Hobbesianism of poets who, unable to assume that their imaginations were immune to the contamination of matter and action, accepted the condition and used poetry more or less openly to resist the abuses and excesses of political reality. The first and most open form of this resistance is of course satire.

Now satire is notoriously hard to define, being in history and temperament a kind of anti-genre, a catch-all mode where nearly anything goes. The best modern critical practice has emphasized the 'positive' elements of the satirist's outlook and intentions, justifying his bad manners, his violence, his scurrility or obscenity by seeing these as the signs of an admirably serious and intense commitment to truth and virtue. This is right and important, but it can lead to confusion. Once you start talking about Dryden, Swift, and Pope as the intelligent, humane, morally serious men they certainly were, you may be on the way to trivializing their works, taking them as urging the obvious, 'normal' ethical values of their times (which is not entirely true) and treating such values as equivalent to the literary force of the works as experienced (which is a disastrous error). We seem to have trouble believing that someone who lived before our own dark times can mean it when he reports that life is full of vileness, that the integrity of 'spirit' is usually a hoax or a tragic illusion, that the centre of most lives is an empty space enclosed only by the elaborations of personal and cultural style. (It is the trouble *Lear* poses to those who want Shakespeare to have been a sad, good Christian at his heart.) The critical fate of Swift is instructive: in reaction to Victorian horror some modern scholars have found a sound, sensible Anglican moralist behind the mask, but one may rather prefer Thackeray, who at least had the wit to be horrified and think it meant something serious.

Perhaps we could say that the satirist speaks for virtue without expecting that speech will make it prevail in the actual world. It seems naive to assume that satiric castigation of vice expects to reform vicious men. Few bad men are made good through reading satire, and I doubt that many men inclining toward evil have been saved from the brink by literary means—such are I suppose rescued, if at all, by the timidities and anxieties and blessed little scruples that sustain the moral life more commonly and often more securely than deliberation and reasoned choice. Though satirists understandably claim that they mean to reform the world by exposing its unconfessed vices, it seems more realistic to consider their art as descriptive drama, expressing the *inner* counter-workings of benevolence and malice, hope and despair, through which ethical self-consciousness defines itself. The satiric work, like any other, is imaginatively alive only to the extent that you can find in it a man thinking and feeling, and since even decent men are capable of occasional bitterness, self-seeking, envy, or hatred, satire may enact the sublimation of such unlovely emotions into ethical attitudes that retain some of their primitive force even as their bearing on the original object satirized is widened and depersonalized.

Satire is thus thoroughly Hobbesian, in my playful sense, in that it supposes no essential difference between the 'world' it describes and the 'self' that does the describing—both self and world are fallen moral estates, even though the satiric self struggles for its own regeneration. At any rate, satire implicitly questions the assumed distance between imagination and public reality. The satirist speaks as a man who *knows* vice and folly in the world, who has had close experience of politicians and statesmen and knows that most of them are villains whose exposure is urgent. If one view of satire sees it as weakness revenging itself on the aggressions of the strong, still weakness aims at a kind of strength for itself that the strong would have to recognize and give ground to; the satirist doesn't laugh at corrupt power behind its back but rather, in his bravest and most admirable mood, attacks it with means it might yield to, force like its own. Sadly, this is more fantasy than fact—as in some Steigian dream of glory, the satirist casts himself as a tough guy giving the bullies their lumps, a warrior (as Pope put it) drawing his sacred weapon in a heroic last-ditch defence of truth and freedom. But it is a potent fantasy all the same, one which predicts most 'modern' definitions of the artist and his public role and which—as the history of literary censorship indicates—the public powers were not always to take as empty bluff.

It was in Augustan satire that subsequent political poetry was to find its training ground. Here the disaffected citizen stands up to a secular power that has lost most of its religious sanctions and much of its imposing focus in the quasi-heroic figure of the monarch. Where Dryden and Pope see admirable rulers more as kindly (if raffish) uncles or doting maiden aunts than heroic supermen, their *enemies* tend to take on the size and weight of the old epic man: calling this transformation 'mock heroic' shouldn't obscure the fact that Shaftesbury and Shadwell and Cibber represent a shift of literary attention that reflects a shift of political power. The villains aren't kings or heroes but men of lesser name, ultimately of no 'name' at all in the epic sense, as one enters the realm of the bureaucrat, the functionary, and the manipulator, where power is dispersed into anonymous, invisible hands. Augustan satire divides in mid-century, with Johnson and Churchill preserving the form and tone of the established genre while some different poetic modes relocate the imagination's relation to public life; after looking at Dryden and Pope as political poets, I will consider two famous eighteenth-century poems of 'solitude' as latent political statements and indications of the need for new political and poetic forms as Augustan satire wore itself out.

1. Satire and Political Doubt: Dryden's *The Medal*

It has evidently been decided that *The Medal* is something less than Dryden's finest work. It has 'a few concentrated passages' (Mark Van Doren); it is 'less brilliant' than *Absalom and Achitophel* since it lacks that poem's 'edge' (George Sherburn); it is 'a simpler poem, as brilliant in its language, but without the scale of allusion or the depth of characterization' of *Absalom* (Martin Price). No one quite dismisses it, but no one explains just what's wrong with it, what it is that puts one off a little. Objections do come readily enough to mind. Measured against Dryden's other big works of controversy in the 1680's, *The Medal* lacks a 'structure' comparable to the parody-fables of *Absalom and Achitophel* and *Mac Flecknoe* or the allegorical design of *The Hind and the Panther*, or even the sustained mood of personal reflection of *Religio Laici*. And its occasion looks rather trivial by the measure of such works: Shaftesbury was a beaten man by 1682, acquitted of sedition but discredited and disgraced in the eyes of all but his most fanatic Whig followers, and it may seem needlessly brutal to kick him when he's down. Besides, Dryden's treatment of him as Achitophel was so exhilaratingly conclusive as to make new attack seem redundant and fruitless. Where *Religio Laici* and *The Hind and the Panther* were to open new controversial ground from new positions, *The Medal* represents no such advance.

All such objections have their point. And yet *The Medal* seems to me a very interesting and very good poem, one which may make evident a problem Dryden faced in writing political satire that isn't so clear elsewhere. The satirist, according to a familiar theory, finds in his own literary activity proof that truth and justice differ from their public representations in his society; he is a little like the later artist of the avant-garde, who also challenges the normative assumptions of a society and justifies his challenge (if he can) by proving that *his* 'reality', the new work of art, is richer and more authentic than the public reality it rejects or mocks. To be sure, traditional satire speaks for a conservative moral and political lore, what we have forgot to our peril, where avant-garde art expresses some radically progressive impulse, what we've not yet thought of; but both cases stress the disparity between what the artist wants and what he thinks the world is apt to give him, if left to its own resources and habits.

The Medal has for its subtitle 'A Satyre Against Sedition', which seems to show that Dryden works from the normal satiric position, an abhorrence of (in this case) political acts that demonstrably violate legal, moral, and religious standards of right. The poem does much to support this professed claim for political verities, but it is not what we hear most strongly at the beginning:

> Of all our Antick Sights and Pageantry
> Which *English* Idiots run in crowds to see,
> The *Polish Medal* bears the prize alone:

A Monster, more the Favourite of the Town
Than either Fairs or Theatres have shown.

This is the voice of the man of taste, equally above the vulgarity of fairs and supposedly more sophisticated entertainments. The scorn cuts not only at Shaftesbury's medal but at the mass-taste that creates and pursues political vogues as thoughtlessly and transiently as it does fashions in amusement. The remoteness is so emphasized as to leave you wondering (despite '*our* Antick Sights') if this isn't some Chinese Visitor speaking, for whom Polish Medals are no more exotic and bizarre than English Idiots. At any rate, the poem begins not by establishing a responsible position on political issues but with an implied condescension toward all politics, which is seen as a kind of show-business even more contemptible than the real thing.

This is not to say that *The Medal* presents Dryden as a man incapable of strong partisan feeling, or without a reasoned idea of how the state should be managed. For many readers, I'm sure, it is just its vehemence that makes the poem seem one-sided and a little boring, without the complicating urbanity of tone that makes the great moments of *Absalom and Achitophel* and *Mac Flecknoe* so impressively shifty.[1] But if Dryden's mastery of murder-by-indirection is the hallmark of his satiric art, one may still want to respect the force of the blunter method of *The Medal*, the directness that at a considerably quieter pitch makes *Religio Laici* his most consistently sustained long poem and fitfully illuminates the *longueurs* of *The Hind and the Panther*. The great portrait of Shaftesbury early in *The Medal* establishes invective as a brilliant and telling mode of poetic rhetoric:

Oh, cou'd the Style that copy'd every grace
And plough'd such furrows for an Eunuch face,
Cou'd it have form'd his ever-changing Will,
The various Piece had tir'd the Graver's Skill!
A Martial Heroe first, with early care
Blown, like a Pigmee by the Winds, to war.
A beardless Chief, a Rebel e'er a Man,
(So young his hatred to his Prince began.)
Next this, (How wildly will Ambition steer!)
A vermin wriggling in th' Usurper's ear,

Bart'ring his venal wit for sums of gold,
He cast himself into the Saint-like mould;
Groan'd, sigh'd, and pray'd, while Godliness was gain,
The lowdest Bag-pipe of the Squeaking train.
But, as 'tis hard to cheat a Juggler's Eyes,
His open lewdness he cou'd ne'er disguise.
There split the Saint: for Hypocritique Zeal
Allows no Sins but those it can conceal.
Whoring to Scandal gives too large a scope;
Saints must not trade; but they may interlope.
Th' ungodly Principle was all the same;
But a gross Cheat betrays his Partner's game.
Besides, their pace was formal, grave, and slack;
His nimble Wit outran the heavy Pack.
Yet still he found his Fortune at a stay,
Whole droves of Blockheads choaking up his way;
They took, but not rewarded, his advice;
Villain and Wit exact a double price.
Pow'r was his aym; but, thrown from that pretence,
The wretch turn'd loyal in his own defence,
And Malice reconcil'd him to his Prince.

This elliptical, knotty verse needs first to be seen and heard as at
unit, so that the extension and ironic recoil of each couplet is fell
as a rhythm, a continuing wave-motion against which to measure
the force of the separate jokes as they break upon the mind, as the
moral fable moves towards its necessary end. Dryden makes you
hear couplet rhetoric as having the force of intellectual and moral
continuity, the persistence of a single consciousness that registers
the crazy antics of the object; and here that consciousness shows
itself, in its almost entire reliance on a native, plain-spoken Saxon
idiom, as a considerably less elegant and 'European' sense of
things than the Dryden of *Absalom and Achitophel* exhibits.

Such an effect is hard to talk about if one conceives of criticism
only as the discovery of unexpected meaning, the text's exfoliation
into complex richness when the critic turns the heat on. (We
should of course admire such criticism, and practise it when we're
able.) Here, as in Pope's lines on Sporus or many of Milton's best
accounts of Satan, rhetorical energy is pretty single-mindedly

expended in underlining what is clear from the start—that Shaftesbury is a bad man and Dryden loathes him. Even his wit, which in the *Absalom* portrait allows Dryden to weave a thread of regret for wasted talent through the contempt, here has little complicating effect; a clever man can obviously outrun the 'heavy Pack' of pompous Puritans Shaftesbury tried to throw in with, but their gravity wonderfully frustrates his frantic attempts to thrust his way through 'whole droves of Blockheads', who are far better equipped to pursue self-interest than a *witty* villain, with his susceptibility to images of physical impotence, can ever be. This impotence is indeed the underlying figure. From the original absurdity, the soft, eunuch thing memorialized in bronze that falsely imposes on it the furrows of sober, statesman-like delibera-tion—an ironic minification of the 'deep scars of thunder . . . intrenched' on Satan's face (*PL*, I, 600)—Shaftesbury is sub-jected to a series of increasing physical outrages. He is a pigmy blown to war, a vessel out of control, a wriggling vermin, a self-made icon that splits from its inner flaw, a bagpipe groaning and sighing with the painful effort to blow loudest, a puny wit humi-liated by burly blockheads—it must indeed have been wretched-ness that turned him loyal 'in his own defence'. The importance of 'wit', here a self-serving cunning grotesquely denied any realizing of its conceits in *action*, is deftly pinned down.

Dryden thus questions the connection of wit and works, the possibility of Shaftesbury's political arts being translated into political accomplishment. The tasteless, fraudulent art of the medal itself neatly captures the essence of its model, in a way the engraver never intended:

> Never did Art so well with Nature strive,
> Nor ever Idol seem'd so much alive;
> So like the Man; so golden to the sight,
> So base within, so counterfeit and light.   (6-9)

The paradox is deadly. Insofar as the medal misrepresents his real appearance and character, it is a victory of art over nature. Yet a man whose nature is false, whose character is never out-wardly confessed, is truthfully represented by just such false art. Behind Shaftesbury looms the vastly larger figure of another im-perfectly artful rebel doomed to impotent failure, Milton's Satan, the confused spirit of self whose unprincipled wit rises against creative order out of sheer compulsion to be negative. Shaftesbury is of course pitifully not up to such *magnificent* evil, but he does his feeble best:

> Ev'n in the most sincere advice he gave
> He had a grudging still to be a Knave.
> The Frauds he learnt in his Fanatique years
> Made him uneasie in his lawfull gears.
> At best as little honest as he cou'd:
> And, like white Witches, mischievously good.
> To his first byass, longingly he leans;
> And rather would be great by wicked means.   (57-62)

The figure of impotence now takes the form of habitual necessity; the bowl, an object without will, can only follow the bias built into it, and Shaftesbury ends the helpless captive of what he began by being. Like Satan he is to be seen as at once a deliberate villain and a moral exemplum without control of his fate—he *could* be good, and yet it is ordained that he *won't* be. His malevolent art, at a further remove, can be seen as something his will doesn't govern, and yet he remains also a figure in the moral foreground, whose will co-operates with his fate. If this is a theological complexity of some size in *Paradise Lost*, it is also, in Dryden's diminished version, an index to the difficulty of thinking about public men who are also villains, a difficulty that needs to be resolved.

At this point, where the implications of art and fact most richly blur together, crucial decisions about Shaftesbury's status as imaginative object have to be made. For Dryden, naturally, he was first of all a real public man with private disabilities that could be exploited (with the essential dishonesty of analogy) in attacking the political cause he led. But *The Medal* aspires to more than persecuting him as moral villain and representative Whig. Politics is not just an opportunity for invective, gratifying and liberating as that can be; it would spoil the fun if Shaftesbury were generalized out of his existence as a particular satiric victim, but the poem also needs a voice that can indicate larger, more dispassionate kinds of awareness too, moods in which political issues can, without ceasing to exist and matter, seem to point beyond themselves to a more general moral drama. When you see in him a conflict between will and fate, as I think Dryden invites you to do, you may also begin to see a relation between Shaftesbury's individual nature and the features of crowd rule Dryden so hates and fears. *The Medal* is a great polemic against popular government, and one owes Dryden the courtesy of taking his antipathies seriously. We can't assume, that is, that he began by disliking Shaftesbury and went on to dislike all Whigs, Monmouth's rebellion, and the whole theory of limited monarchy just because these happened to be associated with the bad Earl himself. It would be futile to speculate about priorities; all one can say is that immediate animosities and broader theoretical objections come together here, and that Dryden's problem as poet was to find a way of combining polemic animus with serious, if fragmentary, concern for political theory.

The general nature of Dryden's theory is clear enough:

> Almighty crowd, thou shorten'st all dispute;
> Power is thy essence; Wit thy Attribute!
> Nor Faith nor Reason make thee at a stay,
> Thou leapst o'er all Eternal truths in thy *Pindarique* way!
> *Athens*, no doubt, did righteously decide,
> When *Phocion* and when *Socrates* were try'd;
> As righteously they did those dooms repent;
> Still were they wise, whichever way they went.
> Crowds err not, though to both extremes they run;
> To kill the Father and recall the son.   (91-100)

Popular democracy, with its reckless adherence to expedient impulse, is for Dryden both an intellectual absurdity and a blasphemous contravention of eternal truth: 'This side to-day, and that to-morrow burns;/So all are God a'mighties in their turns' (109-110). It looks as if he cares less about the particular effects of political actions—he can't very well mean that recalling the son is as *bad* an 'extreme' as killing the father—than about some larger offence to principles of order and continuity in government, some excess virtually of *style* (as 'Pindarique way' and its rude fourteener line announce) through which mob passion reveals its inherent viciousness. In particular matters of policy and action, the monarchy Dryden advocates could after all change its mind too; Halifax, who had no love for the mob and whose Character of Charles II so strikingly parallels Dryden's portrayal of him as King David, suavely admonishes that if Charles 'had sometimes less firmness than might have been wished, let the kindest reason be given, and if that should be wanting, the best excuse', and there is a whisper of the same affectionate malice in Rochester's 'The easiest Prince and best bred Man alive'. Not the failure of principle in individual political acts but something larger and less obvious is at stake.

To be fair to *The Medal* one must both enjoy the violence of Dryden's *ad hoc*, *ad hominem* invective and see beyond these immediate pleasures to the habits of mind the poem implies as the basis of its politics. There should be no question of critical pieties here. The poem is no better if you can find some 'general attitudes' in it, and I don't suggest that satire simply dresses up large issues in lively local particulars. But *The Medal* raises larger questions than ones about the character of Shaftesbury and his followers, and these questions can make clearer the idea of politics the poem pursues. What strikes me most strongly in the poem is a view of action, busy-ness, business, that turns up repeatedly, whatever the satiric topic at hand. There is something odd about the view, and I want to examine it in some detail.

In the long portrait of Shaftesbury already quoted, Dryden dwells (as we saw) on purposeless activity, or activity denied its intended ends. The images show Shaftesbury's impotent passivity, the way his career has been determined by outside forces; he is powerless not just because he can't achieve the kind of power he wants but because he is temperamentally unable to define and pursue *any* goal through self-determined action. His political life is a succession of changed plans, switches of side, failed intentions that lead to new and equally hopeless projects. The medal may hideously fix a (false) version of his features, but it can never fix his 'ever-changing Will'. At one point Dryden imagines him worshipping a God who seems oddly relaxed and composed to be adored by such a volatile mind:

> For thine, (if thou hast any) must be one
> That lets the World and Humane Kind alone;
> A jolly God that passes hours too well
> To promise Heav'n, or threaten us with Hell. (277-280)

But this, in reaching out to jokes elsewhere about Shaftesbury's profligate hedonism, is no inconsistency. This God, like his worshipper, really has nothing in mind; his purposes are too self-centred and internalized to find any practical object. Shaftesbury is in effect a *fallen* image of such a deity, less easy in his self-absorption, still pursuing aims he hasn't the sense to see as illusory. But this God is the perfection of a mind for which no action is possible, and this is Shaftesbury's mind.

Moral outrage at such negation of human possibility is easily come by, but I think it would be mistaken to suppose that Dryden ridicules Shaftesbury (and by implication *any* strongly ambitious but unprincipled public man) just because he doesn't know what he wants to get or be. In practice Dryden might like him better if he had principles or useful, humane political goals he pursued sensibly and steadily; but so obvious a homily is an inadequate counterpoise to the weight of the satiric assault, the vehemence of Dryden's invective. The alternative, strange to say, is to think that Dryden in some sense (not the same sense) shares the indifference to action of Shaftesbury's God; perhaps Shaftesbury's crime is not just that he lacks principles, bad as that is, but that he seeks to *do something*, when the best course, even for men who have principles and most certainly for those who don't, may be to do nothing.

Shaftesbury's God has some interesting resemblances to Charles II, as Dryden and others admiringly portrayed him, and certainly *The Medal*, at the moments when it comes closest to stating the desirable alternative to democratic chaos and the self-serving political adventuring that fosters it, leans towards images of inaction and passive repose that play against the aimless animation of Shaftesburian 'wit':

> What Fools our Fathers were, if this be true!
> Who, to destroy the seeds of Civil War,
> Inherent right in Monarchs did declare:
> And, that a lawfull Pow'r might never cease,
> Securd' Succession, to secure our Peace.
> Thus Property and Sovereign Sway, at last
> In equal Balances were justly cast. (112-118)
>
> Such impious Axiomes foolishly they show;

94

For in some Soils Republiques will not grow;
Our Temp'rate Isle will no extremes sustain
Of pop'lar Sway or Arbitary Reign:
But slides between them both into the best;
Secure in freedom, in a Monarch blest.
And though the Climate, vex't with various Winds,
Works through our yielding Bodies, on our Minds,
The wholesome Tempest purges what it breeds;
To recommend the Calmness that succeeds.   (246-255)

Thus in-born broils the Factions would ingage;
Or Wars of Exil'd Heirs, or Foreign Rage,
Till halting Vengeance overtook our Age:
And our wild Labours, wearied into Rest,
Reclin'd us on a rightfull Monarch's Breast.   (318-322)

In each case the present disorder, which Dryden at least pretends to think is about to burst into open insurrection, is associated with *past* disorders and their resolution in the symbolic person of the monarch, who reconciles all dispute as a parent soothes the quarrels of his children. (In the second passage Dryden also invokes the Englishman's odd belief in the healthy severity of his climate, itself an appeal to idealized memory and the stability of folk-wisdom.) The implied future in each case reenacts the past. We too will secure our peace in equal balances, slide between extremes into the best, recline on the Monarch's bosom. It will happen because it has already happened; past and future are not only continuous but coincident, and such an idea of history—not what is temporally 'past' but all that is contained in the immanent whole of 'national' existence—is for Dryden a more satisfying resolution for his poem than any reiteration of moral principle or divine imperative could provide.

Now if you believe, or want to, that the future is the past, you are not likely to have much hope for what individual or collective will and imagination can achieve by way of affecting history. Nor does Dryden seem hopeful:

We loath our Manna, and we long for Quails;
Ah, what is man, when his own wish prevails!
How rash, how swift to plunge himself in ill;
Proud of his Pow'r and boundless in his Will!   (131-134)

The touch is light, but this looks like the doctrinal centre of the poem. The political idea that individual men are bad judges of what is good for them collectively attaches itself to philosophical and religious ideas about the inadequacy of will as ethical instrument and salvational device. This conjunction underlines Dryden's hostility to business and commerce as represented (167-204) by the 'great Emporium' which is London:

> Their Shops are Dens, the Buyer is their Pray.
> The Knack of Trades is living on the Spoil;
> They boast e'en when each other they beguile.
> Customs to steal is such a trivial thing,
> That 'tis their Charter to defraud their King.
> All hands unite of every jarring Sect;
> They cheat the Country first, and then infect.

The author of *Annus Mirabilis* has come a long way, though the moral peril of commerce is no surprising point in a satire against Whiggery and Puritanism. But it is more than a local thrust—to be 'busy' at all, in any sphere, may risk the moral fate of Shaftesbury, with his representative misapplications of energy and will, errors that link him with the behaviour of the seditious mob:

> Thou leapst o'er all Eternal truths in thy *Pindarique* way!

> But this new *Jehu* spurs the hot mouth'd horse;
> Instructs the Beast to know his native force.

> Happy who can this talking Trumpet seize;
> They make it speak whatever Sense they please!

> Then, *Cyclop*-like, in humane Flesh to deal,
> Chop up a Minister at every meal;
> Perhaps not wholly to melt down the King;
> But clip his regal rights within the Ring.

> What else inspires the Tongues & swells the Breasts
> Of all thy bellowing Renegado Priests,
> That preach up thee for God; dispence thy Laws;
> And with thy Stumm ferment their fainting Cause?
> Fresh fumes of Madness raise; and toile and sweat,
> To make the formidable Cripple great.

In each excerpt, political action reveals itself as a violent disturbance to some implied ideal of repose or seemly order. The last passage is especially rich in dramatized jumble and hurly burly, and it suggests, for all its apparently neat 'neo-classical' laying out of rationalized metaphor, that Dryden's finest effects can depend as much upon mixing and confusing figures and sets of associations as upon sorting out and ordering them. Here the 'formidable Cripple' is laboured over not just by medical men but by bellowing priests who are also judges and crooked vintners doctoring up old, vapid wine. Shaftesbury, who a few lines before was the 'Mercury'—both volatile spirit and the highly toxic remedy for venereal disease—that 'the pox'd Nation' felt in 'their Brains', becomes in turn the false god and lawgiver, the raw fermented grape juice that conceals vapidity, and the formidable Cripple himself. 'Formidable' carries its root meaning of 'inspiring apprehension and dread'—it is dreadful to see such great abilities maimed and wasted, but it is also dreadful to think about him getting well, overcoming his disability and achieving the greatness he so much wants, even though we *hope* the 'toile and sweat' is in his case a foolish waste of effort. The metaphorical density suggests that activity, 'doing' of this sort, may only confuse the mind, stirring up trouble by spreading intellectual incoherence.

The Medal, then, treats political activity as a special case of a larger restlessness that may inhere in human nature but which Dryden sees as wastefully subversive of order and repose, comfortable submission to an almost parental authority. His hostility to crowd rule has ample parallel in contemporary political theory, but it manifests itself, as Bernard Schilling observes of *Absalom and Achitophel*, as an appeal to a political 'myth' about kingship embodying things as they comfortably 'are' (that is, *were* and *will be*) rather than in any distinctly defined theorems about the ideal state. Dryden's political satires bring poetry into the area of practical politics, 'affairs of state' in their full particularity; no major poet before or since has dared leave so thin a partition between art and full-scale polemic. But once this area is entered, something hampers the complete *identification* of poetry and politics. Schilling puts it that 'the reasons for going on with the existing scheme of things are poetic reasons, offered in the place of a fully developed rational argument as to the right political system';[2] but these terms seem a trifle out of focus even for *Absalom*, and certainly so when extended to the more direct and vehement method of *The Medal*. (The difference between 'rational' and 'poetic' discourse may depend more on tone and rhetorical stress than on logical coherence—may not the apparent cool neutrality of 'rational argument' in philosophy, for instance, mostly urge the speaking presence of a disinterested man whose propositions will *therefore* have the force of 'reason'?) It's not that Dryden substitutes poetry for rational argument; rather he reveals that rational pleadings have emotional springs—in this case that the anti-democratic politics of *The Medal* expresses personal anxiety, a state of mind that may mix fear of estrangement from the security of 'parental' authority with a poet's simple wish that the world stop interrupting his work. But whatever its motive, the structure of Dryden's politics depends on reductive transformation. The inchoate many become one; distractingly separate parties and identities fuse into the unitary figure of King-Father-Lawgiver; politics itself, with its necessary, complex play of conflicting wills and interests, gives way to something surprisingly like the identification of state with society that Hegel would postulate as the end—both aim and cessation—of political theory.[3]

My reading of *The Medal*, in short, comes out just about where one might expect it to—with the impression of a mind weary of politics, sceptical of the possibilities of action and disputation, anxious for calm and order and agreement in things as they are. This is the Dryden who got on personally and professionally under Cromwell about as well as under Charles II, who welcomed the advent of a Catholic monarch yet survived 1688 in a reasonably equable state of mind, to work busily in the calmer medium of translation until the end of the century. It's the Dryden of Schilling's 'conservative myth', the Dryden whose 'commonplace mind' T. S. Eliot found room for in the major poetic tradition (though one hopes he meant 'commonplace' to include an interest in what is common, available to all men), the Dryden whose imagination grasped for moments of resolution and achieved order whenever they seemed at hand:

> No Civil Broils have since his Death arose,
> But Faction now, by Habit, does obey;

And Wars have that respect for his Repose,
    As winds for *Halcyons* when they breed at Sea.
                    (*Heroick Stanzas* to Cromwell, 1659)

At home the hateful names of Parties cease
And factious Souls are weary'd into peace.
    . . . .
Oh Happy Age! Oh times like those alone
By Fate reserv'd for great *Augustus*' throne!
When the joint growth of Arms and Arts forshew
The World a Monarch, and that Monarch *You.*
                    (*Astraea Redux*, 1660)

Thus to the Eastern wealth through Storms we go,
But now, the Cape once doubled, fear no more:
A constant Trade-wind will securely blow,
And gently lay us on the Spicy shore.
                    (*Annus Mirabilis*, 1667)

Henceforth a Series of new time began,
The mighty Years in long Procession ran:
Once more the God-like David was Restor'd,
And willing Nations knew their Lawful Lord.
                    (*Absalom and Achitophel*, 1681)

. . . If still our Reason runs another way,
That private Reason 'tis more Just to curb,
Than by Disputes the publick Peace disturb.
For points obscure are of small use to learn:
But *Common Quiet* is *Mankind's concern.*
                    (*Religio Laici*, 1682)

Equal to all, you justly frown or smile,
Nor Hopes, nor Fears your steady Hand beguile;
Your self our Ballance hold, the Worlds, our Isle.
                    (*Britannia Rediviva*, 1688)

(It is admittedly a career of bad guesses and disappointed hopes.)
The concluding major chord is Dryden's pleasant poetic vice—
even the grotesqueries of *Mac Flecknoe*, his darkest comedy, lead
to the image of Flecknoe sinking (in mid-declamation) to the
underworld, a happy restoration of at least gravitational order

even though Shadwell remains to carry on immortal war with wit.

But this talent for hopefulness is far from cheery, simple-minded optimism. The *Secular Masque* (1700), with its tart if affectionate farewell to 'a very Merry, Dancing, Drinking,/Laughing, Quaffing, and unthinking Time', welcomes the new century with a warning that action has no lasting effect, that history is a record of frustrations and failures:

> All, all of a piece throughout:
> > Thy Chase had a Beast in View;
> Thy Wars brought nothing about;
> > Thy Lovers were all untrue.
> 'Tis well an Old Age is out,
> > And time to begin a New.

Though it will take up different hunts and wars and amours, the new age isn't likely to accomplish much more than the old. The final stage-direction is significantly to a *dance* of huntsmen, nymphs, warriors, and lovers—dance is movement without progression or practical result, action formalized into its own repetition, energy poised in an image of agreement and mutual respect.

But in *The Medal* such moments of poise can't wholly control Dryden's love of invective and imaginative violence. The historical and psychological roots of satire have been located in the primitive 'curse' as practised first by Archilochus, traditionally thought the father of satire—the curse being the most direct and uninhibited mode of verbal aggression, language which means to *kill*.[4] In its treatment of Shaftesbury and the Whigs, *The Medal* is the clearest case of such an aggressive impulse in Dryden, clearer than *Mac Flecknoe* and *Absalom and Achitophel* for lacking any consistent allegorical or parodic superstructure to complicate its hostility toward the object. If Dryden is sceptical about politics or any form of individual or group action, preferring to accept things as they were and will be, still these feelings are formulated in verse that is anything but bland and unruffled. The treatment of the Whigs is rhetorically active, violent, lethal, as it is in the brilliant vituperative prose of Dryden's dedicatory 'Epistle'. To forget the essential rudeness of his style—a very British rudeness that is only intensified by a nominally polite urbanity of manner

—is to miss the whole point. But that aggressive, offensive rudeness expresses more than serene superiority to its victims:

> Thy military Chiefs are brave and true,
> Nor are thy disinchanted Burghers few.
> The Head is loyal which thy Heart commands,
> But what's a Head with two such gouty Hands?
> The wise and wealthy love the surest way;
> And are content to thrive and to obey.
> But Wisdom is to Sloath too great a Slave;
> None are so busy as the Fool and Knave.   (179-186)

This manages to combine approval of 'the surest way'—profitable acceptance of the existing regime—and impatience with
sloth and the rich living that makes hands gouty. The fools and
knaves, whose activity is so contemptibly misdirected, seem for a
moment almost enviable—if only we could be as busy as they
are, it might go better for our cause. It shows again how hard it
is to reconcile Dryden's 'ideas' with the actual effect of his best
verse. The point here *should* be that busy-ness is vulgar and
dangerous, that we may all be content to thrive and obey without
stirring things up further; but this idea collides with a fundamental suspicion of having it too easy—the fools and knaves may
be getting the jump on us.

It is as if Dryden, the master of styles and forms, surely the
most various talent in English literature, yearns for a *release* from
styles and forms, a pacification of his own witty vitality in some
state of peace and repose. *The Hind and the Panther* was to be his
last significant act of poetic controversy, and one almost suspects
that he wrote the most boring poem he could manage as a kind
of triumph over his own imaginative energy. Be that as it may,
The Medal is of two minds about its own purpose. As a statement
of political position it is clear and coherent: order and stability
are best, and Shaftesbury and the Whigs deserve at least poetic
killing because they would replace public stability with the violent,
pointless ebb and flow of personal and collective ambition and
whim. To 'kill' in this imaginative way is consistent with the
political and moral thesis, since killing someone means making
him inactive, easing him of the demands of his 'wit', bringing
him into a personal repose that reflects the desired public condi-

tion. In this sense Dryden's aim might be called the abolition of politics, or even the abolition of life itself.

But it would be absurd to follow a political theory that far, and Dryden does no such thing. The poet of *The Medal* is an active political man, a controversialist with a point of view and a general programme quite as strenuously desired and urged as those of his enemies. In short, the poem sustains the paradox most decent men feel about politics. It is somehow distasteful and demeaning and we would gladly be rid of it, and yet it is irresistible in its power to generate strong feelings and give them gratifying play, gratifying if only because they prove we're still alive, after all. It may even be ennobling in its provision of extra-personal, seemingly unselfish ends for our moral natures to pursue and sacrifice to. *The Medal* shows how commitment to politics can interact with intelligent scepticism about its nature and purposes. For all its complicating undertones of cynicism and doubt—indeed, *because* of them—it is one of our clearest poetic images of a healthy political life.

2. The Decline of English Politics, 1688-1789

Sir Lewis Namier, without whose monumental work there could be no understanding the politics of the eighteenth century, neatly epitomized the fate of public involvement under the early Georges by contrasting some words of advice given to Robert Pitt and to Edward Gibbon by their fathers. What should motivate the aspiring young parliamentarian? 'In 1706 it was "faithful service to your country"; in 1760 "service of one's friends".'[5] Between the two ideas of service stands a history of politics dwindling into the pursuit of personal interest, as principles, public causes, and even party loyalties give way to the manoeuvres and intrigues of men whose primary motive was profit and place for themselves and their associates.

Namier's massive documentation of his view affords some stirring vignettes of the new mentality in action. There is the case of Chauncey Townsend, M.P., a linen-draper risen to the dignity of general merchant and victualling contractor, who, 'having in a letter to James West, on 26 June 1754, enumerated the services he had rendered to the Administration in elections at a cost to himself of £6000, explained with regard to the reward he ex-

pected: "Mony support I allways declined when hinted—half
Gibraltar was my object".' (Depressing to say, he only meant
half the supply contracts for the garrison.) Or consider the Duke
of Newcastle's remarks about Zachery Fonnereau, M.P., who
had deserted Newcastle's cause to support the Earl of Bute: 'he
owned very plainly that it was interest. . . . I suppose his price
is some valuable remittances to Minorca, etc.; when a man knows
himself that he is bought, one has nothing to say to him.' This
admirable moral reflection is a little deflated by the discovery that
Fonnereau's price had in fact been a share of the Gibraltar contracts that Thomas Walpole, *to whom Newcastle wrote these remarks*, had himself held under Newcastle's own patronage.[6]
Soame Jenyns, Dr. Johnson's old aversion and an M.P. for thirty-
eight years, summed things up sensibly enough in his *Thoughts
on Parliamentary Reform* (1784):

> [Members of Parliament] are seldom, very seldom, bribed
> to injure their country, because it is seldom the interest of
> Ministers to injure it; but the great source of corruption is,
> that they will not serve it for nothing. Men get into Parlia-
> ment in pursuit of power, honours, and preferments, and
> until they obtain them, determine to obstruct all business,
> and to distress the Government; but happily for their coun-
> try, they are no sooner gratified, than they are equally
> zealous to promote the one, and support the other.[7]

It was clearly an age with few illusions about its pursuit of
self-interest, and, as Namier is careful to point out, the system
had some unexpected advantages. Rotten and pocket boroughs,
for example, the symbols of infamy for a later generation of
political reformers, were by no means inevitable sources of evil in
practice; Burke learned that an Opposition Member was much
freer sitting for a pocket borough than for the City of Bristol,
whose merchant-electors required him to court Government
favour for them, and the rotten boroughs, under Government
management, opened Parliament to capable 'professional' ad-
ministrators and statesmen and to the energetic and often civic-
minded new-rich, helping to preserve the House from total
domination by unqualified or indifferent members of the old
landed gentry.[8] Then too, power based on money, with its way

of changing hands and fostering a certain flexibility of status, has some advantages when compared with power based on rigid distinctions in birth and station; men entered Parliament to promote their careers in the civil service, the armed forces, and the church, and if it is disconcerting to read of the council of war aboard H.M.S. *Neptune* on September 25, 1757, at which seven of the eight officers present were, had been, or would be M.P.'s, or to hear the Bishop of Oxford bemoaning his political impotence ('The small property I have in Oxfordshire is either in the hands, or in the neighbourhood, of persons whom I cannot influence. . . . I have no preferments to give the clergy. I cannot promise or threaten to behave to them according as they vote'),[9] there is still some merit to a system in which power and status *can* be pursued with hope of success. And as Namier dryly remarks, there is something to be said for a Parliament whose members, for whatever dubious reasons, have a strong interest in commerce and finance and surprising expertise about the technical details of economic questions.[10]

On the whole, however, eighteenth-century England was a dreary political scene, one in which it was hard for serious men to associate the human purposes of public activity with any existing partisan cause. For Dryden, with his scepticism about secular enthusiasms and commitments, opposition to Whiggery coincided well enough with loyalty to the monarchy and its political position; you could support the King and know that your theoretical and practical objections to popular rule were accommodated by such allegiance. But 'causes' even under William III and Anne quickly came to mean self-identification with particular leaders and cliques,[11] as Swift's early career as political hack-writer shows well enough. Marlborough's continental wars were something less than universally popular national causes, and the great debate over the Hanoverian Succession was largely a matter of back-stairs hugger-mugger between rival palace factions, Harley, St. John, Godolphin, Marlborough, Walpole, and their coteries of politicos, pamphleteers, and ladies-in-waiting. After 1688 politics gradually lost the 'dramatic' potentialities it held for an earlier age, the capacity to enlist and represent strong feelings about national policy and the rectitude of individual leaders. As Pope suggests in *Windsor Forest*, an age of commercial expansion and national self-respect is no time for fussing over small points of doctrine or programme. Namier observes that

> After the spiritual and political upheavals of the preceding age, this was the time of England's inner consolidation, when common sense and ready toleration—in other words, insistence on a conformity of a singularly unexacting type —effected a reconciliation in this country such as France was never to reach after her great Revolution.[12]

It was an age when the great attachment was not between a man and his principles or his leaders but, in a good Lockeian way, between a man and his property. But a time of inner consolidation soon enough becomes a time of aimless indulgence and moral inertia, in which the Byzantine complexities of 'personal' politics become fathomless even to such magisterial manipulators as the great Newcastle:

> Altogether 148 men were returned at the general election of 1761 who had not sat in the House at the dissolution; in drawing up a list of them Newcastle omitted four, added five out of ten seats which were vacant, inserted the name of a man who had sat in Parliament since 1715 . . . , and having made three mistakes in addition, finished under the impression that he had 149 entries, though in reality there are 150 entries containing 144 valid names. . . . He ended by placing 101 as 'friends' and 43 as 'others'; but of the friends 40 are queried, and of the others 9. In short, at the end of a general election which he had managed himself and to his own satisfaction, he admittedly did not know what to expect from more than one-third of the new Members.[13]

Here, as Henry Adams might say, was chaos itself. In the face of such rich indeterminacy, one gains affectionate insight into a man like William Aislabie, Member for Ripon from 1721 to 1781, whose durability may have had some connection with the apolitical temperament his admiring biographer records: 'the contemplation of the beauties of nature, and rural occupations, formed his chief and unceasing delight.'[14] When politicians assume the sensibility of poets, what in the world shall poets do?

3. Satire and Political Despair: Pope's *Epilogue*

It is always, of course, more than a matter of what the times are like—Pope would mainly have been Pope whenever he lived. The fierce moral and intellectual pride, the disposition to sort out mankind into friends one loves (even unreasonably) and enemies one despises (whatever they do), the near-paranoid need to know what people think of you and to suppose that it's mostly unflattering, the passion for manipulating and misleading other minds, the fundamental association of consciousness with physical and moral pain, none of these is peculiar to the age into which Pope was born. But when he addressed himself to the public, political scene of England in the 1730's, his personal characteristics came into rich engagement with satiric objects that were peculiarly ready for a mind like his.

His 'official' view of politics at the beginning of this period is stated in Epistle III of the *Essay on Man*, where, after an account of the primitive sources of government and its development (and frequent corruption) as human history progressed, and an eloquent celebration of political order as a *concordia discors* ('the World's great harmony'), he remarks:

> For Forms of Government let fools contest;
> Whate'er is best administer'd is best.   (303-304)

The ominous ring of this was perfectly evident in his day, even though the context is a plea for charity, urging concern for the rectitude of one's own life rather than suspicion of other people's principles; and hostile comment moved him to some defensive marginal comments:

> The author of these lines was far from meaning that no one Form of Government is, in itself, better yn another . . . but that no form of Government, however excellent or preferable in itself, can be sufficient to make a People happy, unless it be administered with Integrity. On ye contrary, the Best sort of Governmt, when ye Form of it is preserved, and ye *administration* corrupt, is most dangerous.

There is no reason to suspect insincerity in this point, with its respectable roots in Aristotle's *Politics*, and it would be sophomoric to require Pope to state a preference between a good form badly administered and a bad form well administered, which is what his enemies in effect were asking. From this position he could criticize the contemporary political condition, in the *Moral Essays* and the Horatian satires, without in any way questioning the fundamental rightness of the post-1688 political settlement; we ought not to examine the *form* of government but rather government's effect upon human happiness, and here, Pope would make it clear, the current incumbents were hopelessly inadequate, because profoundly corrupt. It is essentially the position of Dryden, a plea for directing political energy not to radical revision of the system but to cleansing the existing temple of its moneylenders and Pharisees.

Pope's antipathy to the administration of Walpole and the Whigs is amply documented in the satires of the 1730's, which, whatever the immediate critical focus on manners or morals or literary and intellectual imbecility, are never without an underlying political relevance. But while no one would question their success as poems, they fail to engage the political enemy in fundamental controversy—there is no decisive battle on doctrinal ground. The satires convince us that there are bad men in high places, unsurprisingly enough, but their badness is mostly attached to failures of personal integrity and moral taste, not underlying misapprehension about policies or principles. To this extent Pope, unlike Dryden, has no secure general position of his own. His allusions to actual politics can do little more than suggest that things would look up if only *his* friends—the 'Chiefs, out of War, and Statesmen, out of Place' (*Sat.* II, i) whose retirements he was so proud to share—could get back in again. (As a matter of fact, they had more poetic use where they were, since in retirement they could always be invoked as a sympathetic audience for the sober reflections on mutability that make the satires so morally charged and dignified.) Pope was in some danger of seeing in politics only what his enemies saw there too—a basic pursuit of office and interest.

At the end of this period in his career Pope wrote a pair of great political poems, the two dialogues of the *Epilogue to the Satires* (1738), which constitute his farewell to poetry as an art of public suasion. But in saying good-bye to satire he achieved his greatest success in the genre, and in despairing of politics he made his most impressive statement about politics, one which disturbingly relates the special circumstances of Augustan political corruption to any circumstance in which politics betrays the human purposes it ought to serve.

The two poems are established as dialogues by Pope's invention of a 'Friend' whose urbane, disillusioned mind seeks to restrain and rebuke the poet's own passionate concern for the state of the public world. The abrasive interaction of these two voices creates some remarkable effects, as in this exchange in 'Dialogue II':

> [FR.] The Priest whose Flattery be-dropt the Crown,
> How hurt he you? he only stain'd the Gown.
> And how did, pray, the Florid Youth offend,
> Whose Speech you took, and gave it to a Friend?
>   P. Faith it imports not much from whom it came,
> Whoever borrow'd, could not be to blame,
> Since the whole House did afterwards the same:
> Let Courtly Wits to Wits afford supply,
> As Hog to Hog in Huts of *Westphaly*;
> If one, thro' Nature's Bounty or his Lord's,
> Has what the frugal, dirty soil affords,
> From him the next receives it, thick or thin,
> As pure a Mess almost as it came in;
> The blessed Benefit, not there confin'd,
> Drops to the third who nuzzles close behind;
> From tail to mouth, they feed, and they carouse,
> The last, full fairly gives it to the *House*.
>   FR. This filthy Simile, this beastly Line,
> Quite turns my Stomach—P. So does Flatt'ry mine;
> And all your Courtly Civet-Cats can vent,
> Perfume to you, to me is Excrement.   (164-184)

The Friend's reasonable, ironically polite disapproval ('pray') is first parried by 'Faith it imports not much', the offhand indifference of someone comfortably above a distressing subject. But this serene superiority vanishes in the fierce obscenity that follows, obscene not merely in reference but in the intensity and obsessive detail with which the image is pursued. (The Friend in fact initiated the image himself, but his 'be-dropt' and 'stain'd the Gown' are tactfully equivocal and sly—his obscenity can blandly be disowned if anyone takes offence.) The occasion scarcely justifies such fury, reasonably speaking—politicians do worse things than borrow one another's speeches. The analogy between noble statesmen and hogs would cut more insolently if it were merely hinted, and Pope's almost pedantic concern for stating every nasty detail, thus magnifying the petty offence out of all reasonable proportion, takes him disturbingly far from the tone of gentlemanly insinuation with which the speech began. By most tests of social and poetic decorum, the Friend's protest is just. It really is a filthy simile, and P.'s final rejoinder seems distinctly petulant and lame.

But of course such objections don't question the passage's success as poetic 'drama'. Rather, they define the imaginative energy being expended to escape ordinary motions of decorum and good sense, which the Pope of the *Epilogue* finds intolerably hampering to a free response to public corruption. The passage is a revealing collision between blunt moral speech and a more equivocal, temporizing style of judgment that may seem shamingly close to anyone's normal political vocabulary. At the beginning of 'Dialogue I' the Friend complains about Pope's infamous lack of political tact, and his own voice nicely catches the 'sly, polite, insinuating stile' of the 'artful Manager' Horace which he recommends to the poet:

> To Vice and Folly to confine the jest,
> Sets half the World, God knows, against the rest;
> Did not the Sneer of more impartial men
> At Sense and Virtue, balance all agen. (57-60)

Desirable social equilibrium requires that sense and virtue be kept in their place; Pope in effect gives himself a taste of his own medicine, as his surrogate self 'P.' is made to endure lectures about balance and poise not unlike those he gave the world in the *Essay on Man* and the *Moral Essays*. The Friend isn't imperceptive—he knows the difference between Vice and Virtue, Folly and Sense, and one imagines a knowing simper as he says 'impartial'—but it's enough for him to relish in private the amusing discrepancies between official and real virtue. He could be taken as virtually a caricature of the Dryden of *Religio Laici* or the underlying quietism of *The Medal*, preferring 'common quiet' to unruly public disputes about unreal issues. In him we seem to have Pope's mature assessment of the cool, disengaged urbanity of an Addison or a Shaftesbury, which is also an assessment of a youthful ideal of his own:

> Leave dang'rous Truths to unsuccessful Satyrs,
> And Flattery to Fulsome Dedicators. . . .
> 'Tis best sometimes your Censure to restrain,
> And charitably let the Dull be vain:
> Your Silence there is better than your Spite,
> For who can rail so long as they can write?
>
> (*Essay on Criticism*, 592-599)

FR. presents himself as a realist. His theme, like the professed theme of Pope's elusive contemporary Mandeville, is the inevitable and useful imperfection of things as they are. His voice, at times indulgent and avuncular, at times maliciously feline, at times shrill with shock at P.'s plain dealing, is the familiar voice of intelligence debilitated by too much knowledge, sophistication that marks not moral subtlety but Gerontion-like moral paralysis.

The Friend is more than a straw man, however. Both he and P. are versions of Pope himself, or of any man aware of the conflict between his social identity and his secret image of himself as autonomous moral hero. The dialogue form articulates the inner debate between that sceptical self that 'knows better', which like FR. stands by one's indiscretions murmuring 'alas' with the sympathetic disapproval that identifies our elders and betters, and that other self which, passionately committed to its own free perception of truth, allows no concessions. I am sure that Pope could see perfectly well the essential theatricality of both 'selves', but the *Epilogue* moves not toward reconciliation of such extremes, as do so many of his earlier poems, but toward something like acceptance of P.'s view in all its extravagant exaggeration.

The two dialogues develop various modes of response to the politic voices of FR. Until late in the poem the mode of 'Dialogue I' is ironic in the textbook sense: P. pretends to defend 'the dignity of Vice', and the terms of the defence expose the speciousness of justifying things as they are. If, as FR. insists, the crimes of the well-born and high-placed are no concern of satire, the job still remains of keeping clear the necessary differentiation of classes. The vulgar imitate the crimes of their betters with intolerable cheek: Cibber's son 'Swear[s] like a Lord', Ward 'draw[s] Contracts with a Statesman's skill', Bond and Peter Walter 'pay their Debts [and] keep their Faith like Kings' (that is, not at all). The joke is clear enough. It is indeed bad for the lower classes to copy the behaviour of the great, but not because they may thus become *better* than they should be. In this topsy-turvy society the highest are not the best (*aristos*) but the worst. Plebeians may have quite as much natural inclination to vice, but in their proper condition and station they are denied the know-how. For them to learn the *style* of accomplished evil from those who are naturally gifted would make general an efficient viciousness that may otherwise be confined to the small world of aristocrats and statesmen, where one expects it and is prepared to resist or at worst endure it.

But the indirections of irony fail to undermine the Friend's complacency, and towards the end of 'Dialogue I' P. is driven to a more open mode of speech. Virtue is classless, he at last admits, and so it needn't concern the satirist: 'She's still the same, belov'd, contented thing' whether she 'dwell in a Monk, or light upon a King.' (But note the barbed difference between those two verbs.) Vice, however, has greater delicacy; she is 'undone, if she forgets her Birth,/And stoops from Angels to the Dregs of Earth'. The bitterness of 'Angels' marks a change of tone; conversational give-and-take fades away in the concluding lines (145-172), the chilling vision of the Triumph of Vice. The everyday world is revealed as a hellish nightmare, ordinary human activity blurs into ugly parodies of itself as cultivated irony is abandoned and the poet's voice trembles with visionary rage. The Friend's 'politic' view of a public reality sustained and ordered by opposing evils has been a delusion all along; society collapses as nobles sacrifice their honour and commoners their families, and established religion abdicates its function as 'grave Bishops' bless the Goddess of Vice: 'hers the Gospel is, and hers the Laws.' It isn't quite clear whether gospel and laws are *now* being taken over by her, or whether the poet discovers that behind the veneer of law and spiritual authority Vice has always lurked as hidden manipulator. But whether revolution or revelation, the Triumph of

Vice is a moment of seemingly final despair for positive civic intelligence and its hopes for a continuous human future.

The oxymorons of Vice—innocence is shame and villainy sacred—are only blunter versions of the moral evasions and mystifications which FR. has been advocating from the start. At the end of 'Dialogue I' the debate between FR. and P., the political man and the moral hero,[15] has been transcended:

> Yet may this Verse (if such a Verse remain)
> Show there was one who held it in disdain.

This final couplet can't, by the strictest logic, be spoken by either participant in the dialogue, for both of whom the foregoing has been real conversation, sentences and not 'verses' in a poem. They didn't know their dialogue was a fiction, but Pope did and here admits it—indeed insists on it. Behind FR. and P. stands another mind, one which closely resembles P.'s and yet knows that P. is a character in a poem; and this mind doesn't hesitate to shatter the dramatic illusion when possessed by the anger and disgust P. has generated. Feeling takes precedence over formal consistency when the stakes are high. Pope himself asserts his independence of a corrupt political and social reality; his lonely voice in effect rejects the world in order to maintain his moral integrity. Like Coriolanus, he reacts to the felt disparity between his moral ego and public possibility by arrogantly banishing the world in a splendidly heroic and supremely absurd gesture.

But if Pope is P., the heroic clown, so to speak, he is reluctantly, painfully, also FR. To write a poem at all is in some sense to pursue accommodation, talking in the hope that someone will hear and be moved to agree. If the conclusion of 'Dialogue I' is Pope's version of Coriolanus's brave insistence that 'there is a world elsewhere', then 'Dialogue II' re-enacts his awful discovery that there is finally no such thing. Again P. begins in the mood of ironic indirection. The satirist would be a hunter of vice, but in the face of FR.'s knowledgeable explanation of the game laws the dignified possibilities of the role fade, and P. is left as a kind of poacher, ruefully asking if there isn't *some* prey he may legally take:

> Must great Offenders, once escap'd the Crown,
> Like Royal Harts, be never more run down?

> Admit your Law to spare the Knight requires;
> As Beasts of Nature may we hunt the Squires?
> Suppose I censure—you know what I mean—
> To save a Bishop, may I name a Dean?   (28-33)

(FR. presently offers him as fair game Jonathan Wild, ten years hanged.) As in 'Dialogue I', however, irony fails to accommodate the seriousness of the case, and after a revealing confession that he finds it easier to honour great men when they're out of office, P.'s voice again assumes the inflection of the serio-comic moral hero:

> I follow *Virtue*; where she shines, I praise:
> Point she to Priest or Elder, Whig or Tory,
> Or round a Quaker's Beaver cast a Glory.   (95-97)

The ludicrous effect of that last image is not to be minimized. By 'cultivated' standards this involuntary morality comes close to absurdity, and Pope knows it. But to express such intense conviction one can only shrug off ridicule and keep on talking:

> Enough for half the Greatest of these days
> To 'scape my Censure, not expect my Praise:
> Are they not rich? what more can they pretend?
> Dare they to hope a Poet for their Friend?   (112-115)

Such insistent arrogance signifies more than personal egotism. The 'I' of the poem isn't just the man but the man as poet, with claims to virtue and dignity of person that derive from the craft and its moral history. It is a claim Dryden makes only indirectly, through haughtiness of tone, in his own satiric confrontations with public corruption; for Pope, finally, indirect demonstration of moral authority, through style, isn't enough—where Dryden could present himself as a concerned citizen who was only incidentally a poet, Pope here must insist on his status as poet almost to the exclusion of any personal involvement in the public world.

This new role expresses anxiety as well as pride. Poetry is a rather unsubstantial weapon and public vice a Protean object, and the exaggeration with which P. defines his poetic identity hints at uncertainty and defensiveness:

Ask you what Provocation I have had?
The strong Antipathy of Good to Bad.
When Truth or Virtue an Affront endures,
Th' Affront is mine, my Friend, and should be yours.
Mine, as a Foe profess'd to false Pretence,
Who think a Coxcomb's Honour like his Sense;
Mine, as a Friend to ev'ry worthy mind;
And mine as Man, who feel for all mankind.   (197-204)

According to this rather stubborn rejection of moral subtlety, there is Good and there is Bad, and their antipathy is as natural and inevitable as magnetism. Moral categories demand large letters, perhaps, but the touch seems a little strained; 'antipathy' is feeling *against*, a negative, defensive emotion, and P.'s idea of himself as a Promethean figure feeling for all mankind suggests how far he has been driven from the ironic modesty that is the Horatian satirist's normal air:

FR. You're strangely proud.
            P. So proud, I am no Slave:
So impudent, I own myself no Knave:
So odd, my Country's Ruin makes me grave.
Yes, I am proud; I must be proud to see
Men not afraid of God, afraid of me:
Safe from the Bar, the Pulpit, and the Throne,
Yet touch'd and sham'd by *Ridicule* alone.   (205-211)

This is impressively lofty, of course; like Coriolanus he seems 'a thing/Made by some other deity than Nature,/That shapes man better'. But here, as in *Coriolanus*, the liberating assertion of pride as a moral good has to contend with ironies the poet is fully aware of. Even if bad men really *are* touched and shamed by ridicule (and we rather suspect they're not, or not much), ridicule alone is pretty easy to shrug off, compared with the substantial penalties of the civil and ecclesiastical powers whose demise is being mourned. The poet's pride is a minimal sort of thing; to have even the slightest distaste for servility is to be 'strangely proud' by the standards of this world, and the tone is rueful in its arrogance. P. has reached the situation in which irony threatens to collapse inward and become literal statement—there has to

114

be someone to say 'But it's *not* odd to be concerned about your country's ruin', and it is just this healthy sanity of response that P. can't count on.

Still, the positive force of the satirist's lonely pride is clearly rendered. If he has been *driven* into this ultimate position, this is only to say that the ground he now occupies is the centre of his case, which need no longer be qualified or compromised. He has, at whatever cost, broken loose from the inhibiting styles of concession and cynical adjustment that govern the public world at its potential worst. Satire is a 'sacred Weapon', the 'sole Dread of Folly, Vice, and Insolence' in a world whose institutions are too feeble or corrupt to enforce significant order. The satirist, no longer able to speak simply as a man among men, now assumes the role of God's deputy, trying not by persuasion and reason but by sheer intensity of will to make an impious society correct the imbalance between its values and divine ones. His instrument is 'to all but Heav'n-directed hands deny'd', and his target is the falsity of official distinctions, 'All that makes Saints of Queens, and Gods of Kings'. And his heroic intensity affords him a vision of the triumph of Virtue to counteract the vision of Vice in 'Dialogue I':

> ... diadem'd with Rays divine,
> Touch'd with the Flame that breaks from Virtue's Shrine,
> Her Priestess Muse forbids the Good to dye,
> And ope's the Temple of Eternity.   (232-235)

The permanence of art is eloquently stated. Immortality rewards imaginative virtue, and while it is figurative immortality—fame —rather than literal, still the petty achievements of the worldly can never earn it. The true moral scale transcends time and death, to which even the officially mighty are subject, and the poet speaks for a power that is ideal and eternal:

> Let Envy howl while Heav'n's whole Chorus sings,
> And bark at Honour not confer'd by Kings;
> Let Flatt'ry sickening see the Incense rise,
> Sweet to the World, and grateful to the Skies:
> Truth guards the Poet, sanctifies the line,
> And makes Immortal, Verse as mean as mine.   (242-247)

But Pope understands the ironies that adhere to any heroic identification of self with natural virtue. The grand tone can't disguise the fact that this assertion of the artist's unique moral dignity is also a confession of practical defeat. Artists, Pope would be the first to insist, have their significance in a community, in relation to an audience, and for him a community of cultural understanding was at least roughly congruent with certain social and even political affinities and functions. But the heroic stature P. conceives for himself is clearly, again like Coriolanus's, a function of alienation. (Indeed, a man grows more mysterious and poten- tially awesome—more 'heroic'—as he is able to divest himself of dependency upon or loyalty to other people, who then figure as external limitations upon his freedom.) Pope's satirist-spokes- man would not need to glorify his role so insistently if every other form of virtue hadn't vanished from his field of awareness. He simply has no peer to talk to. The select, understanding inter- locutors to whom the *Moral Essays* and the other *Imitations of Horace* were largely addressed have been replaced by the anonymous and hopelessly compromised 'Friend', who in the ways that count is no friend at all. Dialogue has become oration, even harangue, addressed to anyone who will listen, and this provides a final twist of bitter comedy:

> Yes, the last Pen for Freedom let me draw,
> When Truth stands trembling on the edge of Law:
> Here, last of *Britons!* let your Names be read;
> Are none, none living? let me praise the Dead,
> And for that Cause which made your Fathers shine,
> Fall, by the Votes of their degen'rate Line!
>   Fr. Alas! alas! pray end what you began,
> And write next winter more *Essays on Man*.   (248-255)

The grand tone has grown almost too grand. ('Pens' and 'Votes' in this context are perilously close to the kind of anticlimax Pope ridiculed in *Peri Bathous*.) And the discovery that the good men are all dead—that the celebration of virtue must be an elegy— produces a faltering of the voice ('none, none') that resembles the classic double-take of farce.

The Friend's concluding rebuke fixes the problem for inter- pretation. One wants to agree that P. has gone too far; such extravagance is probably not only uncivilized but futile. To reject politics *in toto* is to reject the possibility of human adjustment on any but an authoritarian level, and poets scarcely command that kind of authority. But Pope has not invented the voice of FR. simply so that good sense and prudence may have the last word. To Pope's Augustan mind there is always something absurd about the idea of perfection in human form, and not even his own desire for perfect virtue is exempt from amused objections; but if experience teaches such cautious disbelief in perfection, virtue is nevertheless one sphere in which it may be worth pursuing, at whatever Gulliverian risks. However one reads the Fourth Voyage, it is certain that Swift doesn't *want* the Houyhnhnms to represent perfect rational virtue as lifeless horror; if we feel that Gulliver sacrifices everything 'humanly' worth having in the pursuit of perfection, that may only show that we have learned to love our weaknesses more than we love truth. But of course we *have* done that, and it's late in the day to change sides. The point is that both Gulliver and Pope's P. find virtue achievable only in utter rejection of worldly subtleties and sophisms, that both are theoretically right to do so (the world being what it is), but that both end up seeming obsessed and mad to an eye that views them from any part of that rejected world. Compelled to choose, who would not prefer the Gulliver of Book IV to the Gulliver of Book I, or P. to FR.? But who would not resist such compulsion?

Luckily the choice in Pope's case isn't the end toward which the work impels you. The folly that is part of the truth about P.'s position isn't to be taken as proving any final conclusion about the case. It is one thing to be a fool because you *are* one, in all innocence, and quite another thing to *choose* to be foolish because you can't bear the sophistical evasions of practical wisdom. P. is Pope's demonstration of how a corrupt society drives the good man to despair in stewarding his goodness; but Pope himself falls a little short of P.'s purity, enough at least to permit the invention of FR. as antagonist and the assignment to him of some telling resistances. P. is Pope, a Pope provisionally freed from the irksome necessity of being judicious and equitable in his assessment of the public scene, free for a moment to be irresponsible to everything except his own deepest conviction of moral necessity; FR. is Pope too, then, but in his poetic role are combined and punished just those elements of 'civilized' behaviour which necessarily yet tragically thwart the full realization of one's best impulses. Pope the man could never quite live up to the passionate moral conviction of P.—his biography is full of the troubles he got into by trying—but in the figure of P. he shows both his understanding and his defiance of the unhappy wisdom that R. P. Blackmur once formulated in more modern terms: 'We are never equal, so far as we have one, to our view of life. Our lives are but a parody of our best selves.'

It is significant that the *Epilogue*, Pope's richest display of moral energy in engagement with politics and power, should also be the poem of his that most seriously and dismayingly questions the possibility of the imagination affecting the public world. For P. there simply is no political mode of virtue; even his own good cause has been so implicated in corruption that it can survive only if internalized, made an aspect not of the dialectic of issues and parties but of the poet's stubbornly 'personal' sympathies and affections. If good politics is the effective embodiment of ideas about public benefit, ideas given shape and substance in the policies and achievements of groups of men, then in the P. of the *Epilogue* Pope shows us such ideas stripped of any public realization and shrunken back to the lesser status of private 'ideas', objects only in the interior theatre of the poet's mind. Here they, of course, become all the more compelling, since they're about all the mind has to concern itself with, the only sureties the moral sense can hold on to; but such a condition is awfully close to some old-fashioned metaphors for madness, as Pope's tough mind well recognizes. He was to write nothing of significance for the next five years, before rousing himself for the final magnificent effort that is the Fourth Book of the *Dunciad*, with its mournful farewell not just to politics but to the whole possibility of civilized order on traditional models. The *Epilogue*, to play with a teleological view of a poetic career, is the crucial and difficult dissociation from hopeful action and public engagement that cleared the ground for the essentially tragic mood of the *New Dunciad*.

4. The Politics of Solitude: Gray's Churchyard and Goldsmith's Village

If politics in Pope's *Epilogue* is internalized, the literary process preserves at least the shape and form of activity, even violence, in the mind's way of possessing its ideas; if Pope finally despaired of politics, his despair was no passive, acquiescent thing. But the dominant poetic mood of the middle of the eighteenth century was anything but active and violent, as is well known to the reluctant readers of period anthologies, which leave you with the depressing picture of a rural landscape crowded with lugubrious figures, none of them seeming to know the others are there too, busily writing poems called 'A Hymn on Solitude', 'Ode to Evening', or 'The Pleasures of Melancholy'. By the testimony of their verses, at least, these poets never read newspapers, went to parties, or held a steady job, and it is hard to think of an age whose literature—apart from resolute Augustan diehards like Johnson and Churchill—shows less contact with public experience. F. R. Leavis puts it that

> when we think of Johnson and Crabbe, when we recall any example of a poetry bearing a serious relation to the life of its time, then Gray, Thomson, Dyer, Akenside, Shenstone and the rest belong plainly to a by-line. It is literary and conventional in the worst senses of those terms. It keeps its monotonous tenour along the cool sequestered vale of Polite Letters. 'Sequestered', significantly, is among the words one finds oneself underlining most frequently . . . ; it vies with 'mouldered' (or 'mouldering'), 'contemplation', 'pensive', and 'votary' (the poetic world is something for special cultivation—apart and solemn, belonging, as it were, to a sabbatic cult).[16]

This is telling and essentially right, but I'm not sure that 'poetry bearing a serious relation to the life of its time' is best exemplified by Johnson and Crabbe, fine poets though they are. What seems to me so admirable about them both is precisely a refusal to accommodate their idea of poetry to the 'life' of the times, as they opposed and in effect denied that life by writing in a style which would even then have seemed quaint and old-fashioned. Surely 'life' had then been coloured by a literary sensibility that was itself trivial and corrupt, so that the life of the time was in fact more accurately expressed by the fashionable cultist verse that Leavis and everyone else finds so boring.

The problem, I think, is to understand the state of mind that could generate and find pleasurable use for such idioms and moods, while granting that the poems themselves are mostly dead for ever. An adequate answer would have to draw many bad poems into an essentially sociological frame of analysis; having a frivolously low tolerance for bad poems and no sociological aptitude whatever, I will content myself here with two 'period' poems that are by no means bad, seeing what they may suggest about my main theme.

Significantly, Leavis echoes Gray's *Elegy* in criticizing the poetic by-line the later eighteenth century derived from Milton by way of the Pope of *Eloisa to Abelard*; and yet the *Elegy* is (with Collins's 'Ode to Evening') one of only two poems in this mode that Leavis specifically exempts from his general censure. This suggests the obvious truth that the *Elegy* is a success, one of the very few eighteenth-century non-satiric poems that remain alive for modern readers. For Leavis it remains alive in spite of its belonging to the 'meditative-melancholic' mode, being in fact braced by the presence of an Augustan taste and tact:

> The positive Augustan in him enables Gray to achieve a strong conventionality; his churchyard meditations have, as it were, social substance; his commonplaces are weighted by the idiom of a literary culture that laid peculiar stress on the normally and centrally human as manifested on the common-sense social surface of life. It is significant that Johnson exempted the *Elegy* from his general disparagement of Gray's verse. . . .

No one else could 'get' Gray so beautifully in a few phrases; it is exactly true that the *Elegy* is sustained by the 'social substance' of the Elegist's meditations, that the poem, in articulating the dramatic presence of a solitary, socially disengaged mind, remains always conscious of a felt social identity that no opting for isolation could quite quite erase in the eighteenth century. But the social substance of the *Elegy* seems to me interesting, even peculiar, when looked at in more detail.

In those famous opening stanzas, the solitary Elegist is hardly distinguishable from the place, the 'atmosphere', he occupies:

The Curfew tolls the knell of parting day,
The lowing herd winds slowly o'er the lea,
The plowman homeward plods his weary way,
And leaves the world to darkness and to me.

Now fades the glimmering landscape on the sight,
And all the air a solemn stillness holds,
Save where the beetle wheels his droning flight,
And drowsy tinklings lull the distant folds;

Save that from yonder ivy-mantled tow'r
The mopeing owl does to the moon complain
Of such, as wand'ring near her secret bow'r,
Molest her ancient solitary reign.

The stress on departure, evanescence, diminishment, is clear enough, especially in the curious effort it costs the Elegist to get his rhythm and syntax sufficiently energized to generate a poem. Only in its last line does the first stanza even minimally escape the drugged iteration of disjunct declarative statements, and not until stanza three does the complete coincidence of phrase with line-unit yield to some rhythmic complication. The poem only barely manages to begin, only just overcomes the inertia of the mood. The images make of nightfall a kind of death, when human activity and natural animation virtually cease; this, however, is evidently the right moment for such a poem, when the observer's personal identity fades into the dwindling landscape, when he and the darkness (l. 4) share one another's nature, when he himself is no more the wanderer who molests the owl than he is the owl herself, 'mopeing' just as he will later be listless, mutt'ring, drooping, forlorn, hopeless, and burdened by some nearly inexpressible secret. It's only in solitude, when other people have gone home or become invisible bodies in graves, that the mind achieves a fully 'poetic' relation with its objects, which are not present objects at all but subjective moods and *imagined* memories—he can only pretend to remember the dead villagers, whose living selves he never knew.

And yet, as Leavis implies, the *Elegy* also seems in some way to recognize the world outside the churchyard, the public world Gray indicates with capitalized abstract nouns—Ambition, Grandeur, Honour, Flattery, Knowledge, Luxury, Pride, and the rest. These are of course the shabby villains all eighteenth-century moral poems love to hiss, but their familiarity doesn't explain why Gray needs them there. Whatever his real feelings about dead rustics, it seems that he can only support them in the poem as contrasts to something else, the city-world where talents are perverted or destroyed by having avenues too readily open for their exercise, in contrast to the country, where talent seldom finds any avenues at all. In one of his fine Marxist moods Empson said that the *Elegy* was about the pathetic but unchangeable fact that Gray's England had no scholarship system; the poem thus was to be seen as a rather tricky apology for the *status quo*, praising renunciation and isolation as though they were natural conditions, to show that 'we ought to accept the injustice of society as we do the inevitability of death'.[17] This is very helpful in identifying and understanding the pervasive *lowness* of the *Elegy*'s tone, a lowness that suggests not real meditation, which after all requires some mental action, but something closer to paralysis of mind and will—a reluctance to insist upon one's own existence for fear of disturbing the way things are, which could be read as a reluctance to disturb even the rigid form of society itself.

But the question is *how* the public world of wealth and power is evoked in the poem, and whether the Elegist's dismissal of it—which with Empson we may read as covert or unconscious acquiescence in its existence—seems adequately founded on a serious grasp of its nature. Now Gray and the Elegist are far from scorning the best possibilities of political action:

> Th' applause of list'ning senates to command,
> The threats of pain and ruin to despise,
> To scatter plenty o'er a smiling land,
> And read their hist'ry in a nation's eyes,
>
> Their lot forbad. . . . . (61-65)

—which is to say openly that the villagers were sadly forbidden the largest and most gratifying exercise of virtuous talent, after which the counter-reflection that they never had a chance to be grandiosely *wicked* either comes as something of a let-down. But the willingness to represent the public world only in personified abstractions works against the complicating power of such a concession. We can of course assume that personification had more force for Gray's contemporaries than for us; the device—as often in Thomson and Collins, and indeed Blake and Keats—really can condense and clarify the 'feel' of experience, the relation of sensuous objects to the psychological shape they impress upon the receiving mind. But Collins's Evening or Keats's Autumn is conceived *as* a vehicle of sense data, whereas the Elegist's personifications originate as moral abstractions which are then given some minimal human outline:

> Let not Ambition mock their useful toil,
> Their homely joys, and destiny obscure;
> Nor Grandeur hear with a disdainful smile,
> The short and simple annals of the poor.   (29-32)

Sensuous responsiveness is not the Elegist's *métier*; he finds natural objects most available for poetry when they are comatose or dead and his own mind is correspondingly dulled and passionless, and a similar incapacity seems to interfere with his perception of just what it is about the city-world that he wants to rebuke with his celebration of simplicity. The 'hoary-headed Swain' will later describe the dead Elegist in a significantly uncertain way:

> Hard by yon wood, now smiling as in scorn,
> Mutt'ring his wayward fancies he would rove,
> Now drooping, woeful wan, like one forlorn,
> Or crazed with care, or crossed in hopeless love. (105-109)

As in scorn, *like* one forlorn—you just can't tell whether such melancholy postures are sincere, accurate reflections of inner feeling. And I suppose the remark in the Epitaph that the Elegist 'gave to misery *all he had, a tear*', could suggest emotional puniness as well as lack of funds.

My view is that in the *Elegy*, whatever his intentions, Gray found a beautiful poetic equivalent for emotional poverty, the failure of feeling and imagination to generate responses strong enough to seem equal to experience as 'healthy' minds know it. In the earlier 'Ode on a Distant Prospect of Eton College' Gray sadly observed of the innocent schoolboys that 'Thought would destroy their paradise', and the *Elegy* itself describes a ruined paradise and suggests that it was thought that destroyed it. The Elegist is a kind of eighteenth-century Hamlet, The Man of

Feeling who so intrigued Sterne and bemused Henry Mackenzie, his native hue of resolution sicklied o'er with the pale cast of thought, cultivating marginal, private kinds of emotional stimulation (sympathy) out of the failure of stronger responses to the concerns of the active, busy world. An epigram like 'the paths of glory lead but to the grave' (36) shows thought producing not politically usable ironies about glory but a perception about death that levels any functional distinction between glory and obscurity —*all* paths lead but to the grave, as the churchyard itself proves. In *The Invention of Liberty* Jean Starobinski suggestively reformulates a familiar and relevant eighteenth-century emotional predicament: one felt the power of the pastoral idyll's suggestion that harmony between man and nature was still possible, yet one knew that the real countryside (as in Crabbe) revealed only 'an inexhaustible inventory of misery'. Resolving the predicament required finding *another* nature, 'intact, wild, remote, where men were scarcely to be seen. It was necessary to abandon social ideals, to become a traveller, an exile, contemplating the world in isolation.'[18] In such sublime aloneness, surrounded by mountains and storms or whatever, weakness of inner resources somehow felt right—the largeness of that nature excluded human participation anyway, so it really didn't matter that your own passion and will had been minimal to begin with. Thought first persuades you that your life, anyone's life, life itself, is finally insignificant —and then in the right setting you discover that this isn't just a 'thought' but a strangely consoling natural fact, consoling because it at least shows you're not going mad by entertaining such thoughts.

These are of course not the particular terms of the *Elegy*, where 'nature' is not sublime and the Elegist's isolation not quite so theatrical as that of the professional Exile or Wanderer. In Gray's world emotional poverty justifies itself not as a comforting contrast to nature but by perceiving in the dying landscape an *identity* of self and nature. The poem takes much of its tone and manner from the convention that makes rural experience a means of seeing city experience in a new light—the poet had to be versed in country things because they either shamed or wonderfully epitomized the values of city and court. And part of Gray's purpose is to shame urban pretentiousness by showing that it's doomed to the same mortal necessity that has filled the country churchyard with tombstones: *Et in Arcadia ego*. But I hear another motive, perhaps even a stronger one, in the poem. Being where the Elegist is, in rural solitude, has its own value quite apart from moralizing about Pomp and Power:

> Far from the madding crowd's ignoble strife,
> Their sober wishes never learn'd to stray;
> Along the cool sequester'd vale of life
> They kept the noiseless tenor of their way.   (73-76)

Certainly it's good to think that sober wishes won't go astray here as they may do in more stimulating places; but the last lines alter the case. The cool sequestered vale is not just a refuge from something bad outside. It's also an image of inaction and repose desired for their own sake, a 'noiseless' state where feeble passion and declining will can feel at home, a normative, biologically imperative tranquillity the Elegist himself has achieved by the time of the Epitaph, when he 'rests his head upon the lap of earth', 'the bosom of his Father and his God', like any tired child. Gray does know that death comes hard even for simple rustics who haven't much to lose. 'This pleasing anxious being' has inherent value whatever one's rank. But the image that sums up this persistence of life also fixes it in death—

> Ev'n from the tomb the voice of Nature cries,
> Ev'n in our ashes live their wonted fires

—as if life somehow became more important, or important for the first time, by contrast with its end. (A main point here is the importance of being mourned, stirring feeling in someone else as if to replenish a world which has lost *your* feeling.) If the rich die as inevitably as the poor, then the poor are as anxious to be remembered as the rich, which at least shows that the Elegist doesn't find social distinctions very solid.

It seems that Gray, despite the poem's professed criticism of the world of power, never found public, social abuses real enough to figure as actual dangers to the emotional privacy he so much preferred. The dead villagers never 'knew' what cultivated people know, and at first this seems a tragedy:

But Knowledge to their eyes her ample page
Rich with the spoils of time did ne'er unroll;
Chill Penury repress'd their noble rage,
And froze the genial current of the soul.   (49-52)

But later we're asked to be glad that 'their sober wishes never learn'd to stray' from their peaceable kingdom, and there is something rather tricky stirring here, I think. Words like 'rich', 'noble', 'genial', suggest that the villagers missed something exciting and humanly desirable, but perhaps in the long run nobility is better repressed. Genial currents of the soul *should* be frozen, since feeling only gets you into tragic trouble. The more you know of emotional energy, the more painful death is going to seem as a contrast, and it is both prudent and more responsive to the meaning and value of death to make your life a preliminary kind of dying. The poem ends with the Elegist joining the dead he has talked about, as he imagines his own grave and invents memorial feelings for those who survive to mourn him. And his Epitaph is rather evasive: 'No further seek his merits to disclose,/Or draw his frailties from their dread abode' points at least two ways. By concealing his living talents and defects he cultivates an anonymity that 'democratically' obliterates his painful living sense of superiority to the simple rustics. Death creates the egalitarian society that living politics can never achieve. But also and more generally, the Epitaph admonishes the kindred spirits who read it to remember that talent and achievement need to be forgotten if the living are to accept death, personal extinction, as the good it is. Country-people ought to die, they do die, it's their nature to die; whereas storied urns and animated busts represent the bewildering *surprise* death is to a world intent on power and achievement. It may be true that no one, great or humble, ever resigned 'this pleasing anxious being' without regret, but somehow the poor and simple die better, with the minimum of fuss, while the rich and powerful demand obsequies and monuments to show that their importance and fame survive, which is to say that the most significant part of them, in their own estimation, hasn't died at all.

An elegy is of course a poem about death itself, but it is also a demonstration of how death is best observed and commemorated

—no literary elegy is ever without a certain reflexive consciousness of its own status as memorial object. Gray's churchyard is
itself a kind of monument, but one that has comfortingly lost its
relevance to particular personal fates. This is its distinction from
storied urns and animated busts, which in a sense remain the
private property of individual dead men. The country churchyard, like the ruined castles and abbeys that dot the lansdcape in
so many eighteenth-century poems and paintings, is a sign of
cultural amnesia, so to speak, the loss of one's particular awareness of a particular past. To look at ruins, Starobinski remarks,
may be to find 'history' blurring into an essentially 'aesthetic'
perception that has no discernible relation to the idea of time as a
record of human action but rather finds time a mystery like the
creative mystery behind a work of art.

John Byng (later Viscount Torrington), one of those compul-
sive eighteenth-century travellers who kept elaborate 'philosophical diaries' of their journeys, put the mood with disarming precision when he wrote: 'to me castles and monasteries in decay are
the daintiest speculation'. It is a remark that reeks of literature,
of course, and it is good to know that Byng could take a blunter
line about homelier matters like his personal comfort: 'The dinner
was better than I expected in this filthy Inn (The Wheat Sheaf)
which to the miseries of a cold alehouse, joins the charges of a
London tavern: for 2 small Tench stew'd in a black Sauce were
charged 7 shillings.'[19] But the characteristic speech and behaviour
of an age usually has literary models, and Byng's 'daintiest speculation' is both characteristic and revealing. One speculated about
ruins because they are mysterious, combining human designing
and constructive effort with a non-human process—what Wordsworth in a similar mood called 'the unimaginable touch of time
—that beautifully modifies and enriches the effect of human art.
(The 'aesthetics of irregularity' in fact assumed that the human
artist should anticipate some of the effect of temporal process
upon originally more regular forms, as in 'Gothick' and the
ready-made ruins for setting up in the back garden.) But 'daintiest'!—for Byng and his age ruins had something less than the
violent dramatic force they would exert upon Henry Adams and
Dorothea Brooke Casaubon in the next century. Such shattering
experiences are produced by the imagination's attempt to *re-enact*

the history that has led to the ruined present, and Gray's solitary Elegist avoids re-enactment quite as much as he avoids initiating new action. The churchyard is a monument, but the lives it memorializes have in effect weathered into anonymity, and it would be painful to try to imagine them back into particular identities. (A 'mute inglorious Milton' is easier to contemplate than a *real* Milton, since he won't suddenly get divorced or write *Samson Agonistes*—he requires only the attention and concern you invented him to evoke in the first place.) Pain itself is a sign of activity, and this Elegist shuns it as he does all other forms of action.

The *Elegy*, of course, sets out to explore the relation between simple and sophisticated lives; it is a political eclogue, as Empson suggests, but its effects are curious. The Elegist detaches himself from the social and educational station implied in his cultivated, 'literary' mode of speech and achieves, by meditating upon the fate of simple folk, what Neil H. Hertz in a perceptive commentary calls a 'relation of shy familiarity' with peasants and rustics. In return, the rustics accept him—see the hoary-headed swain's remarks—as an eccentric but familiar figure for whom they can feel a certain puzzled affection. The Elegist, as Hertz says, can only evaluate his own solitude by relating it to *some* society—for Gray solitude has little of the intrinsic value it will have for Wordsworth. His position 'enables him to view, in distant perspective, both the "madding crowd's ignoble strife" and the more sober but limited lives of the villagers'.[20] But Gray sustains such relations, I think, only by enlarging 'society' to mean any minimal human encounter, however remote from mutual understanding and shared purposes. The Elegist can *join* the villagers only in the grave, where his identity and merits can be as unpublicized and seem as unpretentious as theirs. Above ground they were at least potentially involved in the compromising business of life, of which the public, city society is only the awful extreme case; there are Hampdens, Miltons, and Cromwells in both worlds, and while their blessed lack of opportunity preserved the village versions from the fate of their city counterparts, I suspect that for the Elegist it's their being *dead* that makes them so comfortable to think about.

In short, I take the *Elegy* to mean fundamentally that *any* mode

of 'life' is finally unacceptable. The short and simple annals of
the poor are better than the more pretentious records of Ambition
and Grandeur just because they *are* short and simple, reducing
the bothersome details of a lifetime to the least possible number
of words. The Elegist rejects the world of action and power not
because he prefers the simple life of humble people *as* life, but
because it is the closest thing to no life whatsoever. His own
solitude, with its passive receptivity to whatever is at hand and
its preference for objects and moods with little or no animation,
is a preparation for his own death, which he imagines not only as
annihilation of personal consciousness but as obliteration of his
individual existence even from the memories of those who survive
him. He becomes his own epitaph, itself a mysterious, enigmatic
'ruin' of what was once a whole human personality, to lead any
future 'kindred Spirit' to a similar consoling fate.

What such a reading might signify about Gray himself is not
strictly a concern for criticism; we know him to have been a shy
and retiring man, a scholar who 'produced' only notes and frag-
ments, a poet who finished few poems, an academic recluse whose
social relations were largely conducted through letters, but the
Elegy's status as autobiographical document may safely be left
problematical. What is certain is that the *Elegy* is his one assured
poetic achievement, and with the 'Ode to Evening' (as Leavis
rightly insists) one of the two unquestionable masterpieces of the
late-Augustan melancholy-meditative style. And it is significant
that Gray rejects public vices—the city world of Politics, ambition, pride in status—not because they interfere with superior
human possibilities but because they have come to seem covert
metaphors for life itself.

The *Elegy* is the greatest eighteenth-century poem of solitude
because it is the most uncompromising in seeing what the pursuit
of solitude implies, the least reticent about what may happen
when one loses interest in human society. (Its closest literary relative is not a poem but Mackenzie's imitation of a ruined novel,
The Man of Feeling, which seems only an absurd exercise in
literary fashion until you begin to think out the implications of
the failure of self it so insistently dwells upon.) Goldsmith's
Deserted Village (1770), which also represents a solitary mind
contemplating the public world from a country location, shows

how similar poetic materials can produce a significantly different conclusion. *The Deserted Village* is much the more 'dated' work, and I don't suppose one now can take Goldsmith as seriously as Gray; but those qualities of style and outlook that make the poem seem sentimentally unreal are aspects of a whole effect that made sense to the eighteenth and nineteenth centuries, and it needn't be wholly beyond our sympathetic grasp.

One problem for us is Goldsmith's relentless tenderness, which kept generations of schoolmarms warm on winter mornings:

> Sweet Auburn, loveliest village of the plain,
> Where Health and plenty cheared the labouring swain,
> Where smiling spring its earliest visit paid,
> And parting summer's lingering blooms delayed;
> Dear lovely bowers of innocence and ease,
> Seats of my youth, when every sport could please . . .

(Here I omit some 25 lines, no real offence against so leisurely a voice.)

> . . . These were thy charms, sweet village; sports like these,
> With sweet succession, taught even toil to please;
> These round thy bowers their chearful influence shed,
> These were thy charms—But all these charms are fled.

This lilting anapaestic music, with its innocent and rather Irish charm, may not quite disarm resistance to the heaping up of 'sweets' and 'charms' and 'lovelies', the impossible ideality of the claims made for agrarian simplicity. This is no way to talk about a community of real, fallen souls. But of course Goldsmith is not talking about people and their complex existences but about *memory* and its power over fact. The 34-line first sentence, with its tender catalogue of village scenes and pastimes, works like a flash-back which dissolves into a very different present; the past tenses aren't narrative conventions but signs of a historical disaster, a clash between memory and present awareness that 'turns the past to pain' (82) when you fully recognize where you are.[21] Goldsmith's speaker is a traveller come home after 'many a year' to settle down and do some showing off for his stay-at-home friends, 'tell of all I felt, and all I saw' before he 'die[s] at home at last' (92-96); but it turns out that 'at last' and 'at home' don't accord so comfortably, since the village is no longer the home he left.

So far the drift of the poem is touching but hardly remarkable. Growing old always involves losing one's past; everyone knows you can't go home again. Even if Auburn were still alive and bustling, its charms would hardly be what they seemed in his youth. He stands as a pretty conventional type of the melancholy traveller—'in all my wanderings round this world of care,/In all my griefs—and GOD has given my share' (83-84)—who is only too ready to strike the poignant note, as when he characterizes himself as a hunted hare who 'pants to the place from whence at first she flew' (94). (Even the little sexual shift to 'she' stresses his sense of victimized weakness.) We idealize what we have lost, commonly enough, and within any particular loss we easily discern the larger pathos of 'Experience' itself creating psychological homelessness, the root meaning of 'nostalgia'. To this extent *The Deserted Village* is about the painful discovery that time interferes with possession of one's personal history—Goldsmith mourns something like the loss of identity that Gray's Elegist welcomes in death.

But of course *The Deserted Village* has a more obvious and more important concern than this. Something happens when the Traveller contemplates the scene he has 'returned' to:

> No more thy glassy brook reflects the day,
> But choked with sedges, works its weedy way.
> Along thy glades, a solitary guest,
> The hollow sounding bittern guards its nest;
> Amidst thy desert walks the lapwing flies,
> And tires their ecchoes with unvaried cries.
> Sunk are thy bowers, in shapeless ruin all,
> And the long grass o'ertops the mouldering wall.   (41-48)

Here personal grief is nicely transferred onto the natural scene, so that the bittern is a 'solitary guest' like the Traveller, and the sluggish 'choked' brook and the lapwing's obsessed, 'unvaried' cry participate in his own mood. But a larger feeling stirs in the last couplet quoted, a lament for past glory that aspires to some of the depth and scope of the Old English elegies. The shapeless ruin and the mouldering wall aren't quite to the scale of an abandoned *village*, and they hint at a mythic grandeur in Auburn Lost that Auburn Regained could never claim. The poem exists at the point where 'memory' ceases to be a record of biographical fact; individual history melts into a larger history whose implications are more general.[22] Goldsmith's main purpose is to make social metaphor, and the last three-quarters of the poem reveal almost nothing more of the Traveller as a particular person.

For modern readers this transformation has its difficulties. For example, the elegiac passage just quoted ends with a somewhat jarring couplet:

> And trembling, shrinking from the spoiler's hand,
> Far, far away thy children leave the land.

This is not just identity struggling to cope with an external world that denies the memories by which identity asserts itself—this is someone else's fault, there's a 'spoiler' who ruins villages and drives the rustic folk away. Such an attempt to personify the impersonal forces of social and economic change now seems quaint and crude, but there's something admirable about trying to attribute bad times to human malice or error, instead of resigning yourself to 'conditions' that are beyond anyone's control or influence. Goldsmith was willing to risk other kinds of objection, including considerable ridicule for his insistence that Depopulation was a present sociological fact, that enclosure of common land had disastrous economic consequences and marked a grave decline of responsibility and moral generosity in the landed class. In dedicating the poem to Sir Joshua Reynolds, himself a sceptic about depopulation, Goldsmith regretfully refused to defend his views against the objections he rightly expected from Mandevillian theorists who thought luxury the basis of national prosperity: 'the discussion would take up too much room, and I should prove myself, at best, an indifferent politician, to tire the reader with a long preface, when I want his unfatigued attention to a long poem'. For him the poem was a political act, and as such its integrity and public intelligibility presumably mattered more than any display of psychological coherence in the narrator.

Here, of course, is where *The Deserted Village* and Gray's *Elegy* part company. And one may rather admire Goldsmith's spirit— his Irish insistence on the value of lost causes—in pursuing poetry's connection with a public life that Gray more reasonably found unavailable to a 'poetic' sensibility. If Goldsmith was wrong about depopulation as a gross demographic fact (the whole population of England was of course mushrooming in the eighteenth century—people were going not to America but only to Manchester), he was perfectly right in thinking that a stable agrarian society was dying and that this would cause trouble before long; England came closer to revolution in the 1790's than has always been understood. And it was good of him not to settle for just another poem about solitude and nostalgic melancholy, the fashionable stuff the magazines were full of. In short, he was not essentially mistaken about the public condition the poem sought to publicize, and (like so many eighteenth-century poets) he had himself been poor and hopeless enough to know what the private effects of public disorder could feel like. But, quite simply and obviously, his literary instrument wasn't suited to the expression of *both* personal suffering and its relation to politics and power. Even at his best, the tone never quite escapes a mild schizophrenia:

> Ill fares the land, to hastening ills a prey,
> Where wealth accumulates, and men decay;
> Princes and lords may flourish, or may fade,
> A breath can make them, as a breath has made;
> But a bold peasantry, their country's pride,
> When once destroyed, can never be supplied.   (51-56)

Here a fine and sober rhetoric, convincingly implying a general wisdom based on a fund of particular instances, slips in the last couplet into generality of another sort, based less on experience than the easy maxim-making of special pleading. The implications of princes flourishing and fading like simple flowers, wealth growing virtually *out of* the decaying substance of ruined men, seem too large and serious to be accommodated by a point about a 'bold peasantry', which wrenches things back into the limiting frame of sociological argument—as though the images of decaying and fading meant only that simple peasants are more important and somehow more persistently real than great men.

It would be ridiculous to claim that the poetic habits we lump together as 'neo-classical' or 'Augustan' forbid convincing expression of personal suffering. But as rendered by Pope or Johnson or Goldsmith himself, it is suffering *distanced* and made intelligible by the intervention of a somewhat generalized diction, a rhythm conditioned by the couplet pattern into a psychologically 'closed' set of expectations, a speaking tone and implied moral mood that may show variations between Pope and Johnson (with Goldsmith somewhere in between) but is always relatively dignified, unsurprisable, prepared for the worst and grateful for exceptions, always aware that the event must be made available to an audience and that the poet's own response may at any moment be challenged or questioned by someone sceptical or unconvinced. The habit of personification works well enough when you need a fleeting suggestion of how the mind grasps and responds to a natural object, but not so well (as we saw in Gray) when used as moral shorthand, when the poet's concern is not with sensuous effects but with distributing human nature under the ledger-headings of moral accounting. Gray's Ambition, Grandeur, Honour, Pride, and the rest mostly express indifference to the public world they divide into segments, urging us not to work up moral indignation about that world but rather to forget about it, since there's no health there.

Goldsmith, however, wants to keep such concern alive, and when, at the climax of *The Deserted Village*, this motive leads him to personification, the results are depressingly out of key with the intention:

> Even now, methinks, as pondering here I stand,
> I see the rural virtues leave the land:
> Down where yon anchoring vessel spreads the sail,
> That idly waiting flaps with every gale,
> Downward they move, a melancholy band,
> Pass from the shore, and darken all the strand.
> Contented toil, and hospitable care,
> And kind connubial tenderness, are there;
> And piety, with wishes placed above,
> And steady loyalty, and faithful love.   (397-406)

The poem's point is that economic 'rationalization' has consequences in human suffering, and so we need to observe human figures suffering such consequences. But here personification works to depersonalize feelings Goldsmith earlier took some pains to give affectionate human embodiment: the parson 'passing rich with forty pounds a year', the schoolmaster ('twas certain he could write, and cypher too'), the 'village statesmen' pontificating over their ale and stale news. All these are types, perhaps, but ones with considerable representative value. (A stable society like a rural village in fact makes 'typical' roles available and encourages you to adopt them, so that busy people won't have to waste much time figuring each other out.) But while Goldsmith can charmingly represent the villagers as they were before the calamity, he can't show them suffering their destruction in any immediate and moving way. It would be pleasant to think that it's the *social process* that creates this concluding distance—things have gone so far that one can barely imagine their former reality at all. But we can be pretty sure that any such effect is an accidental irony at best, a result of Goldsmith's general literary taste and not of his grasp of the subject at hand. The saintly parson of Auburn has to become 'piety, with wishes placed above', if he's to seem important enough for cultivated readers to take seriously. Even with an authentic human meaning to express, Goldsmith can't quite trust it to operate without 'literary' certification in stylistic elegance.

Gray and Goldsmith differ in that the latter preserves a somewhat old-fashioned, 'Augustan' concern about the effects of public process while the former finds that process only an antipathetic presence defining the limits of what is poetically important and interesting. But the poems, in primary motive, differ less than they seem to. Starobinski classifies both the *Elegy* and *The Deserted Village* as cases of 'pastoral dirge', a mode in which the idyllic relations between country perfection and city corruption are broken, at the point where 'the internal requirements of truth and fatality demand the death of the idyll (if necessary through the deaths of the idyllic characters)'. Here the outward reference of pastoral, the distant city whose flawed, 'political' nature ordinarily measures the value of solitary withdrawal, *fails* to absorb the feelings that solitude gives rise to. When politics, with all the misimaginations of self it implies, is no longer a strong enough figure of antagonism, the old dialectic can only be transformed into a confrontation between the solitary self and *death*. The solitary man considers not other men, or their collective embodiment in social and political institutions, but tokens of mortality, church-yards or deserted villages (both monuments to buried, lost lives), some ruined form of a past whose human purposes and feelings have been forgotten, whose meaning can only by validated by the death of the solitary contemplating mind itself, as it *enters* the oblivion it has pondered and found inscrutable but wholly compelling.

To be sure, in *The Deserted Village* there is resistance to the idea that poetic inspiration requires solitude so that it can seize upon lost connections, failures of strength, as its proper subject. Goldsmith, who could be unhappy but never very productively introspective, would of course not have thought losses and failures alone the proper subject for poetry. In *The Traveller* he invents (or rather adapts from literary vogues) a speaker who feels 'remote, unfriended, melancholy, slow' mostly so as to ponder the state of political and moral 'Freedom' without the limiting prejudices of nationality—the sub-title is 'A Prospect of Society'—before he concludes that private, 'domestic joy' matters more than that part of a man's existence that 'government' affects. In *The Deserted Village* a very similar Traveller returns to his starting point but as a changed man, sophisticated by his experience of other, larger worlds; as Gray says in the *Elegy*, simple people don't write poems, and so people who do write poems can't quite claim fellowship with them. The speaker in *The Deserted Village* is dangerously near to being someone for whom villages in decay are the daintiest speculation; the poem thus records his learning *not* to aestheticize his experience (including his memories) but rather to keep some passion alive by treating his experience as a 'political' symbol for the experience of other, simpler men. But his poetic style, and the sensible, 'middle-class' understanding of established conventions of art and life it implies, keep him from finding a secure location for *himself* in the poem. He can see the ruined villagers, and the process that has ruined them, only from a distance that blurs the particularity of both the process and its victims. His generous feelings remain imprisoned within the linguistic frame of the existing order. It would take a new language, a new definition of the political situation, to get the poet's feelings solidly *into* the poem and strip personified social abstractions down to their naked human skin:

> Pity would be no more,
> If we did not make somebody Poor.

*   *   *

It did not take long for a poetry open to political and social concerns, the poetry of Dryden, Pope, and their lesser contemporaries, to yield the fashion to poetry that (like Collins's) insulated itself from public subjects entirely or (like Gray's) admitted public referents only as remote, cautionary presences on a horizon from which one was constantly withdrawing. The imaginative avoidance of politics is itself a response to politics, however, and it is less than surprising to find such poetry in an age whose public life was as settled and undramatic and frankly corrupt as that of the later Augustans. The official mood of the century was more or less the sedate acceptance of the universe recommended by Addison in *Spectator* 381:

> An inward chearfulness is an implicit praise and thanksgiving to Providence under all its dispensations. It is a kind of acquiescence in the state wherein we are placed, and a secret approbation of the divine will.

It takes only a little fudging to secularize these terms, taking 'state wherein we are placed' as the political state itself, whose dispensations of places have some of the benign force of providence. But if this was the official mood, it was not inevitably the mood of the century's greatest imaginative moments, which are often moments of moral peril or defeat, when the mind confronts an external chaos that threatens something like the destruction of personality, as in the *Epilogue to the Satires* and *Dunciad IV*, the 'Digression on Madness' and Gulliver's last voyage, and corresponding incidents and tones in *Clarissa*, *Rasselas*, Gibbon, and *Tristram Shandy*. These are great moments because they dramatize a strain between madness, death, or cultural collapse, and an opposing perception of 'order' that resists such finalities. And that opposing order is quite as much public and political as it is personal and ethical. Gray's *Elegy* shows such an opposing political order on the verge of disappearing from the poet's field of mind, and *The Deserted Village* shows it being kept in sight only

137

at considerable sacrifice of clarity and coherence. Romanticism was to be as much a discovery of new political modes, and a new involvement of poetic imagination in politics and myths that express it, as it was to be anything else.

NOTES

[1] The best account of Dryden's major satiric mode is Reuben A. Brower, 'An Allusion to Europe: Dryden and Tradition', *ELH*, XIX (1952), 38-48.

[2] Bernard N. Schilling, *Dryden and the Conservative Myth* (New Haven, Yale University Press, 1961), p. 238. For a discussion of the political implications of *The Medal*, see Alan Roper, *Dryden's Poetic Kingdoms* (London, Routledge & Kegan Paul, and New York, Barnes & Noble, 1965), pp. 87-103.

[3] 'When the given order is taken as rational, idealism has reached its end. Political philosophy must henceforth refrain from teaching where the state ought to be. The state is, is rational, and there's the finale. Hegel adds that his philosophy will instead counsel that the state must be recognised as a moral universe. The task of philosophy becomes that of "reconciling men to the actual".' Herbert Marcuse, *Reason and Revolution: The Rise of Hegel's Social Theory* (London and New York, Oxford University Press, 1941), pp. 182-183. The whole of Marcuse's chapter, 'The Political Philosophy', is pertinent, especially in warning against finding in Hegel sanction for the modern totalitarian state, a warning that would apply to Dryden too.

[4] See Robert C. Elliott, *The Power of Satire* (Princeton, Princeton University Press, and London, Oxford University Press, 1960), pp. 3-15.

[5] L. B. Namier, *The Structure of Politics at the Accession of George III*, 2nd ed. (London, Macmillan, and New York, St. Martin's 1957), p. 18.

[6] For Townsend and Fonnereau, see Namier, *Structure of Politics*, pp. 49-50.

[7] Namier, *Structure of Politics*, p. 214.

[8] Namier, *Structure of Politics*, p. 89; Namier, *England in the Age of the American Revolution*, 2nd ed. (London, Macmillan, and New York, St. Martin's, 1962), pp. 4-5.

[9] Namier, *Structure of Politics*, p. 31, p. 68. Compare George Grenville's distinction between 'bishoprics of business for men of abilities and learning, and bishoprics of ease for men of family and fashion', and Namier's remark that 'pluralism was, to a large extent, the ecclesiastical equivalent of sinecures in the State—the Church could not but reproduce the dominant features of the national structure' (*Crossroads of Power*, p. 185).

[10] Namier, *Age of the American Revolution*, pp. 33-35.

[11] See Robert Walcott, *English Politics in the Early Eighteenth Century* (Oxford, Clarendon Press, 1956), for an analysis of elections and parliamen-

tary sessions between 1701 and 1708 that shows interesting similarities to Namier's findings about the mid-century and later.

[12] Namier, *Crossroads of Power*, p. 17.

[13] Namier, *Age of the American Revolution*, pp. 173-174.

[14] Namier, *Age of the American Revolution*, p. 220.

[15] My calling FR. the 'political man' and P. the 'moral hero' should not obscure the fact that each is a parody, an overstated version of the role he plays; I think that Martin Price, in his interesting discussion of the *Epilogue* in *To the Palace of Wisdom* (New York, Doubleday, 1964), p. 176, misunderstands my original formulation of this point.

[16] F. R. Leavis, *Revaluation* (London, Chatto & Windus, 1936), pp. 105-106.

[17] Empson, *Some Versions of Pastoral*, pp. 4-5.

[18] Jean Starobinski, *The Invention of Liberty 1700-1789*, tr. Bernard C. Swift (Geneva, Skira, 1964), pp. 159 ff. Starobinski's whole treatment of the relation between idyll and real rural nature is very instructive.

[19] *The Torrington Diaries*, ed. C. Bruyn Andrews, abr. ed. (London, Eyre & Spottiswoode, 1954), p. 243, p. 151. Literature and life come memorably together in Byng's remark that 'the way to enjoy Tintern Abbey properly, and at leisure, is to bring wines, cold meat, with corn for the horses; (bread, beer, cyder, and commonly salmon, may be had at the Beaufort Arms;) spread your table in the ruins; and possibly a Welsh harper may be procured from Chepstow' (p. 40).

For the vogue of travel and its relation to contemporary aesthetic tastes, see Paul Fussell, Jr., 'Patrick Brydone: The Eighteenth-Century Traveler as Representative Man', *Bulletin of the New York Public Library*, 66 (1962), 349-363.

[20] Neil H. Hertz, 'Poetry in an Age of Prose: Arnold and Gray', in *In Defense of Reading*, ed. R. A. Brower and Richard Poirier (New York, Dutton, 1962), p. 67.

[21] For the relation between memory and present social fact in *The Deserted Village*, see Raymond Williams, 'Nature's Threads', *Eighteenth-Century Studies*, II (1968), 53-56; after some hesitation, I have not revised my interpretation in the light of Williams's admirable essay, which deals in its own way with perceptions somewhat like mine.

[22] Raymond Williams ('Nature's Threads', pp. 53-56) objects that this 'negative identification' of the poet's personal history of suffering with 'the facts of a social history beyond him' confuses things, making him describe the land as blighted just when it was really being tidied up and used more productively; the confusion is there, but it seems to me to make the poem more interesting and moving.

CHAPTER FOUR

The Revolutionary Imagination

In what Northrop Frye would have us call the Age of Sensibility, poetry withdrew from a public life it found corrupted and corrupting; one of the chosen tasks of the new age was to make connections between poetic imagination and the politics of unrest and revolution. The English Romantic poets I shall be discussing —allowing for their great differences of temperament and interest —tried to find, and sustain belief in, some equivalence between internal' and 'external' revolution. In what sense could a radical politics objectify the energies and aims of a radical aesthetics? I assume that the Romantics themselves took the primacy of imagination as a given; while revolutionary politics and their own new ways of seeing and feeling might both manifest the same evolution of spirit, still for them the poet started not with the external, public condition but with the movement of his own mind in new and exciting patterns. Romantic literature can hardly have *created* the revolutionary politics of modern Europe; revolutions are created mostly by ordinary people's economic woes feeding into the ambitions and dreams of ideologues and would-be leaders. But whatever the case, the Romanticist's prior concern for his own mind and feelings was fortunate, preserving him as it did from an idea of self that could figure in public affairs only as a passive spectator or victim, as in Gray and Goldsmith.

For the Romantics, then, the public poem was a crucial imaginative act, a way of locating consciousness so as to associate it with the movements of revolutionary power, participating in the political drama and not just observing and recording it. The task had its dangers. The failing of imaginative power was an obsessive concern for Wordsworth and Coleridge, who experienced the disaster themselves, and it was never far from the ironies of Byron and the anxieties of Keats, even though they were themselves spared middle age. The matter was particularly important, I suppose, because the youthful commitment of mind to public process, the linking of imagination and revolution, left one vulnerable to the feeling that decline, when and if it came, wasn't just a sad but inevitable biological wasting but a betrayal of the ideological energy that had illuminated one's youth with a rich sense of involvement in other lives. And conversely, one could never be sure that political disillusionment wasn't a frightening signal of spiritual and imaginative atrophy, rather than maturity's wiser assessment of youthful excess. One didn't have to be a Chateaubriand to lose libertarian passion; but it took Chateaubriand's kind of vulgar egotism not to be profoundly shocked and depressed when it happened.

Much Romantic poetry sought a commitment of creative mind to public causes, and it seems right that activist poets of our own day should find Blake and Shelley compelling models of feeling and technique, and that their revolutionary 'myths' should so occupy the minds of serious literary scholars. But if it is important to know how Romantic poets approached public subjects, one must also recognize the difficulties they faced in integrating imagination and political enthusiasm. Perhaps the greatest difficulty, and the one I shall be most concerned with, is the tendency to achieve such integration by 'aestheticizing' one's concern for immediate social and political reality, transforming it into some symbolic paradigm that the mind can possess and manipulate more easily that the intractable stuff of the public world itself.

1. Blake: The Mythologist as Agitator

No reader of Blake can doubt that he was intensely and productively interested in the social and political aspects of his world. David Erdman has extensively explored his political attitudes and responses to public events, and Jacob Bronowski has outlined his poetry's bearing on the social and intellectual conditions of a society on the threshold of modern economic and technological rationalization.[1] That these are important perspectives becomes evident at one's first look at a poem like 'London', with its immediate and profound horror about what urbanization does to spirit:

> I wander thro' each charter'd street,
> Near where the charter'd Thames does flow.
> And mark in every face I meet
> Marks of weakness, marks of woe.

In every cry of every Man,
In every Infant's cry of fear,
In every voice: in every ban
The mind-forg'd manacles I hear.

How the Chimney-sweeper's cry
Every black'ning Church appalls,
And the hapless Soldier's sigh
Runs in blood down Palace walls.

But most thro' midnight streets I hear
How the youthful Harlot's curse
Blasts the new-born Infant's tear
And blights with plagues the Marriage hearse.

There's no mistaking the governing feeling, and of course no one has mistaken it. But even at the risk of rehearsing the obvious, it may be worth seeing how the poem creates a personal location from which to indict a society terrorized and morally deadened by institutional repression.

The speaker is an urban version of someone like Gray's Elegist (or Eliot's Tiresias), a solitary, reflective mind examining a scene that is not its native habitat and pondering the significance of anonymous, essentially dead lives. He speaks as a wanderer who changes places without any fixed plan or purpose of his own, and the state of mind that generates the poem is evident only when you penetrate a tonal surface that is curiously impassive and matter-of-fact. His words *mean* horrible things, to be sure, but the horror is in the scene and it needs little stress in the telling; it is enough to present, with some of the detachment of the social scientist, a virtually quantitative report. 'Every' is the recurring word, as though a statistical reckoning had been made and found to yield an improbably consistent result, with a shift in the last stanza to an account of the observation that 'most' yielded the uniform conclusion—whether 'most emphatically' or just 'most frequently' isn't stated. Blake's language for describing urban dissociation acknowledges and at one level mimics the cold mechanics of a depersonalized social awareness. People are reduced to their faces and then further reduced in the last three stanzas to mere sounds, bodiless signs of distant, generalized cases of suffering.

Such detachment is of course only a preliminary effect. It masks a rhetorical emphasis that points away from descriptive analysis toward the agitator's passion for reform or even revolution—the impatience with elegant variation in the almost clumsy repetition of 'mark' and 'marks' in the first stanza, the hammer-blows of 'every' in stanza two, the quickening effect of initial metrical truncation in six of the last eight lines. The same fervour produces the dream-like blurring of sense categories in stanza three, where auditory phenomena have visual effects, a cry 'appalling' ('darkening', the church itself is not horrified) the church and a sigh dripping down palace walls. For this observer, the evidence of suffering isn't remote and ignorable noise but immediately visible and almost tactile, 'pall' (like the soot the sweep stirs up) and 'blood' being substances and not mere ocular signs of agony.

The strain between dispassionate surface and subliminal moral vehemence is epitomized in the final stanza, a formed, almost anecdotal detail that is at once realistic, like some vignette out of Defoe or Hogarth or Mayhew, and symbolically resonant with the terror and pathos of the whole condition being indicted. The harlot's curse is first of all just that, a curse—she damns and blasts her crying baby and summons a plague to take the institution of marriage itself. (It could be either the casual or forced marriage of the poor that then abandons mother and child to their own devices, or the respectable, bourgeois marriage from which she and her kind are excluded by economic disability.) She is first of all *real*, that is, and the fussy locution 'youthful Harlot' seems almost to mock the cautious formality behind which gentility shelters its helpless embarrassment at the spectacle of vulgar misfortune. (One imagines that a century later Gladstone thought the girls he befriended in the streets were 'youthful harlots' and not 'young whores'.) But she is also the symbolic epitome of the weakness and woe the poem inwardly rages against, and of their consequences for society. Her curse, the life that reduces her to impotent if sincere blasphemy, in a larger sense does blast the prospects of innocent children—when they grow up to be people like her they'll have plenty to cry about—and blight the healthful possibilities of marriage, since her mere existence is a gross parody of sanctified mutuality in love and a living rebuke to those who assume that lawful respectability distinguishes people who matter from those who don't. Blake's reservations about contractual marriage are well known, but we may be sure he drew the line at prostitution, which is after all a contractual relation too, if one that both parties are able to carry out rather more expeditiously. Marriage and harlotry may be equally undesirable to Blake, but I think he here expects us to be shocked by the conjunction of positive, sanctified sexual union (the ideal of marriage if not always its actual nature) with literal 'social disease' and symbolic social death.

The poor harlot shows how feeling and spontaneous life can be reduced to the passionless routines of economic progress, getting and spending, so to speak; just so, abstract law tries to impose its fictions upon the substance of the human community, invisibly marking off the limits of control and ownership upon the streets and, as a final absurdity, the fluid Thames itself. But the dreadful fact is that the fictions work; the manacles of legalism and economic necessity, though only mental forgeries, do bind men and women and children to roles that corrupt or drain their living spirit. The poem offers no practical remedy, but the identity the poet achieves in speaking the poem gives at least a hint of hopeful counter-action. Although the streets are chartered he wanders through them freely enough. If the people he encounters are so marked by suffering as to seem unresponsive to anything except their own misery, he himself is not so spiritless—he indeed has no identity except that enforced upon him by their plight, no object but them for his concerned attention. A man who can hear the mind-forged manacles in every voice is himself not yet bound by them, and if mind can put men in bondage, another kind of mind may be able to release them. 'London' is a powerful, even heroic, poem because it shows isolated moral awareness asserting, without self-praise or self-mockery, that its own existence is sufficient rebuke to a thoroughly corrupt public condition. For such a voice to formulate a 'programme' or call for followers would seem superfluous and somehow demeaning.

It took no visionary powers to see that England was in a bad way in the 1780's and '90's, and I have risked saying obvious things about a familiar poem to suggest that it was not Blake's peculiar way of seeing his world so much as his thorough grasp of his verbal medium that makes a poem like 'London' so much better and politically more dangerous than the satires on public affairs and laments for lost national innocence that were being written at the same time. Blake's political feelings were of course strong and unconcealed, enough so to get him into serio-comic trouble with the law in 1804, when he was tried (and only with some luck acquitted) for 'having uttered seditious and treasonable expressions'; and his earlier association with the radical circle of Priestley, Price, and Paine is sufficient proof of 'activism' as times went then. His excitement about popular revolution is obliquely evident in *Tiriel* (probably written in 1789, though never engraved), with its implied comment on George III, and more openly, indeed aggressively, in *The French Revolution* (unengraved, 1791), *The Marriage of Heaven and Hell*, *Visions of the Daughters of Albion*, *America* (these three dated 1793), and *Europe* (1794). And his withdrawal into the endless drafting and redrafting of *The Four Zoas* and the composing and engraving of *Milton* and *Jerusalem* coincides at least roughly with the decline of the French Revolution into the new oppressions of Napoleonic empire; Blake was accused of uttering pro-Bonaparte sentiments during the invasion scare of 1803, but it seems unlikely that he did so, or that he ever saw Napoleon as anything but a Urizenic menace to the Revolution and its promised future.[2] But if revolutionary fervour and subsequent despair about the re-establishment of tyranny mark general stages in Blake's imaginative and emotional life, they do not account for the poetry in any direct way.

'London' is intensely alive with an immediate and practical rage, like some other great *Songs of Experience*—'Holy Thursday', 'The Chimney Sweeper', 'A Little Boy Lost'. But in some of Blake's best poems the passionate awareness of the destructive effects of a rationalized social order is more obliquely expressed. Blake had great compassion for suffering, especially the suffering of children, and a fine ruthless contempt for autocrats and exploiters, but he normally looked beyond present evils to ultimate moral issues, as in 'The Tyger', with its formidable challenge to unravel the mysterious relations of energy to virtue, and 'The Human Abstract', one of his finest and most demanding poems:

> Pity would be no more,
> If we did not make somebody Poor:

And Mercy no more could be,
If all were as happy as we;

And mutual fear brings peace;
Till the selfish loves increase.
Then Cruelty knits a snare,
And spreads his baits with care.

He sits down with holy fears,
And waters the ground with tears:
Then Humility takes its root
Underneath his foot.

Soon spreads the dismal shade
Of Mystery over his head;
And the Catterpiller and Fly,
Feed on the Mystery.

And it bears the fruit of Deceit,
Ruddy and sweet to eat;
And the Raven his nest has made
In its thickest shade.

The Gods of the earth and sea,
Sought thro' Nature to find this Tree
But their search was all in vain:
There grows one in the Human Brain.

This has the gnomic air of a riddle; we seem to be children
listening to a patient, explanatory voice leading up to some simple
but important discovery we must finally make for ourselves, some
moral lesson thinly concealed in the fable. But there is something
smug and nasty in that voice. The opening lines in fact mimic
and mock the prudential, self-congratulatory morality of conventional religiosity: 'we' exercise Pity and Mercy on 'somebody'
(*anybody* will do), one of those other, less privileged people
proper children are taught to feel sorry for, vaguely, as they enjoy
their own comfortable lives. At one level, the first stanza tells
simple truth: the ethical virtues, ethics itself, are necessary only
because this is a fallen world, where poverty and misery tragically
do exist but can't be relieved except by the exercise of what compassion one can muster up. But of course, like any other virtues,

Pity and Mercy have a way of becoming their own reward; Blake knew as well as Hobbes or Mandeville that most people practice compassion because it makes them feel good, and the obvious implication is that we have adjusted the socio-political machine to *create* misery and poverty so that we can congratulate ourselves for our concern. The static social order sustains itself, in the name of charity, upon a secret but active determination to deny other people spiritual freedom and economic substance. To the child who asks why there are poor people, the bland voice of Moral Instruction answers: 'So that we may be good Christians, dear.'

From this harsh beginning the poem develops an allegorical homily about evil growing out of the uneasy stability of a secular order based not on positive vision but selfishness and 'mutual fear', those 'private vices' that in Mandeville's mocking sociology sustain 'public benefits' in the modern political state as it really is. The smug hypocrisy of practical moralists can sustain its equilibrium only so long, since our selfishness tends to expand beyond the restraining boundaries of other people's selfishness. Then order can be supported only by Cruelty, a calculated, cunning repression that masks as pitying concern offering the 'fruit of Deceit' it has nurtured with its crocodile tears; the tree of Humility bears the dark foliage of Mystery, which feeds the devouring vermin of a false priesthood more nourishingly than it sustains the laity with its ruddy and sweet-seeming fruit. What cynical theorists see as the 'natural' equilibrium of opposing evils in the political state can't in fact sustain itself without the pacifying frauds of institutional piety, persuading us that truth hides in unfathomable darkness and that it is thus enough for ordinary men to imitate the feigned humility of their spiritual teachers, acquiescing in a 'spiritual' order they don't see to be the created fiction of calculating, self-serving cruelty and rational repression.

The last stanza brings the allegory into focus with the 'Human Abstract' of the title. I take 'the Gods of the earth and sea' to be a satiric formula for the self-styled lords of creation who would master the secular order of things, the kings and ministers of state who have always sought 'natural' sanctions for their autocratic desires and methods. Even in 'nature' (remembering that for Blake the word usually signifies the fallen, unregenerate external world) there may be no model for successful tyranny; but in the Human Brain, the seat of reductive, mechanical reason and its cunning calculations, the Tree of Humility and Mystery has been flourishing all along. The phrase 'human abstract' combines several points of Blakeian doctrine: the power of intellectual abstraction is peculiarly human and the symptom of man's Urizenic fall from the imaginatively integrated state that was his divine origin and remains to be redeemed from the bondage of Lockeian, Newtonian conceptualism; men's 'abstraction' (both indifference and diversion of attention) from the reality of other men's desires is what sustains a fallen society like the England of Pitt and George III; the tendency to systematize conduct into 'abstract' formulas like 'Pity would be no more,/If we did not make somebody Poor' draws the mind away from immediate and genuine sympathy with suffering; finally, the image of 'man' provided by abstract reason unsurprisingly stresses the primacy of reason itself, substituting for the 'Divine Image' of Innocence a lifeless mechanical object abstracted from its passionate centre. All such meanings combine to mock our own self-regard—are *we* not bloodless mannequins just as we suppose all those 'somebodies' are upon whom we practice our pious pretences? Maybe 'we', too, batten on the fraudulent fruit we offer to others; maybe priests have no monopoly on profitable mystification.

In comparison with 'London' or 'The Tyger', 'The Human Abstract' may seem a little unfinished, not completely reduced to dramatic and 'visionary' wholeness. There were evidently other attempts to write an Experience counterpart of Innocence's 'The Divine Image': 'I heard an Angel singing' (Rossetti MS.) contains what was to become the first stanza of 'The Human Abstract', and the rejected plate of 'A Divine Image' looks like an earlier attempt at the same theme. Plate 11 of *The Marriage of Heaven and Hell* gives an account of priesthood's origin in the attempt 'to realize or abstract the mental deities from their objects' and provides a useful gloss. The design of 'The Human Abstract' shows Urizen (looking startlingly like Santa Claus) glumly plucking at his rope-like bindings at the foot of a tree, and similar scenes are described, often with strong verbal similarities to 'The Human Abstract', in plate 5 of *The Visions of the Daughters of Albion* (1793), plates 11, 25, and 28 of *The Book of Urizen* (1794), and plates 3 and 4 of *The Book of Ahania* (1795). The pious cruelty of the tyrannical father-king was obviously much in Blake's mind during those revolutionary years, and he worked hard at finding the right poetic context for it, in his own mind perhaps never quite succeeding.

But 'The Human Abstract' seems to me the right version. Its oddly flat allegorical method provides the 'mythical' portentousness and the detachment from a single narrative consciousness that the prophecies achieve only with greater, more cumbersome effort. Blake's revolutionary myth, with its repressive fathers, lamenting mothers, and victimized children, draws extensively upon infantile and regressive archetypes, as any dream of innocence restored will do; to say this is no condescension to Blake, or to innocence, but an acknowledgment of how powerfully he was in touch with a primary motive of the will to freedom. It is just this basis in infantile awareness that is acknowledged and exploited by casting the poem's grim ironies as instructive nursery story rather than as epic myth.

The Prophetic Books themselves, and the great symbolic system they play variations on, may show not so much a decline in Blake's poetic powers as an inevitable but depressing attempt to expend those powers upon an impossible conception of what poetry can do. In the Lambeth Prophecies of the 1790's and the fascinating epic monstrosities that followed, you see Blake breaking up and recasting the individual perceptions of the great songs, trying to shape them, according to the political and epistemological programme adumbrated in *The Marriage of Heaven and Hell*, into some final, definitive statement of all that his imagination persuaded him was the truth about religion, moral history, and the psychological bases of power. It was a heroic enterprise and there are great moments in the prophetic works, dense though they often are to the point of incoherence. T. S. Eliot's unpleasant essay demonstrates how easily resistance to Blake's system can come to sound snobbish and patronizing, and that won't do; but I must agree that the system itself, as distinct from the feelings and insights it brings together, has too much of the improvisational and arbitrary about it to be as impressive as some modern exegesis makes it seem.

What the system aims at, of course, is a man's full and complete possession of his own beliefs, and it is hard to object to that. It is the aim of any adequate religion, any serious philosophical enterprise, any satisfactory intellectual life at all. Blake's own relation to the system it would be an impertinence to question or object to. But one may question the impulse to construct full accounts of reality, imaginations of plenitude, even as one acknowledges their usefulness. It is one thing for Blake to want to articulate a full-scale myth; it is quite another for us to accept that myth as more important than the coherence of the literary works that express it, or than the *life* it means to represent. The urge to master the system and think it what is most important about Blake seems a little like wanting to own all the Oz books or write sequels to *The Lord of the Rings*. One recognizes and respects the appeal of intellectual plenitude, but if not kept in check, it can lead to an over-valuation of completeness and order at the expense of the contingent *disorder* one mostly lives with.

J. Hillis Miller shrewdly associates the prophetic books with Emily Brontë's 'Gondal' poems, which lack the fullest kind of religious expressivity:

> A religious belief, to be valid, must become the form of a collective belief, and permeate the culture of a group. The validity of Emily Brontë's visions depends on their being kept private. Their purpose is to create an inner world excluding other people and the real world.[3]

Blake of course presents himself as a prophet, one who has in mind the conversion of humanity to the light, but there *is* something private and exclusive about the system. Evidently he needed to keep re-casting and complicating his myths lest they be too easily available to unvisionary minds. He seems at some level to have feared that his system, if too easy to grasp, would seem only something like the systems of religious fabulists like Spenser and Milton, rather than absolutely radical and original inventions of his own idiosyncratic imagination. At any rate, some such exclusiveness does operate in many readers of Blake. The exegetes take satisfaction in unfolding its inner coherence and symmetry, and the enthusiastic neophytes are sometimes a little surprised and annoyed to find that one has read him too—it had felt like a secret—and sometimes reluctant to expose their sense of him to discussion and critical testing. The pleasure of solving puzzles and knowing secrets may be a little out of place in dealing with someone who hated mystery as Blake did.

In short, I see in Blake an ultimate contradiction between the impulse to convert the world to simple imaginative truths and a growing impulse to address the world only in a hermetic language of private symbols—which in effect is to cease addressing 'the world' at all. The danger of radical positions—it is also their attractiveness—is that they make self-dramatization so easy. This is no danger in stupid men, but it has perils for intelligent ones (Byron is a good case), who can't help noticing and feeling uneasy about the heroic postures their politics lead them into. Blake was of course a sublimely intelligent man, but he became increasingly an obsessed man too, as his political and artistic intentions were more and more frustrated by the world's indifference to what he was up to. He was spared the Byronic experience of self-doubt and self-ridicule, but it is hard not to think that his later absorption with full-scale 'prophecy' was a kind of self-dramatization that hampered his genius and interfered with his own prophetic purposes. I don't suggest calculation on his part, but eccentricity can become its own purpose and reward without meaning to; the older Blake was not just a heroic artist persisting in his vision in defiance of corrupt politics and debased aesthetic values, he was also—as Crabb Robinson's journal and his own letters suggest— a kind of professional 'character', a man well able, in whatever innocence, to satisfy other people's taste for interesting eccentricity.

In both his later life and his later poetry (the pictorial work, of course, never ceased to develop marvellously) there is an aestheticizing of moral passion, a transmutation of radical politics and social criticism into personal roles and artistic forms that become more their own objects of concern than successful vehicles for the ideas and feelings they were invented to express. Blake spent some ten years, on and off, conceiving and writing *Jerusalem*, and some five years more engraving its 4,500-odd lines; the result may have the status of personal property quite as much as that of art, and its status as art may refer more to the effort invested in making it than to its intended relevance to its mighty subject. It is as though engraving had ceased to be the revelation of meaning once hidden beneath the surface of things but now forced into visibility by the artist's corrosive imagination, and become only a kind of obsessive pastime like stamp-collecting or model railways when pursued to the exclusion of virtually everything else. Engraving becomes not the discovery of meaning already there but the *creation* of meaning through the intensity of the artist's effort and the self-referring intricacy of the product, and this the younger Blake would have known how to despise.

I don't mean that we should despise *Jerusalem* ourselves, or any of the other, less obsessive prophecies. Some will have time and interest enough to read and master them, others won't; if this is a remark one couldn't conscientiously make about *King Lear* or *Paradise Lost*, neither is it to say Blake shouldn't have bothered. I do believe, however, that the over-valuation of the prophetic writings may obscure something more important about Blake, the astonishing way in which his best short poems (and *The Marriage of Heaven and Hell*) bring both prophetic vision *and* technical and intellectual control, 'wit' in the best sense of the word, to the service of moral redefinition of a corrupt public order. This can best be demonstrated, perhaps, by looking at a few Songs of Experience that are not immediately about the contemporary public world but have strong, if oblique, relation to it. I want to show, if nothing more, that the habit of referring everything Blake wrote to its possible 'symbolic' function can obscure or distort the force of exciting and difficult poems.

Take the simple song 'Ah! Sun-flower':

> Ah, Sun-flower! weary of time,
> Who countest the steps of the Sun:
> Seeking after that sweet golden clime
> Where the travellers journey is done.
>
> Where the Youth pined away with desire,
> And the pale Virgin shrouded in snow:
> Arise from their graves and aspire,
> Where my Sun-flower wishes to go.

This is too often read as some sort of lament for sunflower, youth, and virgin alike, seeing them as cruelly thwarted by external restraints upon their sensuous freedom, represented by the 'sweet golden clime' upon which all three fix their yearning imaginations; some readings even have the poem promising them a heavenly reward for their constancy, a glorious resurrection after death. This seems to me a very confused version of what the poem says and what we'd *expect* Blake to say in such a case; we know he disapproved of sexual and other kinds of repression, and flowers in poems are ordinarily good, innocent things, but such a reading makes the poem trivial and saccharine, and this can hardly be right.

At the risk of sounding simple-minded, let me suggest first that we seldom listen hard enough to Blake's rhythms, and that effects of 'sound' are often important cues to meaning in his lyrics. 'Ah! Sun-flower' is based on an anapaestic metre, with initial iambic substitutions in lines 1, 2, and 7. Anapaestic metre is fairly unusual in *Songs of Experience*; only three other songs use it consistently, with a fourth, 'The Sick Rose', a curious mixture of anapaests and iambs. Elsewhere the metre identifies a speaker who fails to see the whole point of his experience ('Nurse's Song', 'My Pretty Rose Tree') or who learns the point only as the poem destroys his innocence ('The Garden of Love'); the sing-song sway of the anapaest is obviously suited to creating a childish, nursery-rhyme tone. 'Ah! Sun-flower' is no nursery-rhyme, but we may wonder a little about the speaker. We may notice too that there is no discrepancy between the anapaestic pattern and normal English pronunciation *except* in line 3, where metrical stress can be preserved only by a painful sacrifice of natural accent:

Seeking after that sweet golden clime

—which suppresses the initial accents of both 'seeking' and 'golden' and turns the line into the doggerel of school-room recitation.

Such an effect is less than weighty evidence, but there is a way of reading the poem that would take it into account and suggest a considerably more interesting and I think more Blakeian meaning. If the disturbance of metre is heard as a signal to beware of taking the sentimental, consoling possibilities of 'sweet golden clime' too seriously—to resist the rather tinny music produced by trying to preserve the anapaestic norm here—then the poem comes into a different focus. It may be risky to participate too readily in the speaker's sympathetic concern for the sunflower, whose point of view after all might reasonably be thought a little limited. The flower is rooted in earth and able to travel only vicariously, by keeping its face turned to the moving sun. It has only a fanciful idea of freedom, which it understandably but inadequately conceives in the 'golden' terms of the sun it yearns for. Just so, I suggest, the youth and the virgin accepted (before it killed them!) the idea of restraining desire that society and religion imposed upon them, substituting for gratification a thin and insubstantial hope of future spiritual reward for virtuous inhibition. They can only 'aspire' after they are dead in the body, rooted in earth like the sunflower, and they may have no better chance of reaching that story-book heaven than the sunflower has of reaching the sun. The syntax, which has the vagueness of vision and perhaps also of ill-suppressed indignation, would thus in the fifth line make 'where' equivalent to 'the place toward which' the youth and virgin aspire, to match the 'where' in lines 4 and 8; they don't arise *in* the sweet golden clime but in a place from which they can still only aspire to go to it, like the sunflower.

In short, the poem doesn't console unfulfilled desire by imagining its eventual reward, the great golden pay-off for which it has saved up. The rather bland sympathetic tone covers a bitter protest against the pious fraud of persuading desire that it is better off unfulfilled, and the anapaests are Blake's parody of the Sunday-school lessons by which a dead social order imposes its self-protective moral 'wisdom' on passionate life. 'Ah' may be not a gasp of sympathetic concern but a sigh of half-mocking exasperation and sadness.

'Ah! Sun-flower' has (I think) been misunderstood because of the habit of reading Blake as if a poem were only a framework of 'symbols' with little or no involvement in a developing drama of rhythm, syntax, and speaking tone. And this kind of reading is encouraged by too trusting an appeal to the symbolic grammar of the system. 'The Clod and the Pebble' is a case of a troublesome, subversive lyric drained of its force by too automatic reference to symbols elsewhere in Blake:

> Love seeketh not Itself to please,
> Nor for itself hath any care;

But for another gives its ease,
And builds a Heaven in Hell's despair.

So sang a little Clod of Clay,
Trodden with the cattle's feet:
But a Pebble of the brook,
Warbled out these metres meet:

Love seeketh only Self to please,
To bind another to Its delight;
Joys in another's loss of ease,
And builds a Hell in Heaven's despite.

Because there are clods of clay elsewhere in Blake who seem to speak a wisdom endorsed by the poet, *this* clod's praise of humility and self-abnegation has been taken as Blake's 'real' position on the issue.[4] But such a reading must ignore not only Blake's assignment of the last word to the Pebble but the greater rhythmic energy of the Pebble's stanza, the pronounced stresses, for example, on 'only', 'bind', 'Joys', and (due to the caesura) 'Hell', that much exceed their counterparts in stanza one. The poem quickens in the ear after the clod stops talking, which suggests complications of meaning.

The clod sings a conventional Christian love-ethic, self-sacrifice for the sake of another's pleasure; this it calls building a heaven, just as the Gospels do, in our present understanding of them. (But 'If thou humblest thyself thou humblest me', the Jesus of Blake's *Everlasting Gospel* would say reproachfully.) But there's really no other doctrine the clod could sing—under the feet of cattle what can you do *except* praise self-sacrifice? ('The cut worm forgives the plow', as the 'Proverbs of Hell' sardonically remark.) The clod justifies a condition it is helpless to change; and for all its praise of selflessness, the song shows some concern for self, a need to believe that the existence you have is the best one possible. But where the clod aims at improving the pleasure of others, the pebble insists that if pleasure is worth giving to others it is worth having oneself. It is free to choose, and in its delight (the point of the rhythmic quickening) it sings an apparently shocking doctrine of selfishness. Yet its version of love—aggressive, demanding, self-assertive—generates a vocabulary of positive emotion ('delight', 'joys') that the clod has no use for. If there is no delight in love for the self, what can it hope to arouse in another (besides gratitude or embarrassment)? 'To bind another to Its delight' may be not to enslave him but to infect him with that delight; 'another's loss of ease' may be good for him if 'ease' means comfortable indifference to the demands of emotional involvement. We aren't ordinarily very responsive to lovers who act like perfect servants, so anxious about our pleasure that they never have any fun themselves.

But if it is better to love in Hell than serve (and serve, and serve) in Heaven, the pebble's 'last word' may not simply be Blake's own. To be sure, if we start with a clod-morality, as Blake rightly assumed we at least pretend to, then it has to be challenged and exploded by the pebble's more lively, open, human answer. But the clod isn't wilfully evil or even stupid; it is the victim of its circumstance, conditioned by helplessness and an incomplete perspective on the world, which includes freer states than its own. The pebble's Hell (thanks to the caesura) is more vigorously 'in' the poem than the clod's Heaven, but no *marriage* of Heaven and Hell is achieved, no durable synthesis of innocence and experience. The poem does show a piety that Blake values being subjected to corrosive ironies, but in man's fallen state such piety is mostly insincere, and Beulah is to be regained only through a testing submission of innocent selflessness to the sceptical energies of experience. In *this* world, at least, the pebble's song is more instructive than the clod's, though we can see this without leaping to finalities Blake here does not intend.[5]

'The Sick Rose' is another subversive lyric which has often been misunderstood. And again the critical task is to resist seeing the poem as a static design of symbols and instead to *hear* in it the play of a mind complexly aware of alternatives to conventional moral terms:

> O Rose, thou art sick.
> The invisible worm,
> That flies in the night
> In the howling storm:
>
> Has found out thy bed
> Of crimson joy:

And his dark secret love
Does thy life destroy.

You can of course take this as mere homily, a routine of stylized moral attributions: 'the rose (innocent beauty) is corrupted by being eaten (loved) by the worm (selfish sexuality)', so that the song makes a shocked comment on the destructiveness of passion. But this admirable moral seems quite un-Blakeian, and one may be excused for looking further. The curiously indecisive rhythm, iambic and anapaestic in turn, seems to hint at emotional complexity within the rather flat and declarative tone. And the plain sense of what is stated has at least one peculiarity: logically, the rose would have been occupying its bed (or been a potential 'bed' for the worm) *before* the worm found it out, and 'bed of crimson joy' seems a strangely elaborate periphrasis for 'rose' in a poem that's otherwise so direct and plain-spoken. And it sounds like an unusual setting for the repose of innocence, to say the least.

The worm itself is wrapped in a rhetorical atmosphere of sinister, lurid mystery—he is invisible, nocturnal, violent, and nastily secretive. Indeed he is made so elaborately diabolical as to seem suspiciously melodramatic, a stage-Mephisto in full regalia. Blake is usually harder on Evil than this. As a counter-irritant to moralistic readings, one might try reading the song as a joke, though not a frivolous or very funny one. The rose, in such a reading, would represent a taste for passion that has got too thoroughly conceptualized, made fancifully melodramatic by something like Lawrence's 'sex in the head'. She lies (in that bed of crimson joy) dreaming with maidenly lubricity of delicious naughtinesses with primordial demon lovers of a distinctly glamourized sort. But there is more to passion than roses dream of; this one, at least, gets more than she bargained for, finding that 'life' as she has known it cannot survive full passionate possession. There may be as much mockery as concern and sympathy in 'O Rose', and the song itself may have as much in common with *The Rape of the Lock* as with *Clarissa* or *No Mother to Guide Her*.

I would not want to argue that this is the 'right' reading of 'The Sick Rose', which is too enigmatic and self-contained to be reduced to allegory, be it sentimentally or ironically motivated. One is both moved and terrified by the rose's destruction, but that response will be trivialized unless one senses the rose's complicity in her own fate, her participation in a 'nature' (or is it also a 'society'?) in which victims in effect co-operate with or even encourage the aggressors who destroy them. A stock feeling gets twisted to the service of a more demanding moral perception, which discerns the unhealthy mixing of sentiment and perversity in 'romantic' revery, and its disabling vulnerability to real passion. And though the subject of 'The Sick Rose' seems quintessentially private by conventional measures, the poem's placement in *Songs of Experience* reveals its affinities with the songs that are more obviously 'public' in bearing. 'London' and 'The Human Abstract' are in their own ways concerned with the sad disparities between conventional thinking and feeling and the real state of things imaginative vision perceives, and the perversions of sexuality are a revealing aspect of the tyranny of institutions and enforced habit.

Poems like 'Ah! Sun-flower', 'The Clod and the Pebble', and 'The Sick Rose' may suggest that Blake's relation to the social and political circumstances that were his subject was poetically stronger and more viable when kept oblique and circumstantial than when made the overt subject of systematic myth-making. Blake's great myth aimed at the synthesizing of innocence and experience, the recreation of unfallen vision, the liberation of the divinity that resides in the human breast; it was a noble and invigorating purpose, and the myth itself has much instructive value, for all its crankish obscurity in actual exposition. But too much concern with the system, which stresses integrative vision, distracts from the poems, which stress actual cases of disruption and moral confusion. Blake is most in touch with his powers when he is engaged with particular moments *within* the great dialectic he dreamed of, when his moral fervour and intelligence and wit come to bear on some situation of incompleteness, some actual revelation of the grievous animosity between repressive habits and imaginations of freedom. Poems like these are dramatic acts of resistance to a coercive moral authority, and they engage us in their revolutionary action at our own peril—to misread them is to blunder into the ranks of the enemy and suffer Blake's scorn, or at best to adopt a muddled neutrality that betrays his own insistence on truth at any cost. It was his particular genius, in a society undergoing the rationalization into compartments and areas that modern 'social science' monumentalizes, to understand that *all* institutions are versions of the same impulse, which he took to be repressive and evil. Though one's objections may be philosophical, political, economic, moral, or stylistic, one resists always the same great enemy, whether he be called Reason, Custom, Authority, Inhibition, Urizen, or Sir Joshua Reynolds. It took Blake a lifetime to tell it all, and the shorter poems do in a way depend on the cumulative body of prophetic writings for their full significance; but granting the necessity of the whole, still the vision and its significance are most powerfully available in individual shorter works or dramatic moments in the longer prophecies, where a particular issue and a particular form of the Protean enemy is engaged and defeated by poetic art itself.

2. Shelley: The Revolutionary as Swain

Blake's career, I suggest, shows how the imaginative pursuit of revolutionary ends can divert moral and political energy to building mythic systems, systems that become self-justifying 'aesthetic' objects rather than the medium of continuing public engagement. A commonplace distinction between concern and anxiety may help here. The politically concerned man, let us say, tries to remember that other men's freedom and happiness are important and aligns himself, in sympathies and if possible in action, with causes that serve them even if the causes seem socially disruptive. The politically anxious man, however, is prey to fears that inhibit his sympathy and powers of action; he may fear what will happen if the state of things is altered, or what will happen if it *isn't*, but in either case no sense of 'participation' is possible. In practical terms political anxiety leads to retreat into 'symbolic' readings of the public condition, seeing any given political event as a predictable and somehow gratifyingly awful example of what 'They' *would* do, a further evidence of how far things have gone. Political attitudes that are denied realization in action take refuge in the elaboration of mythologies, just as attitudes that are entrenched in power do; for the active involvement of consciousness in public events one substitutes awareness of a constructed *model* that is supposed to represent public reality but is more likely to represent only the fears or complacencies of the model-makers themselves. For the anxious man politics takes the form of zealous commitment to slogans and party symbols, the mythical histories, pseudo-philosophies, and bogus prophecies that sustain frustrated revolutionists and smug patriots alike. Such myth-making is inevitable, no doubt, but the test is whether it expresses ongoing concern and intentions of action or has hardened into a substitute for concern and action. This is usually difficult to determine, just as it is difficult to determine the difference between *literary* myths that refer to human possibilities and ones that have been aestheticized into their own justification for being. But in either case the distinction is worth keeping in mind, and it may have critical uses of at least a suggestive sort.

The Mask of Anarchy is a case of a public poem with revolutionary intentions having to face and cope with the fact that its generating consciousness, the poet's mind, is in no position to do more than write a poem. (This is less clear in Blake's earlier poems and prophecies, where it is perfectly possible to associate the speaking voice with a man who is ready to act, one for whom there is indeed no firm distinction between writing a poem and taking action.) Shelley's subject, the Peterloo Massacre, powerfully draws his imagination to politics, class struggle, and violence, and the accident of geographical exile puts him in a very familiar poetic place:

> As I lay asleep in Italy
> There came a voice from over the Sea
> And with great power it forth led me
> To walk in the visions of Poesy. (1)

Sleep is the medium of dream-vision, as in Chaucer, the state in which the mind is absolved from practical matters and left open to a larger awareness of ordinarily hidden significances. Here it also suggests the relaxed inactivity of the 'impractical' man, the poet who has no real business to attend to but is on a kind of permanent vacation in a warm climate; he is far from home, out of touch, and the reports of Peterloo are news from another world, news from nowhere almost, easily translatable into the summoning voice of the dream-vision itself. And his response to that voice is passive. It leads him, and in following—'to walk in the visions of Poesy'—he makes the not very energetic response of the literally disengaged man. Leavis rightly praises Shelley's success in sustaining this effect, making us feel that it isn't the poet but the vision itself we are in touch with.

But *The Mask of Anarchy* professes to be not a contemplative poem, assessing public events from a distance, but an effort at imaginative engagement in those events, one that has reminded many people of Blake. Leavis warns against misconstruing the simple manner and its Blakeian affinities: 'It lies, not in any assumed broadsheet naïveté or crudity . . . but in a rare emotional integrity and force, deriving from a clear, disinterested and mature vision.'[1] This is fair enough; but one needs to remember that the manner of the poem *is* simple, that Shelley creates and carries off brilliantly the *style* of broadsheet naïveté, the dramatic effect of a cultivated poet being driven out of his usual 'literary' manner by his shock and indignation at the event. He speaks as a kind of swain, in Empson's famous sense; and it is his refusal of sophistication and visible poetic trickiness that conveys the effect.

In the great opening stanzas, that is, you feel that the invective against political reaction is *not* invective, not the product of rhetorical selection but the inevitable effect of the things described:

> I met Murder on the way—
> He had a mask like Castlereagh—
> Very smooth he looked, yet grim;
> Seven blood-hounds followed him:
>
> All were fat; and well they might
> Be in admirable plight,
> For one by one, and two by two,
> He tossed them human hearts to chew
> Which from his wide cloak he drew.   (II-III)

At first it all seems to be done simply by saying how they looked —how anyone would have seen them—and what they did. The potential shock of 'human hearts' has to struggle against the phrase's status as neutral description—'human' to distinguish them from other kinds of hearts one might feed dogs with; and the cumulative disturbance of 'smooth', 'fat', and 'wide' doesn't depend on any one of the words seeming unfairly loaded, since the contrast between Murder's expansive, unmarked, fleshly comfort and the sufferings of his victims develops only as the poem unfolds. The visions of Poesy are first of all visions, ways of seeing. If we leap to the connection between Murder and Castlereagh, or assume that Fraud *is* Lord Chancellor Eldon because he wears an ermined gown and is named 'Fraud', we are a little ahead of the words.

We are not, of course, ahead of Shelley, who knows that identities can get made before they're exactly stated. The lines on Eldon show the intricacy within the simple narrative manner:

> Next came Fraud, and he had on,
> Like Eldon, an ermined gown;
> His big tears, for he wept well,
> Turned to mill-stones as they fell,
>
> And the little children, who
> Round his feet played to and fro,
> Thinking every tear a gem,
> Had their brains knocked out by them.   (IV-V)

Eldon was notoriously lachrymose—he was to shed his most famous tears in 1832, for the passage of the Reform Bill—but the words say directly only that Fraud reminded the poet of Eldon because he wore the same sort of gown and cried a lot. Fraud, that is, would remind *anyone* of Eldon who knew Eldon, yet the resemblance could be quite fortuitous. But of course the 'visual' data of poetic vision is only part of its effect; vision arranges its material in significant ways, and the poet didn't see just a figure who wore ermine and wept. He saw a figure *whose name was Fraud* and *who was like Eldon*—both name and likeness were part of the vision, not interpretive additions by the poet himself. Here is the first victory of poetic vision over public fact, the first immunity established for the swain's simplicity. On this basis, the ironies of 'wept well' (he did it cleverly) and the horrible transmutation of tears into gems into millstones, mirrored by the dictional shift to the blunt brutality of 'brains knocked out', can unfold without embarrassment or undue show of vindictiveness.

'Vision' thus, as in the millstone-tears or Murder with human hearts under his cloak or Anarchy's horses 'trampling to a mire of blood/The adoring multitude' (x), sanctions surrealistic violence and moral fury without compromising the explanatory simplicity of the presentation. The poem is a Mask or Masquerade, and the location of 'reality' becomes an intriguing and difficult problem. 'Destructions' (VII) are 'disguised' 'like Bishops, lawyers peers, and spies', which leaves several possibilities open. The disguises may be fictions limited to the vision itself: there were Destructions, which had the impertinence to masquerade as good people like bishops and so forth, who weren't however really implicated. Or, when the force of this at the simplest ironic level is used up, we may locate the masquerade in the real public world, whose hollowness the vision simply exposes: bishops and lawyers are only disguised forms of Destruction, the costumes and masks that evil wears in its daily commerce. The insolence of this view obviously serves Shelley's aim of 'seeing' into the moral falsities of a reactionary society. But in the metaphor of masquerade I sense a further suggestion that drastically complicates things.

The effect of the 'mask' as Shelley presents it is to question just that distinction between self and role that ordinary masquerading depends on. We like to dress up and wear disguises because it's fun to look and (in some part) feel like someone else without having to accept that other identity permanently; if our intentions are darker, we wear disguises to fool other people, have our way with them without letting them know whose way it is. But though Shelley calls his poem a 'mask', it suggests that in public life there is no value to distinguishing the man from the function he performs or the effect he has—Castlereagh *is* Murder, however much he himself might want to insist on his personal decency and human dignity, or on the tragic difficulty of his job. Behind the mask of public identity—statesman, bishop, peer—is there a human face or merely another, impenetrable mask, the frozen 'face' of power and its dreadful effects? This would be to see politics as an absurd pageant, a pantomime that expresses nothing except itself and can't be referred even ironically to anything principled or rational. What seems to be satiric oxymoron— Anarchy is 'God, and Law, and King' (xv)—may turn out to be something more desperate if the formula is inverted; what if God and Law and King are anarchy, meaningless counters in an essentially aimless movement of undirected forces?

Shelley, in short, seems on the verge of acknowledging a radical disillusionment with politics, a despair about there being any possibility of healthful life in an organized society of men. Peterloo is not the result of good men behaving badly on the basis of principles that are honest but mistaken; more dreadfully, it may not even be the result of *bad* men behaving badly, just as you'd expect them to. Rather the event is so paralysing to the mind as to make the question of motive or moral judgment unaskable. Politics is not a series of calculated impersonations but a series of commitments to roles and styles that penetrate behind the 'mask' to destroy any lingering human identity whatever. This is of course a recurring Romantic obsession, as in Byron, E. T. A. Hoffmann, Poe and Hawthorne, to name only a few—the assumption of a role, for whatever purpose, that absorbs and annihilates the self that chose the role in the hope of escaping the insufficiency or ennui of its original state. It is the idea, to reduce it to its most general terms, that education, the deliberate cultivation of experience for its formative effects on the mind and spirit, paradoxically destroys mind and spirit by transforming them into something unendurably new and alien.

I mean to suggest that an idea like this is involved in the governing 'metaphor' of the early part of *The Mask of Anarchy*, not that it's what Shelley wanted to express or even knew might be suggested. The tenor of his thought was ordinarily optimistic and progressive, though of course its terms changed as his youthful Godwinian notions were absorbed into his more mature vocabularies, as for example that of neo-platonism. Rather *The Mask of Anarchy* seems an intriguing case of a poem in which overt political intentions are endangered by a lurking despair about politics which the poet doesn't intend to entertain but which creeps in anyway; and this clash of attitudes causes some confusion in the poem. The *Mask* gets harder to read admiringly as it goes on, as the chilling portrayal of Anarchy and his followers gives way to the prophecy of political reform through non-violent resistance to Castlereagh and reaction generally. In the larger part of the poem, that is, Shelley reaches for the positive note, as though to avoid the failure of nerve he caustically described in those whose radical hopes were too easily discouraged by the Revolution's lapse into Bonapartist tyranny:

Thus, many of the most ardent and tender-hearted of the worshippers of public good have been morally ruined by what a partial glimpse of the events they deplored appeared to show as the melancholy desolation of all their cherished hopes. Hence gloom and misanthropy have become the characteristics of the age in which we live, the solace of a disappointment that unconsciously finds relief only in the wilful exaggeration of its own despair.

(Preface to *The Revolt of Islam*, 1817)

(This makes a nice gloss on the novels of his friendly enemy Peacock, who also saw the theatricality of 'romantic' disillusionment and detected its relation to political despair.) Shelley never really gave up, and one honours him for it, but it is hard not to think that *The Mask of Anarchy* is damaged by the effort to be hopeful and that he was so hard on the 'moral ruin' of so many contemporaries because he sensed or feared it as a possibility in himself.

Certainly the latter part of the poem shows deterioration. Even at the level of verse-rhythm there is a faltering, a failure to see that the rough, no-nonsense abruptness that so effectively discredited Castlereagh and his crew in the opening vision seems merely clumsy when the mood shifts to prophecy and uplift:

> 'Thou art Justice—ne'er for gold
> May thy righteous laws be sold
> As laws are in England—thou
> Shield'st alike the high and low.'   (LVII)

Or, when the prophetic voice seeks a more comely rhetoric and movement, it too often lapses into the sing-song of instructive nursery-rhyme or routine political oration:

> 'For the labourer thou art bread,
> And a comely table spread
> From his daily labour come
> In a neat and happy home.
>
> 'Thou art clothes, and fire, and food
> For the trampled multitude—
> No—in countries that are free

165

> Such starvation cannot be
> As in England now we see.'   (LIV-LV)

The banality of this, in rhythm and in the appeal to comfy domesticity, can be measured by comparison with Blake, who knew how to make the naif's unembarrassed questioning of obvious things heartbreaking:

> Is this a holy thing to see
> In a rich and fruitful land,
> Babes reduc'd to misery,
> Fed with cold and usurous hand?
>
> ('Holy Thursday')

Or, at its worst, the style slips into unconscious comedy that quite painfully betrays this swain's upper-class origins:

> 'Every woman in the land
> Will point at them as they stand—
> They will hardly dare to greet
> Their acquaintance in the street.'   (LXXXVII)

(One has the eerie feeling that Hilaire Belloc has been tampering with that last couplet.) The passive resistance Shelley advocates is pretty thoroughly rooted in the gentleman's code—the tyrants will be shamed into desisting with 'hot blushes on their cheek' (LXXXVI), and their essentially manly soldier-hirelings 'will turn to those who would be free,/Ashamed of such base company' (LXXXVIII). Revolutionary vision dwindles down to a chapel talk to the Fourth Form, and the nightmare of Peterloo seems pretty distant.

Part of the trouble here, of course, is simply that Shelley didn't know how to talk to or about the social class whose cause he so admirably wanted to feel his own; it is a problem well-born reformers have faced before and since, as Shaw likes to remind us. But there may be a deeper uncertainty in the poem, an unresolved question of conception that comes nearest the surface in the following stanzas:

> What art thou, Freedom? O! could slaves
> Answer from their living graves

This demand—tyrants would flee
Like a dream's dim imagery:

'Thou art not, as imposters say,
A shadow soon to pass away,
A superstition, and a name
Echoing from the cave of Fame.'   (LII–LIII)

Although there is as much rhetorical gesture here as distinct poetic definition, it is interesting to try to take the lines seriously. They seem to say that while tyrants are unreal, as dim and unsubstantial as the imagery of dreams when confronted by a living idea of freedom, freedom itself *is* real, not a 'shadow' but (as the following stanzas will assert) substantial like bread and clothes and fire. As polemic device this is effective enough—people are more apt to resist if they believe in the reality of themselves and their desires and think the enemy mere phantoms—but it threatens to muddle the poet's relation to his subject. If the tyrants are finally dreams and images, then the horror of Anarchy ('trampling to a mire of blood/The adoring multitude') is left with nothing to work against. The poem draws its moral charge, so to speak, from our knowledge that the visions of poesy are *not* visions or dreams but horrible facts—real soldiers have slaughtered real, and unarmed, people at Peterloo, and their action is the direct responsibility of real politicians. But Shelley's rhetoric makes it hard to grasp the matter as a living opposition between human demands and needs, on the one hand, and a substantial exercise of power to intimidate and suppress those demands—which is to say that, for all his vehemence of feeling, he is close to denying that the political issue and its terrible consequences really exist.

In my view, then, *The Mask of Anarchy* is almost a model case of how a certain kind of poetic imagination can unwittingly damage its own admirable concern for the public world. Shelley was determined to preserve his radical beliefs and resist the anxiety and despair that can ruin a sensitive mind's involvement with politics; but his remoteness from the experience of the social class he was concerned with is all too clear, most notably in his allowing the revolutionary issue to shift from a concern for suffering and the callousness that causes it to a more 'mythical' opposition between Freedom and Tyranny that has lost touch with its human referents. The other sense of 'mask'—as 'masque', moral allegory refined to courtly entertainment—intrudes itself here. If the poem does not express a total loss of faith in politics, it at best shows such faith sustained only by the mythologizing of political issues, making them rhetorical and symbolic 'properties' in a moral drama whose relation to the actual public case grows increasingly tenuous.

This is not to say that *The Mask of Anarchy* fails as a poem. It in fact is a fine poem, in its earlier part very nearly a great one. The vision of Anarchy and his cohorts accepts the poet's remoteness, geographical and social, from the dreadful reality of Peterloo and makes a poetic virtue of it; the allegorical figures of 'vision' beautifully represent the depthlessness of practical politics, the subsuming of feeling into function that makes 'official' violations of human freedom possible; and the swain-like simplicity and directness of the narrative manner reminds us that only a perverse sophistication can tolerate such horror. But as the poem goes on, the swain becomes a bumbling Old Etonian with Radical Ideas, 'vision' becomes sentimental polemic fantasy, Peterloo becomes not an immediate horror but just another *example* of the mythical war of Freedom and Tyranny that was so irresistible a subject for Shelley in other poems too. In short, he can't wholly keep passion from lapsing into mere political rhetoric, repeating one's commitments out loud to persuade oneself that they're still firm The *Mask* is an *attack* on Anarchy, seeking to attach a bad word to an appalling public condition; Shelley might have expressed his inclinations better, and written a more consistently strong poem, if he had abandoned the old conservative vocabulary of order and disorder and come out *for* Anarchy as the alternative to a hopeless politics.

3. Wordsworth: The Bard as Patriot

In Blake and Shelley, as I read them, revolutionary passion is converted by practical frustration and changing artistic aims into 'aestheticized' versions of its original nature, elaborations of myth that use the public condition for subject-matter but are inwardly as much concerned with the poet's idea of himself as 'revolutionary artist' as with political or social fact. Blake in such a view is something like a heroic figure—a status Shelley may not quite achieve because of a certain effusiveness. (If Blake is the Old Bolshevik of Romanticism, Shelley is an aging upper-class Fellow-Traveller, a little down on his luck but still charming at parties.) But the heroic possibilities of the role work at the expense of a continuing closeness to the subject—the issues become counters in one's personal symbolic grammar, the human agents and victims become figures of private myth, the sense of participating in a great cause is preserved only by translating the cause into an artistic image of itself, whose life and urgency is of another sort. There is nothing morally reprehensible about such a transformation—its alternative may be the atrophy of any public concern, actual *or* symbolic, and that seems worse. Nor is its artistic consequence necessarily ruinous—many intelligent people find Blake's later prophecies his greatest works, and while I don't agree I do see what they mean. But public poetry (in my sense) becomes something else when we begin to suspect that the poem exists for its own sake and not for the sake of the human experiences of politics and social action it seeks to organize and interpret.

In *The Mask of Anarchy* a poet keeps in touch with public reality only through an exertion of will that complicates and to some extent damages the poetic result. It is almost as if Shelley knew in 1819 that the immediate future of radical politics was dismal, as revolutionary energy began to melt and blur into cautious liberalisms; 1848 would be only a false dawn[7] and the radical imagination would for some time have to seclude itself in the British Museum and the shabby backstreets of the Continent. But some sixteen years earlier, a very different kind of poet had expressed political disillusionment by making poetic capital of such uncertainties and anxieties.

In 1802 and 1803 Wordsworth wrote some two dozen sonnets on the current political and military situation, which for an Englishman in those anxious days meant Napoleon Bonaparte—his rule in France, his threatened invasion of England, the effects of his power on Sweden, Venice, Haiti, and Switzerland. Eight of the sonnets were published almost immediately, in *The Morning Post* and *The Poetical Register*. The others first appeared in the *Poems* of 1807, at a time when the subjects were still of at least general concern. The sonnets differ in quality, some being very fine poems and others decidedly poor stuff, which is to say that they may nicely represent a mind too concerned with urgent public subjects to be in consistent control of its poetic medium. Two of them can illustrate this qualitative range and suggest some of the difficulties Wordsworth encountered in turning his art to immediate patriotic purposes:

XXII

OCTOBER, 1803

When, looking on the present face of things,
I see one man, of men the meanest too!
Raised up to sway the world, to do, undo,
With mighty Nations for his underlings,
The great events with which old story rings
Seem vain and hollow; I find nothing great:
Nothing is left which I can venerate;
So that almost a doubt within me springs
Of Providence, such emptiness at length
Seems at the heart of all things. But, great God!
I measure back the steps which I have trod;
And tremble, seeing as I do the strength
Of such poor Instruments, with thoughts sublime
I tremble at the sorrow of the time,

XXVI

ANTICIPATION. OCTOBER, 1803

Shout, for a mighty Victory is won!
On British ground the Invaders are laid low;
The breath of Heaven has drifted them like snow,
And left them lying in the silent sun,
Never to rise again!—the work is done.
Come forth, ye old men, now in peaceful show
And greet your sons! drums beat and trumpets blow!
Make merry, wives! ye little children, stun
Your grandame's ears with pleasure of your noise!
Clap, infants, clap your hands! Divine must be

That triumph, when the very worst, the pain,
The loss and e'en the prospect of the slain
Hath something in it which the heart enjoys:—
True glory, everlasting sanctity.

I use the numbers and titles Wordsworth gave them when he grouped them in Part I of 'Poems Dedicated to National Independence and Liberty' in the edition of 1845; however, I follow the earliest printed texts, that of the 1807 *Poems* for XXII, and that of *The Poetical Register*, 1803, for XXVI. Wordsworth later made some significant revisions, as we shall see.

It is rather startling that a poet, within the same month, could take such radically different views of the same general subject. (There are, in fact, five sonnets on the invasion scare dated October, 1803, and three others that may have been written in that month.) 'Anticipation', which was published almost immediately, has the look of a calculated morale-builder, while 'October, 1803' was suitably saved for the more disinterested circumstance of a volume of poems. But this is no reason to suppose that Wordsworth was distinguishing between the 'occasional' and the 'serious'. Some of the best of these 'Political Sonnets' (as he labelled the group in 1838) were published in the papers, while some of the poorer were held until 1807, and he may have taken 'Anticipation' as seriously as 'October, 1803'. We of course are free to do otherwise.

The trouble with 'Anticipation' begins in the almost incessant exclamatory tone the punctuation makes so obvious. Speech at such a high pitch isn't much different from the unconsidered excitement anyone might feel during a grave national crisis. Even the promising image of drifted snow in the silent sun is cheated of its elegiac possibilities by the exclamation point. The parade of domestic revelry has little reality apart from one's pity for the grandame's stunned ears, and it would be easy to dismiss the poem as one of the loud annoyances that grave public events seem to demand. But bad as it is, 'Anticipation' has a little more interest than that. One does notice, amidst the forest of exclamation points, two sentences that aren't so overgrown. 'The work is done' makes a relatively quiet pause in the florid oratorio of the opening lines, and 'work' has unexpected force in this context.

It can simply and soberly state what the breath of Heaven has wrought: God has worked for our just cause as easily and naturally as he works on snowflakes, blowing them into drifts and melting them; compared with his power, now that it's all over, the enemy seems pretty small and trivial. Or, since (in 'anticipation') it was a real human battle and they are really dead, 'work' reflects the strenuous effort we have invested in killing them and the quiet gratification felt in completed labour, productive and self-justifying activity that it is. There they lie, on British ground, rather like harvested grain at some joyous October festival— when 'work is done', it is right and natural that men join in communal celebration and mirth. In this light, the scene indeed 'hath something in it which the heart enjoys', for not just a battle or a political destruction but a seasonal ritual has been performed.

Now 'Anticipation' doesn't quite *say* all this, but such a counter-meaning stirs, at least, in a poem that would otherwise seem incredibly heartless and obtuse about mass-slaughter. The other unexclaimed sentence, the long concluding one, supports this idea. If it is complacent and cruel to find something 'divine', something 'which the heart enjoys', in 'the very worst, the pain,/ The loss and e'en the prospect of the slain'—'the prospect of our brethren slain', Wordsworth's 1807 revision, makes the smugness smell positively evangelical—still there may be more to it than that. It isn't just that they will sleep in glory and sanctity— heroes always do—but that their death is not merely a personal tragedy but a public ceremony, confirming communal identity and pride in the way that festivals and ritual sacrifices do. This is what I think Wordsworth was trying to say. In 1838 he changed 'pleasure' (line 9) to 'transport' (though he restored 'pleasure' in later editions), apparently in hope of conveying meaningful emotional intensity without the disturbing suggestion of personal gratification. But the poem is too thoroughly cast in the terms of 'pleasure', and Wordsworth can't quite sustain a clear distinction between 'what the heart enjoys' in a serious, ceremonial way and the nagging possibility that these victorious deaths are the occasion for a good party for the grateful and relieved survivors.

The qualities that make 'Anticipation' a mildly effective piece of patriotic polemic, then, are the qualities that keep Wordsworth from fully releasing a potential meaning that is harder and more serious—one that would reveal the painfully complex relation between death as private experience and death as public ceremony. Patriotic anxiety overcomes the reflective instinct. By contrast, 'October, 1803' shows such a complex, hard meaning being achieved. The poet looks on 'the present face of things' in an attempt to see through into 'the heart of all things', where he is appalled to find what seems to be a desolating emptiness. This is a considerable progression. The 'face of things' colloquially suggests the impermanent external form of the world, the public phenomena we must respect, as the only clue to truth we ordinarily have, yet can never quite trust as a reliable figure of truth itself. 'The heart of all things', by an extension of the physiological analogy, is truth inwardly received and verified, the beating source of both 'self' and 'world', the frequent imagistic goal of Wordsworth's spiritual journeys:

> And then my heart with pleasure fills,
> And dances with the daffodils.

> 'Oh! would, poor beast, that I had now
> A heart but half as good as thine!'

>   . . . purifying thus
> The elements of feeling and of thought,
> And sanctifying, by such discipline,
> Both pain and fear, until we recognize
> A grandeur in the beatings of the heart.

But in 'October, 1803' the heart of all things seems vacuous, as 'vain and hollow' as the face of things. The sonnet dramatizes something like a crisis of nerve, triggered by public events but leading inward to a general perception of human desolation and to a particular sense of personal failure and guilt. And as the metaphor of face and heart implies, 'public' event and 'private' response are so closely related as to make such labels seem abstract, crude falsifications of the whole complex experience being expressed.

It is the sonnet's success in connecting and merging seemingly unlike attitudes that makes it so much more impressive than 'Anticipation'. At the start, the poet 'looks' at the public situation; he is a startled observer of Napoleon's single-handed power who states his disapproval in rather snobbish social terms—'of men the meanest too!' Napoleon is an upstart, a nobody; mighty nations sometimes do bad things, but it is astonishing that they should do them as the 'underlings' of such a common, ill-bred person. But there is more here than Blimpish bewilderment. The poet is a man who has responded to heroic 'story', the literary history of human greatness, and the spectacle of Bonaparte threatens his belief in such stories—were all heroes perhaps just vulgar *arrivistes* like him? This is more than an irritating interference with his literary pleasure, since it reaches through his experience of books to his way of possessing his own identity, his ability to believe in and venerate existences greater than himself. His plaintive discovery—'I find nothing great:/Nothing is left which I can venerate'—is vulnerably direct and simple. And it expresses more than practical political anxiety; the emptiness at the heart of things almost destroys his religious imagination, his sense of the governing force of Providence in human affairs. Napoleon represents social anarchy and philosophical meaninglessness— he 'sways' the world not just by influencing its behaviour but by setting it into a purposeless oscillation of doing and undoing, motion without aim.

The sonnet reaches crisis in lines 8-10, where even an apparent bit of rhyme-padding like 'at length' reflects the slow and terrible process of discovering emptiness, the progression from social dismay through aesthetic disillusionment to moral and theological anguish. The tone mixes a flat despair with the agony (the rise of the voice on 'Providence') of resisting despair when it seems inevitable. At this point sonnet convention and the patriotic hopefulness of some of the other Political Sonnets make a turn in feeling seem likely. Surely the face of things and the heart of things are different; surely there is a distinction to be made between the accidents of public reality and the poet's understanding that they *are* just accidents, imperfect, distorted manifestations of eternal writ. With 'But, great God!' we get what looks like the start of such a turn, an affirmation of faith in the midst of apparent chaos; and it seems hopeful when he begins to 'measure back the steps which I have trod', scrutinizing his spiritual history to search out the turning where he lost his way. But the result is not a discovery of truth behind seeming emptiness but rather a *trembling*, both for 'the sorrow of the time' and for the discovery of how 'such poor Instruments' as Bonaparte acquire their power. The 'swaying' of the public world is not contradicted but brilliantly extended to include the trembling poet himself.

Poor Instruments achieve power, he now sees, through the kind of enthusiasm for political innovation and reform that Wordsworth himself felt in the Revolutionary days recorded and criticized in Books IX and X of *The Prelude*. (The great work would have been much in his mind during the anxious times of 1802 and 1803.) The point isn't very clear in the 1807 text I have quoted: 'seeing as I do the strength/Of such poor Instruments' seems to revert to his first mood rather than indicate new awareness. This Wordsworth evidently recognized as an obscurity, for in the *Poems* of 1827 he illuminatingly corrected the line to read 'seeing *whence proceeds* the strength', which introduces a slight stiffness of tone but makes the point clear. He trembles because, retracing his own political history, he finds that the seemingly inexplicable power of Napoleon has grown out of the readiness of people like himself to give themselves to revolutionary causes, to participate (if only sympathetically) in an overthrow of just the social coherence that Napoleon so strangely contradicts. (The older Wordsworth significantly thought of combining these sonnets with the 'Sonnets Dedicated to Liberty and *Order*' of the 1830's and '40's.) The political world, the present face of things, *can't* be dissociated from the heart of all things, because his own heart was in part formed and educated by the passions and enthusiasms that led to Bonapartism. The poet and men like him, good men like Beaupuy, *made* Napoleon. If he is a poor instrument of their intentions, he remains their historical creature, whose strength is the consequence of their original fervour.

Here the sonnet hovers between alternatives, and in its peculiar honesty it chooses neither one. Wordsworth neither accepts nor rejects his political past. Rather, in perfect consonance with the dramatic progression, he *trembles*, responding to opposing pressures without fully electing either. And, through an appeal to 'the sublime' as the eighteenth century had defined it—the psychological state in which the mind is simultaneously excited and terrified by an object too vast and indeterminate for its usual aesthetic categories to grasp—his trembling is justified as the only adequate response to the sorrow of the time, the suffering of other people and his own grief for the present to which the past, *his* past, has led. He does not, however, reject that past as having been wrong; indeed his present ability to tremble confirms the rightness of emotion, the necessity of having felt as he did in the early 1790's. What he has come to, I think, is the recognition of how inextricably private values are involved in public phenomena, and he sees how such recognition shatters the comfortable judiciousness that (for example) 'places' a great man like Napoleon by sniffing at his social antecedents. His experience of Napoleon as a public force reveals the frivolity of honouring greatness in books but scoffing at it in life, and the evasiveness of treating public fact, and one's own responsibility for its being as it is, as though it were all only a 'story' that can be treated with the safe detachment one feels about literary fictions.

'October, 1803' does not 'turn' toward some satisfying emotional resolution, then, but it does lead to a (painful) clarification of the poet's situation. For all his trembling, his final understanding is a great act of mind. These 'thoughts sublime' fill the imagination, even to overflowing. He achieves a perception of process, a coherent vision of apparently disparate feelings that makes his experience intelligible, if tragically so.[8] It is an imaginative synthesis of the kind Wordsworth and Coleridge in their different ways took to be the end and justification of art. To learn and *feel* one's nvolvement in the apparently 'other' world of politics and gross power, to see that both the self and the world are figures of moral history, is to come by way of the combinative powers of the imagination to an experience of simultaneous horror and elevation, the fusing in a single psychological image—here 'tremble' —of seemingly distinct and contrary states of feeling.

Such fusion is what 'Anticipation' reaches for when it speaks of

> That triumph, when the very worst, the pain,
> The loss and e'en the prospect of the slain
> Hath something in it which the heart enjoys.

Here the combination is not adequately achieved, remaining schematic, theoretical, unreduced to the image or tonal inflection that fuses the contraries. And in this schematic form, it translates too easily into the stale and stilted grammar of patriotic reflex, the reduction of conflict to the simple terms of Us and Them. Clearly the writing of these poems posed a problem for Wordsworth. David Ferry speaks of *The Prelude* as showing the poet being

> led 'naturally', by the tutelage of nature, into his political error, or rather into the error *of being political at all*, of putting his faith in man's power to order his world successfully.[9]

That Wordsworth came to think in this way of his youthful involvement in the Revolution is clear; that his eventual disillusionment did not (as Ferry explains) lead to a *total* ironic rejection of the whole experience was a feat of great imaginative subtlety and honesty. But the method of *The Prelude*, which dissociates the poem from *present* political attitudes and anxieties so as to be clearer about the past, is different from that of the Political Sonnets, which undertake to deal directly with the present face of political things. In the sonnets two impulses confront one another: one the relatively new-found conviction that the Revolution had led to political horror and that Englishmen must oppose it, the other Wordsworth's ingrained philosophical suspicion that all 'public' phenomena are mere shows, transitory and insignificant unless penetrated (and in effect destroyed) by the imagination in its hunger for what lies behind the 'symbolic' surface of events.

In some of these sonnets Wordsworth sought to resolve this difficulty through rhetoric, mimicking patriotic oratory as if in the hope that stereotypical verbal gestures could pacify his fear that political concern might not survive the full exercise of imagination:

> . . . work he hath begun
> Of fortitude, and piety, and love,
> Which all his glorious ancestors approve:
> The heroes bless him, him their rightful son.
>
> (VII. *The King of Sweden*)
>
> In our halls is hung
> Armoury of the invincible Knights of old;
> We must be free or die, who speak the tongue
> That Shakespeare spake. . . .
>
> (XVI)

No parleying now. In Britain is one breath;
We all are with you now from shore to shore;—
Ye men of Kent, 'tis victory or death!

(XXIII. *To the Men of Kent*)

If the Churchillian note has its uses and its own kind of dignity, still it is disquieting to find a poet like Wordsworth playing the sloganeer. Happily the Political Sonnets strike other notes too, ones in which the poet's mind dwells more fully on the difficult nature of its own concern for public events, where the tone is not pugilistic or oratorical but personal, reflective, conscious of uncertainty. The poet's concern may settle into a cogent natural image: the evening star (I. 'Composed by the Sea-side, Near Calais') as it expresses both the glory and the uncertainty of England's predicament; the poet 'pensive as a bird/Whose vernal coverts winter hath laid bare' as he contrasts the present deadness of the French scene with memories of Revolutionary excitement (III. 'Composed Near Calais, On the Road Leading to Ardres'); the wonderful vision of Milton's austere patriotism 'Pure as the naked heavens, majestic, free' (XIV. 'London, 1802'). The concern may find its poetic form in the representative detail, as in Sonnet IX ('September 1, 1802'), with its memory of the negress who travelled with the poet from Calais to Dover and whose weary depression and fiery eyes seemed a striking emblem of the cost and spiritual importance of resisting oppression. Or it may all be reduced to the bite and pungency of personal speech in a state of strong feeling:

> I grieved for Buonapartê, with a vain
> And an unthinking grief! The tenderest mood
> Of that Man's mind—what can it be? what food
> Fed his first hopes? what knowledge could *he* gain?
>
> (IV. '1801')

Or the qualifying sense of the imperfection of one's own cause, even if it is preferable to the Napoleonic alternative, may be brought more openly into the argument of a poem, as in the sonnets (XIII–XVII) that invoke the sturdy virtues of Milton's England as a shaming contrast to the national irresolution that lets Bonaparte seem so menacing, or Sonnet XXI, which confesses

England's offences against the world and reveals the poet's patriotism as merely a choice of the lesser evil:

> Therefore the wise pray for thee, though the freight
> Of thy offences be a heavy weight:
> Oh grief that Earth's best hopes rest all with thee!

This last, needless to say, was not published in the papers.

These Political Sonnets are, of course, not all successful as poems, even when they attempt some qualification of simple patriotic fervour. But taken as a group they compose a fascinating portrait of a fine and idiosyncratic mind confronting crisis. The crisis, I should say, is at least as much internal and personal as it is public, at least in the better poems. 'October, 1803' fully and clearly articulates the links between political concern and apprehension about the loss of one's imaginative powers, that great Wordsworthian theme. The political books of *The Prelude* trace in more detail the bloom and blight of Wordsworth's sympathies for the Revolution; and his growing hostility to anything that might upset the *status quo* could be taken as an abandonment of politics altogether, revolutionary or not. But in a curious way his questionings and suspicions of action may keep closer touch with the public world than Blake's elaboration of political passion into myth or Shelley's determination to remain 'committed' even when his imagination of revolutionary realities had weakened. If, as Wordsworth came to feel, political enthusiasm coarsens the imagination or diverts it from its proper objects, still one couldn't know this without having felt such enthusiasm and lived through its painful decline toward crabbed reactionary stasis; and it is Wordsworth's distinction to have been able to make the growth of such disillusionment the subject of poems that relate political experience to the whole complexity of conscious life. Not even Coleridge, whose own imaginative decline took quite different forms, tells us so much about where a fine awareness of things, including political things, leads in the end.

4. The Idealization of Art

No doubt men have always assumed that art and the concerns of practical living are different, but it remained for Romanticism to make the distinction into a fundamental principle of aesthetic and social theory. I have said that poets like Blake and Shelley tended to aestheticize their political feelings, elaborating the mythic import of the work to the point where its own existence as a literary object seems the main focus of attention and effort. This in effect means that the artist's kind of experience, the fullest and most sensitive response to the prevailing conditions of life, is not simply the source and referent of what the artist produces, the work itself, but is subsumed and replaced by the new 'reality' of the work, which now exists independent of its origins in mere life. Raymond Williams, who in *Culture and Society* explores this identification of process and product in detail, puts the matter in a suggestive if knotty way:

> The obstruction of a certain kind of experience was simplified to the obstruction of poetry, which was then identified with it and even made to stand for it as a whole. Under pressure, art became a symbolic abstraction for a whole range of general human experience ... a general social activity was forced into the status of a department or province, and actual works of art were in part converted into a self-pleading ideology. ... In practice there were deep insights, and great works of art; but, in the continuous pressure of living, the free play of genius found it increasingly difficult to consort with the free play of the market, and the difficulty was not solved, but cushioned, by an idealization. The last pages of Shelley's *Defence of Poetry* are painful to read. The bearers of a high imaginative skill become suddenly the 'legislators', at the very moment when they were being forced into practical exile; their description as 'unacknowledged', which, on the theory, ought only to be a fact to be accepted, carries with it also the felt helplessness of a generation.[10]

Poetry, in other words, becomes not simply the record of an unusually open and responsive experience but an essentially autonomous life in itself, behaving as though its own survival depended on triumphing in a competition with mere 'reality'. In such a competition, as Williams implies, art would always seem in its own eyes to be losing—and so *this*, the sense of being ignored by the practical world, became a part of the attitude too, the identifying sign of true art.

Here I have room only for a few loose speculations, but this idealizing of art seems to explain a good deal about English poetry in the nineteenth century. Clearly the poets and poet-critics were the main representatives of the new state of mind, since for the Victorians literary 'art' mostly meant poetry. Fiction was entertainment or (for the George Eliot cultists) lay religion; as Henry James knew, it was hard to persuade English and American readers that 'the art of fiction' was an art at all. 'Literary prose' was mainly an adjunct of political journalism or social science or moral philosophy. Only when one sat down to write a poem did one feel really artistic, and the poems one wrote, when they dealt with public life at all, either adopted the tastes and needs of the adversary society—the 'Light Brigade' sort of thing—or acknowledged only as a menacing circumference to the personal life the social and moral confusions that the novelists and prose writers so heroically strove to understand and explain.

While it is possible to overstress the 'aestheticism' of Tennyson and his age, the addiction to Beauty of those 'world-losers and world-forsakers' whom Leavis castigates at the end of *Revaluation*, it still seems clear to me that Victorian poets had trouble doing justice to public subjects. Arnold is perhaps the classic case of a poet inhibited from a full realization of his powers by an inherited and faulty idea of the poet's role. 'Dover Beach', 'The Scholar Gypsy', 'Thyrsis', 'Lines Written in Kensington Gardens'—such poems give impressively the emotional effect of political and cultural alienation, but without much more than shorthand notations of its public sources. These sources are of course amply and seriously dealt with in Arnold's prose, so that we have the sense of a mind divided between its important *work* and its moments of withdrawal into poetry, art taken as melancholy consolation for one's general circumstance in a bleak and hostile world. Arnold's literary criticism is of two minds about this, of course; poetry is a 'criticism of life', but it usually seems that for Arnold it performed this function by making available consoling and uplifting 'spiritual' alternatives to the worldly materialism of practical life rather than by confronting that life and imaginatively exploring one's own relation to it.

> Others will teach us how to dare,
> And against fear our breast to steel;
> Others will strengthen us to bear—
> But who, ah! who, will make us feel?

Arnold's Wordsworth, that is, is John Stuart Mill's Wordsworth too, and we may be sure that one needn't have had James Mill or Arnold of Rugby for a father to find Wordsworth a guide to the liberation of emotion that life itself seemed to inhibit. But once liberated, what is emotion to do with itself?

Although Blake and Shelley couldn't be sure about it, England's Revolution was to be Industrial and not Political. Material progress was the governing public fact, and the paradox of progress bringing material and spiritual poverty to the larger part of the nation was as apparent to high-minded Tories like Carlyle and Disraeli as to revolutionary socialists like Engels; but the basic ideological and moral issues found little expression in the practical politics of the times. The possibility of a political force that could be both radical and genuinely working-class perished with Chartism in the early 1840's, and the politics of 'Reform' centred upon the gradual enfranchising of the middle class and the refurbishing of the parliamentary system. At a time when the nation seemed unprecedentedly rich in the aggregate, drastic change appeared unnecessary and political passion eccentric—even so thoughtful a man as Bagehot could celebrate "government by discussion' as the best political arrangement, forgetting (as G. Kitson Clark remarks) that cultivated parliamentarianism usually underestimates the importance of crudely expressed ideas and the crude, awkward men who express them.[11] The political mood did quicken some in the 1860's and '70's with the emergence of Gladstone as the energizing conscience of Liberalism, but neither Gladstonian rhetoric nor Gladstone himself gave any very inspiring stimulus to the literary imagination.

In short, 'the continuous pressure of living' in nineteenth-century England included having no politics capable of objectifying the imagination's concern for freedom and disinterested truth, both because official politics was dreary and because the imagination had persuaded itself that *its* truths lay elsewhere, out of an idealized love of its own productions that made their relation to practical life seem essentially and necessarily antagonistic. The 'felt helplessness' evident in Arnold's best poems and at least implicit in Tennyson and Browning and the Aesthetic Movement, was a consequence of feeling that art is irrelevant to public practice. Browning did not speak only for himself when he exclaimed, in the 1863 preface to *Sordello*, 'incidents in the development of a soul! little else is worth study'.

The doctrinaire division of 'art' from 'life' is a historical phase we are only now beginning to emerge from, no doubt, and we are in no position to sneer at our ancestors. But there are few, if any, poems of Victorian England that demand examination in the terms of my present subject. We must I think move to the present century for poetic signs of the recovery of public issues as immediate poetic matter, the restoration of the imagination's concern for the life outside the artist's mind and feelings and belief in the aesthetic autonomy of his works.

NOTES

[1] David V. Erdman, *Blake: Prophet Against Empire* (Princeton, Princeton University Press, and London, Oxford University Press, 1954); J. Bronowski, *William Blake*, rev. ed. (Harmondsworth, Penguin Books, 1954). To these books, and to Northrop Frye's *Fearful Symmetry*, I owe much of what I understand about Blake as a poet generally. I cannot hope to list all the writers on Blake with whom my readings agree or disagree, but I should mention a few whose interpretations, despite disagreements, are enough like mine to give me hope. These include Harold Bloom, *Blake's Apocalypse* (New York, Doubleday, and London, Gollancz, 1963), especially on 'The Sick Rose', 'Ah! Sun-flower', and 'London'; E. D. Hirsch, Jr., *Innocence and Experience* (New Haven, Yale University Press, 1964), especially on 'London' and 'The Clod and the Pebble'; and Martin Price, *To the Palace of Wisdom*, especially on 'London' and 'The Sick Rose'.

[2] Erdman, *Prophet Against Empire*, p. 209, suggests that finally, after Waterloo, Blake lost his faith in the American and French Revolutions, which by then seemed to him mere bourgeois revolts to secure the rights of the commercial class.

[3] J. Hillis Miller, *The Disappearance of God* (Cambridge, Harvard University Press, 1963, and London, Oxford University Press, 1963), p. 157.

[4] Jean Hagstrum, 'William Blake's "The Clod and the Pebble" ', in *Restoration and Eighteenth-Century Studies*, ed. Carroll Camden (Chicago, University of Chicago Press, 1963), pp. 381-388, opposes this view with

evidence for an opposite reading drawn largely from the design of the plate and other passages in Blake.

[5] E. D. Hirsch's generally perceptive reading (*Innocence and Experience*, pp. 216-218) leads him to see 'The Clod and the Pebble' as 'a deeply affirmative representation of the holiness of life and the rightness of the natural order'; but though like other Songs of Experience it may contain the materials out of which such reconciliation can be made, I would insist that as a poem it expresses conflict, *unresolved* antithesis.

[6] Leavis, *Revaluation*, pp. 228-230.

[7] By an interesting irony (pointed out to me by Herbert Lindenberger), *The Mask of Anarchy* was to be a favourite work of the radical poets of the *Jung Deutschland* movement of the 1830's and '40's, particularly Karl Ferdinand Gutzkow and Georg Herwegh; Shelley thus in a way contributed to 1848 and vicariously suffered its great disappointment, long after his death.

[8] I am encouraged by finding in my account of 'October, 1803' some general resemblance to what Geoffrey Hartman describes as the characteristic pattern of the effects of 'imagination' in Wordsworth: 'a moment of arrest, the ordinary vital continuum being interrupted; a separation of the traveller-poet from familiar nature; a thought of death or judgment or of the reversal of what is taken to be the order of nature; a feeling of solitude or loss or separation.' *Wordsworth's Poetry* (New Haven, Yale University Press, 1964), pp. 17-18.

[9] David Ferry, *The Limits of Mortality* (Middletown, Wesleyan University Press, 1959), p. 145; my understanding of Wordsworth owes much to this book.

[10] Raymond Williams, *Culture and Society*, p. 47; my general indebtedness to Williams' treatment of Romanticism will be obvious.

[11] G. Kitson Clark, 'The Making of Victorian England', in *The Victorian Age*, ed. Robert Langbaum (New York, Fawcett, 1967), p. 40. Several points in my paragraph are adapted from Langbaum's deft introduction to this volume.

CHAPTER FIVE

The Modern Poet and the Public World

A notion like 'public world' is especially hard to sustain in thinking about modern literature. Whatever Spenser or Dryden or even Wordsworth took to be the distinction between public and private experience, in our time such a distinction is very dubious philosophically. We see personal relations or even inner psychic divisions as politics, and politics encroaches upon private feeling to the point of bewilderment. 'Inner' and 'outer' are categories that can scarcely survive hard examination, and our idea of the good life, or even the possible life, presumably depends on refusing to make a firm division between what is ours, experience as property, and what we owe the others who constitute our world. If, as Bertrand Russell suggested, the stars are in our brain, then politics must be there too.

But somehow one still thinks that 'public events' have a different bearing on one's life from falling in love or smelling cooking or reading Spinoza. One still wants to say that 'Easter 1916' is a political poem and that *Ash-Wednesday* or 'Sunday Morning' is not. The poems by Yeats, Eliot, Auden, and Robert Lowell I shall be discussing don't, of course, fully represent the variety of modern poetry and its relations to public life—for that, even limiting the discussion to writers in English, one would want to add Pound, Stevens, Frost, the 'Fugitives', Roy Campbell, Hugh MacDiarmid, the Protest poets of the 1960's, and many more. But Yeats, Eliot, Auden, and Lowell do represent four modern generations; each is in a sense *the* poet of his generation, no doubt; and their political attitudes vary, to say the least. The poems I deal with, for all the relative randomness of their selection, may serve to illustrate some promising and unpromising modern views of how art can relate to public events and issues. A simple sketch may be suggestive, even so argumentative a one as this.

1. 'Easter 1916'

Yeats is of course impossible. He wrote more poems than seems

decent for a modern poet to do, and the extent and difficulty of
his prose writings about art and his own mind can be terrifying
to the mere amateur. But one may begin, as others have done, by
positing in him a division between the 'aesthete' and the 'politician', between the reflective man absorbed in magic, symbolic
correspondences, the nature of his own will and affections, and
the active man who was strongly drawn to public enterprises, in
the theatre, Irish nationalist causes, and ultimately a home-grown
Fascism. The merging of such diverse attractions in individual
poems is usually hard to assess accurately. It may be that none of
his poems, even the most remote and mannered lyrics of the
1880's and '90's, is wholly without relevance to some programme
or cause; and even his most obviously political poems draw extensively on the symbols and moods of his private aesthetics. But
if one can't measure the degree to which artist and politician
mingle in a poem, it seems important to insist that they *do* mingle
and that something is missing in a comment like this:

> His political poems . . . are always complicated by his being
> above politics. In 'Easter, 1916' he celebrates the revolt of
> his compatriots but insists also on pointing out what seems
> to him to be its folly:
>
>> And what if excess of love
>> Bewildered them till they died?
>
> The word 'bewildered' is a thoroughly conscientious one
> here. The poem has been castigated because it satisfied
> both the nationalists and the anti-nationalists, but Yeats,
> who had elements of both in his thought, expressed his
> whole position.[1]

The commentator is Richard Ellmann, who must know more
about Yeats than anyone, but it seems just enough 'off' to allow
a qualification. To be 'above politics' is not quite the same as to
have elements of both nationalism and anti-nationalism in one's
thought; this is not above politics but squarely *in* it, just at the
point where it justifies itself by mediating between opposing
motives. Ellmann is caught in a vocabulary that perhaps can't be
avoided when he pairs off 'celebrating' the Easter Rising against
'pointing out its folly', but such terms at least need to be resisted.

The complication here seems to me not some superiority to politics on Yeats's part but rather a recognition that one must distinguish the meaning of a public action from the motives or personalities of the people who perform it, a distinction indispensable to political understanding.

One can approach the complexity of 'Easter 1916' through the paradox of its refrain: 'A terrible beauty is born.' Terror and beauty is a familiar conjunction in Yeats's earlier poems, of course. The beautiful woman whose face is destruction is an almost obsessive presence in 'The Rose of the World', 'The Folly of Being Comforted', and 'No Second Troy', to name only a familiar few; and often enough she represents not just the personal dangers of romantic desire, La Belle Dame Sans Merci, but the descent of fire and ruin upon cities and cultures in some heroic apocalypse:

> For these red lips, with all their mournful pride,
> Mournful that no new wonder may betide,
> Troy passed away in one high funeral gleam,
> And Usna's children died.
>
> (From 'The Rose of the World')

The boundary between personal and public passion is often uncertain in Yeats, and it seems natural enough that in 'Easter 1916' he should put his troubled response to contemporary things in a phrase that recalls earlier and somewhat different applications. Beauty and terror dwell together in revolutionary violence as in love and tragic art, and their conjunction puzzlingly seems natural, a result of 'birth' and not of miracle or cataclysm.

The poem is built on contradiction and uncertainty, and its process throws varying weight on the refrain. The tired contempt of the opening line establishes a very Yeatsian speaker for whom public, social life, the everyday world of routine occupations where 'polite meaningless words' form the currency of speech, is trivial and phantasmagoric: 'being certain that they and I/But lived where motley is worn'. 'They' is enough identification, and amid the grey houses of provincial Dublin at close of day their 'vivid faces' seem bright not with significant, expressive energy but with the fixed garishness of stage make-up, the motley of the actor or entertainer. In the poet, himself one of them, they stimulate only a more calculated theatricality:

> And thought before I had done
> Of a mocking tale or a gibe
> To please a companion
> Around the fire at the club.

If his self-defined identity as clubman and raconteur sneers a little at their clerical routine at 'counter or desk', still the governing feeling isn't mere snobbery but a supra-social revulsion from the banality of all ordinary living. The tone reflects a distaste for life in general that cripples imagination, which even when released from polite meaningless social formula can only express itself in tales and jokes, a glib and formulaic irony that seems no more dignified or significant. In this context 'a terrible beauty' might be read with a slight stress on 'beauty'—the Rising was at least a relief from boredom, transforming a drab routine into something rich and strange, however fearfully so. '*All* changed' comprehends not only 'them', the dull lives that sprang into amazing focus with these great events, but also the poet, who now, not too reluctantly, must seek a new role for himself in this transformed reality.

The poem's second section is a kind of procession, as the poet evokes some of the revolutionary heroes and in effect ticks them off as they pass. (He is interestingly in control, they obey his summons; but this relation will not last.) He knows them and their histories, and yet the contradictions persist: they have 'resigned [their] part[s]/In the casual comedy', and yet their roles remain theatrical as he 'number[s them] in the song', incorporates them in the drama his art creates. They have earned their new roles by what they did in life, but his art of song, whether or not it is to become true heroic song, can claim some share in the transformation.

The problem is that in life they were such difficult, independent figures. Con Markiewicz was more beautiful and heroically suggestive when she was private and peaceful, 'When, young and beautiful,/She rode to harriers'. How can she be part of the 'terrible beauty' when her entrance into politics, the potentially heroic theatre of the poem, in fact betrayed that grace and beauty

into 'ignorant argument' and distorted vocal sweetness into shrill-
ness? Pearse and MacDonagh, poets and schoolmasters, are
equally hard to put into heroic song; nothing in their former lives
suggested a capacity for such an act, and a poet can't feel much
enthusiasm about the truncation of another poet's career, the
dissipation of talent in abortive public violence. MacBride is the
hardest case of all. A 'drunken, vainglorious lout' who has done
the poet personal wrong can only grudgingly be admitted to this
company, and yet he *did* fight, and his character may after all
have been only another illusion of 'ordinary' existence:

> Yet I number him in the song;
> He, too, has resigned his part
> In the casual comedy;
> He, too, has been changed in his turn,
> Transformed utterly:
> A terrible beauty is born.

By now we have been made strongly aware of the poet himself,
and this second paragraph dwells upon the mixed nature of the
patriot-martyrs so as to emphasize the effort it costs him to make
song of such material. Everything in his implied normal temperament, his fastidious, Pateresque devotion to beauty, seemliness,
and grace, rebels at the spectacle of poets taking up arms, women
wasting their sweetness in polemic frenzy, drunken bullies en-
nobled by a cause they can hardly have understood. But—and
here Yeats's usual complex relation to 'reality' comes into play—
he has not committed himself to their existences as real people
in the first place. He had *dreamed* MacBride a drunken, vainglorious lout, not in any simple way known him as that. The
thorough-going scepticism about a world where motley is worn
now supports the truth of their transformation, as if to say 'I
thought them commonplace or worse, but I should have understood that such judgments are unreliable, that behind men's
immediate selves lies a larger, often antithetical drama that historical accident and personal will may distort or conceal.' 'I knew
that One is animate,/Mankind inanimate fantasy', Yeats was to
write in 'A Meditation in Time of War', and it would have been
easy enough for him to reconcile the contradictions by appealing
to his 'system', claiming that a moment of significant violence

like the Rising releases the unsuspected antimasks of seemingly ordinary people.

But in 'Easter 1916' this resolution is hinted at only to be resisted. The poem, of course, can't simply be detached and lifted out of the poetic works of the author of *A Vision*. The Yeats of the great political poems—'Easter 1916', 'Meditations in Time of Civil War', 'Nineteen Hundred and Nineteen', 'In Memory of Eva Gore-Booth and Con Markiewicz', 'Parnell's Funeral', and the magnificent meditations on violence and art in *Last Poems*—remains always involved in the symbolic questionings of 'Among School Children', 'Sailing to Byzantium', and the other great 'visionary' poems, to call them that. The system never explains all, but there are few interesting poems that don't in some way draw upon its ordering capacities. 'Easter 1916' is of the political poems perhaps the least visibly related to the system, but it is there all the same, as a significant influence on the speaker's mode of self-presentation and as a potential *obstacle* to fully grasping the difficult meaning of the event. You can't quite say that Mac-Bride's personal coarseness finally doesn't matter, that it faded away like a dream when the poor man found a way of living into his mythic potential. Yeats bravely admits the temptation of doing just this, but 'dreamed' can mean other things too. It can mean that Yeats thinks it rather foolish for his theories about reality and myth to have confused him into thinking MacBride's loutishness a dream rather than the obvious fact it was. It can suggest that his loutishness was never important enough to be taken as a problem, so that having 'dreamed' it is only an insolent way of putting him in his place. To finish the song it is necessary to include him among the heroes, but not by concealing his faults or the poet's animosity toward him.

At any rate, it does not make things easier to remember Mac-Bride. The emphasis of the refrain might now fall on 'terrible', stressing the intractability of the material out of which 'beauty' comes. The casual comedy, whether dream or fact, has broken down, characters no longer respond to the demands of their former roles, the new 'song' can only accept transformation and try to give it coherent assessment. The third section, however, finds the assessment difficult. 'Hearts with one purpose alone' states the problem. The rebels have set themselves apart from

ordinary men, but through fanaticism or admirable devotion?
Their stony commitment to their purpose, in its contrast to
natural life and variety, could be the mark of moral death:

> The horse that comes from the road,
> The rider, the birds that range
> From cloud to tumbling cloud,
> Minute by minute they change;
> A shadow of cloud on the stream
> Changes minute by minute;
> A horse-hoof slides on the brim,
> And a horse plashes within it;
> The long-legged moor-hens dive,
> And hens to moor-cocks call;
> Minute by minute they live:
> The stone's in the midst of all.

The appeal of this plastic, animated nature is enhanced by the
imagistic economy—we see stream, horse, birds, cloud, each in
more than one way, not as fixed, static 'objects' but as participants
in a fluid, repetitive pattern. Here things come in pairs—horse
and rider, bird and air, hen and cock—and the pairings suggest
intimate mutuality in productive effort. Action and change have
their own order, where even clumsiness—the horse losing his
footing, the birds' ungainly legs—has dignity, endowing even
the ungraceful with a kind of Grace. The stone in the midst of
all surely does trouble this living stream, interrupt its spontaneous flow, hinder its uncalculated exuberance. If the great change
the poem speaks of is an 'enchantment', the word first implies
disturbing violation of natural life.

But the word has another force as well. The natural is limited
to cyclical self-perpetuation, the birds rise only to dive when
called to mate. It isn't necessary to invoke the opening of 'Sailing
to Byzantium' as proof that Yeats could find something unsatis-
fying in incessant change and something compelling about single-
ness of purpose. Enchantment may violate nature, but it reflects
a fascination with mastering and transcending it too, the challenge
nature seems somehow meant to offer human minds: 'Once out
of nature I shall never take/My bodily form from any natural
thing.' 'Minute by minute they live' notes the limits of life even

while cherishing its variety and rich contingency. The stone's indifference is, in human terms, the sign of possession by heroic necessity, and 'in the midst of all' confers on single-mindedness a kind of centrality, a status as reference point dominating the flow of *natura naturans* all around it.

The poet has *not* found a position from which he can securely place and evaluate the public event and its human meaning. Chance and change, contingency and purpose, stream and stone, none of the oppositions reduces to moral syllogism. The stream's vital variety is almost irresistibly attractive, yet its suggestion of phenomenological flux and surface evokes a traditionally opposing symbol of permanence, a mode of being whose substantial, unchanging form preserves itself even at the expense of life. 'The stone's in the midst of all' is so imposing and demanding an image as to deny 'A terrible beauty is born', with its more personal and situational difficulty, its expected place at the end of the section. There is no sustenance for that kind of problem in this intense philosophical air, and the third section is only glancingly about Ireland and the Easter Rising at all.

The transition to the final paragraph in fact comes a little hard. 'Too long a sacrifice/Can make a stone of the heart.' This leaves the point unsettled: to sacrifice the heart by pursuing a single purpose to the point of its abstraction from feeling will turn the heart to stone, but so will too *much* feeling, too intense a devotion exhaust the heart of its saving compassion and responsiveness. Is it turned to stone by disuse, or by over-use? There seems something uncertain, too, in the descent from the large philosophical oppositions of section three to what seems a limiting 'psychological' speculation about the rebels themselves. But the uncertainties (if I haven't invented them myself) seem functional and right. Whatever the process was, they *have* had their hearts turned to stone; they have become monuments, in effect, not people. But the poet has not been so transformed; his own heart remains painfully alive to their action, and his need to ask difficult, unanswerable questions makes the final section a moving record of his persistence in his own human imperfection, his continuing if hopeless search for a role in which 'feeling', with its implication of a single self which feels, can provide adequate participation in the event.

This last section shows the poet trying out various identities in which to face the event and its implications. He first imagines himself as a troubled but practical realist; their sacrifice has not brought the independence they sought, and he wonders when if ever it will suffice. Is there any substantial good in violent gestures which, in the short run, only destroy those who make them? Then he moves from this role, with its obvious limitations, to a sympathetic identification with a mother murmuring the name of her child: 'When sleep at last has come/On limbs that had run wild.' What they did was a kind of playing, of no lasting consequence but deeply affecting to the farther-seeing tenderness of the parental heart; we neither approve nor disapprove but simply love them. This view moves toward hopeful sentimental cliché— 'What is it but nightfall?'—before the poet's sense of tragic honesty protests: 'No, no, not night but death.' They were alive, they had purposes that were not childish, and they have suffered the absolute extinction of the faculties he himself is now exercising. (Extinction may also be transcendence, but any appeal to super-reality here would cheat them and the poet shamefully.) But the political man hasn't been permanently suppressed. He now re-asserts himself in the trivial rhetoric of editorial cliché:

> Was it needless death after all?
> For England may keep faith
> For all that is done and said.

If the poem satisfied both parties, it was not by concealing the worst features of each.

The self-catechism has tried a number of possible conclusions, ways of coming to terms with the rebels and their act, and the inner debate projected is recognizably the Yeatsian 'quarrel with oneself' that makes poetry. The debate is almost embarrassingly open about confessing that any mediation tends toward the senti-mental banality of dead public languages: 'What is it but night-fall', 'for all that is done and said'. The poet's search for an atti-tude is hedged around by the stereotypes of worn-out poeticism and the leader-writer's bag of literary refuse. As Ellmann and others have stressed, Yeats's career hinged on divisions within himself, between the nationalist and the would-be Anglo-Irish aristocrat, the theatrical impresario and the Theosophist, the politician and the parlour mystic, the 'sixty-year-old smiling public man' who was a Senator of the Irish Free State and the 'wild wicked old man' who hammered sexual frenzy, political despair, and a home-made key to all mythologies into the astonishments of *Last Poems*. It is such inner division that the concluding questionings of 'Easter 1916' express, a division that resists the tendency of public languages and attitudes to resolve felt complexity into simple, predetermined conclusion.

There is no such conclusion for this poem, no identity for the poet that can assume the stability of recognizable public roles. The questions lead only to an ultimate question that allows no answer:

> We know their dream; enough
> To know they dreamed and are dead;
> And what if excess of love
> Bewildered them till they died?

It is *not* enough to know they dreamed and are dead—one further question intrudes even upon so bleak and final an honesty, the question that has needed asking all along. Their other identifications in the poem have tried to fix them in manageable roles that separate them from the poet's deepest concern. They were casual acquaintances; 'typical' figures of aristocratic grace, intellectual promise, or vulgarity; stony, statuesque emblems of fanaticism or heroic devotion; children or patriotic saints. To imagine that they were *men*, capable of bewilderment and passionate confusion, victims not of some unimaginable heroic vision but of desiring what they can't possess or even understand, is to face a possibility that makes questions of practical political significance irrelevant and stupid.

Yeats's response to this final question is the only one possible for him, although it contains further ironies:

> And what if excess of love
> Bewildered them till they died?
> I write it out in a verse—
> MacDonagh and MacBride
> And Connolly and Pearse
> Now and in time to be,

Wherever green is worn,
Are changed, changed utterly:
A terrible beauty is born.

A poet can only 'write it out in a verse', claiming no status for himself except that of the humble and in a way mechanical craft of the man who sits and puts down words so that they come out in verses. Nothing allows him to claim any closer relation to them; if excess of love did bewilder them till they died, there is no judgment he can presume to make. Rather he gives us a 'verse' that echoes the vulgarity of patriotic platitude and yet is moving and right. 'Now and in time to be' carries the poem to the brink of a pseudo-eternity that public oratory is always ready to fob off on us, and even a fanatical Fenian might wince a little at yet another wearing of the green. But it takes courage and conviction to let your verse come so close to disaster. The politician's rhetoric, because it is tastelessly, hopelessly a parading of old appeals and pieties, may yet not inevitably be insincere; perhaps there are things that can only be said that way. At any rate, Yeats's poet-self is as helpless as the orator when he tries to connect public events and the aesthetic and moral values that are his own major concern.

But the professional Irishman who tried to read 'Easter 1916' aloud at a St. Patrick's Day rally, though he might (for the first time in the poem) find himself at home with these lines, would be thwarted by the final reappearance of the refrain. The rising curve of the rhetoric falters before the penultimate line, and the completion of the suspended syntax is an anticlimax. Those ringing names, with their associations of heroic promise and failed hopes, are only 'changed, changed utterly', and we are left with the unresolved paradox of terrible beauty. But if this marks ora-torical failure—the politician could have finished the sentence on a triumphant if trivial note that wouldn't smother the rising tone—it, of course, is not imaginative failure. The beauty that is born represents not escape from public terror into aesthetic order but a way of preserving the force of terror while giving it the status of an object being contemplated and known with some of the disinterested concern that one brings to works of art or (more accurately) that works of art enforce upon us. But such disinterest has a place in political contemplation too. 'Easter 1916' teaches a concern for public phenomena that limits their powers to elicit easy and false responses, false definitions of self. If there are finally no responses that are *not* false in some way, then that is worth knowing too, and the knowledge has uses in one's political experience as well as in the private effort to understand and endure one's own nature.

Yeats had certain advantages of nationality. Irish politics were insular and (as in the Dedalus household) quite literally domestic. The Easter Rising was not some remote event known only from its confused edges or from reading the newspapers: it was an action done by friends and acquaintances, and the choice of a side had some of the immediacy and personal peril of taking sides in office quarrels or your friends' divorces. This could and did lead Yeats to overestimate the personal elements in public actions, asking in apparent seriousness whether 'any trade question at the opening of the eighteenth century [had] as great an effect on subsequent history as Bolingbroke's impotence and Harley's slowness and secrecy', and drawing large conclusions from the fact that of his colleagues in the Irish Senate the appointed members (drawn inevitably from the cultivated upper-class establishment) were the most adroit, while the elected members were graceless and embarrassing:

> In its early days some old banker or lawyer would dominate the House, leaning upon the back of the chair in front, always speaking with undisturbed self-possession as at some table in a board-room. My imagination sets up against him some typical elected man, emotional as a youthful chimpanzee, hot and vague, always disturbed, always hating something or other.

But the tendency to see politics in personal terms was also a redeeming habit, since it helped him resist his other tendency, of too readily finding in public events apocalyptic Spenglerian significances that abstracted the events from their human effects:

> The danger is that there will be no war, that the skilled will attempt nothing, that the European civilization, like those older civilizations that saw the triumph of their gangrel stocks, will accept decay. When I was writing *A Vision* I

had constantly the word 'terror' impressed upon me, and once the old Stoic prophecy of earthquake, fire, and flood at the end of an age, but this I did not take literally. It was because of that indefinable impression that I made Michael Robartes say in *A Vision*: 'Dear predatory birds, prepare for war, prepare your children and all that you can reach. ... Test art, morality, custom, thought, by Thermopylae, make rich and poor act so to one another that belief may be changed, civilization renewed. We desire belief and lack it. Belief comes from shock and is not desired.'[2]

This is the mood, though not the tone, of 'The Second Coming', and in its reaching for an idea of modern experience large enough to accommodate tragedy it seems strained and self-conscious, as dated in rhetorical colour as Mussolinian Fascism or chiliastic Marxism. Whatever we now read *A Vision* for, it is scarcely for its power to explain modern political history, and the greatness of 'The Second Coming' lies in its expression of what historical discontinuity feels like whenever it occurs rather than the accuracy of its bearing on a particular moment of time.

In 'Easter 1916' Yeats constructs tragic vision out of experience that was close enough to himself to be called personal; his Irish concerns and loyalties make him speak like a man and not like a cultural theorist. I should put it that his art, to the extent that it is a public art, finds its securest note when it confesses insecurity, questioning the symbolic vision that would reconcile any event, however horrible in itself, to a larger unity. In 'Easter 1916' the poet resists his own beliefs, his doctrines about power and cultural change; and in doing so, he recognizes that public reality is not just a symbolic counter but his own native scene, in which his affections, for all their theoretical modes of disengagement, are inextricably involved.

2. *Coriolan*

'Easter 1916' dramatically preserves the personal and political uncertainty that is both recognized and assaulted by the modern hunger (like Yeats's own) for ideology and total commitment. The poem mediates between public positions—dedicated but parochial nationalism and the 'more responsible' Anglo-Irish hope for some peaceful accommodation with Britain and the modern world generally. But more deeply, I think, it mediates between private ideology, an idea of historical order through which to understand and endure process, and the need to retain freedom of feeling and judgment even at the risk of confusion or inconsistency. T. S. Eliot's *Coriolan* may provide some instructive contrasts. No one, I'm sure, thinks *Coriolan* one of Eliot's best works, and it would be silly to use it for attacking his achievement as a poet. Rather, I'm curious about why it doesn't seem as good in its way as *Gerontion*, *The Waste Land*, *Ash-Wednesday*, *Four Quartets*, or the best short poems. What in *Coriolan* inhibits the fullest exercise of Eliot's great talent?

The poem both benefits and suffers from Eliot's refusal to explicitly attach it to any single public occasion. The method is as usual assimilative, so that 'Triumphal March' takes place simultaneously in ancient Rome, any modern capital, at any time and place where secular power displays its enigmatic face in public. The *société gymnastique de Poissy* and the Vestal Virgins measure the extreme possibilities of value, from trivial to sacramental, but such details are mostly transparent, not interesting in themselves but at most colouring with a trace of irony the central, unlocated abstraction that is the subject: power and its mysteriousness to ordinary, powerless men. This is not a poem much concerned with the detailed surfaces of particular experiences, though it is full of details; something prevents the observed moments from easily unfolding their thematic relevance as moments do elsewhere in Eliot.

The poet does not fail to question both power and ordinary judgment. Power manifests itself in meaningless quantities ('1,150 field bakeries'), and this makes possible some deflating speculations about the 'artful' soldier-hero—is the lack of 'interrogation' in his eyes an imposing sign of self-sufficiency or just pitiful evidence of a small brain in a big body? Yet we can't take much comfort in 'our Ego' whose 'natural wakeful life' is 'a perceiving', since perceiving is represented as a passive, dull-minded acceptance and recording of just such inert data as power presents us with:

> That is all we could see. But how many eagles! and how many
> trumpets!

(And Easter Day, we didn't get to the country,
So we took young Cyril to church. And they rang a bell
And he said right out loud, *crumpets*.)

We are to see a different joke in Cyril's mistake than the parade-
going speaker sees; rather than a 'cute' and understandable
childish false association, the poet asks us to share his own rather
patronizing alarm about the secularization of holy things through
an ignorance not the exclusive property of children. It sounds
like a complaint about the deplorable insensitivity to ritual of the
lower orders, for whom church is only a substitute for day-
tripping. The irony is clearly there, but it's hard to sort out; even
assuming that it would be better for people to take the Mass more
seriously, would this then protect them better from responding
to *secular* rituals like the parade (there's in fact no sign that they
do respond in any very dangerous way), or would it prepare them
better to appreciate the symbolic power of the secular ritual, and
if so, would that be desirable?

We pretty surely are *not* meant to take the incident as showing
health and sanity in the popular mind. Yet a poet less committed
to an external omniscience—the omniscience that intrudes the
Husserlian solemnities about the perceiving ego and the 'still
point of the turning world' business—might think that a citizen
who turns from the vague impressiveness of military display to
an affectionate anecdote about his child sounds like someone not
likely to be taken in by parades and totalitarian mumbo-jumbo.
The voice that says 'what a time that took' may be 'perceiving'
in only a quantitative way and missing fine inner significances,
but it also seems to show an admirable (and distinctly English)
refusal to be too caught up in the rhythm of the event, thus
warding off its invitation to patriotic fanaticism. One would like
to feel surer that Eliot recognized the complex comedy of the
situation—the 'watchful, waiting, perceiving, indifferent' eyes of
the man on horseback encountering the eyes of spectators who
are also watchful and waiting and perceiving and, in their less
theatrical way, redeemingly quite as indifferent to him as he
seems to be to them.

The theme is aborted communication, I take it, the inability of
public ceremony to express a relation between leader and people

and thus articulate the mutual dependencies of an ordered society. The fault lies on both sides. The ceremony is miscalculated in its reliance on the boring manipulation of mere quantities in merely temporal sequence: 'Now they go up to the temple. Then the sacrifice./Now come the virgins. . . .' But (I seem to hear Eliot saying) even a better ceremony would fail with an audience like this one, too much concerned with its stools and sausages and cigarettes to do more than 'perceive' the occasion, be it a military parade or a Christian Mass. The point evidently is not just that mass-ceremonies of the Fascist sort are devoid of genuine communal participation and acceptance of meaning (*were* they, in fact?)—rather it seems that no public ceremony, secular or religious, could penetrate such minds with the 'hidden' spiritual expressiveness one expects and needs from ritual. Evidently politics itself, the range of possible relationships between leader and citizen supposedly represented by public ceremony, must in our time be irrelevant to common humanity.

Now, of course, this may be true, even if one would rather not think so. But it's not a promising attitude with which to undertake the writing of a poem about public men and their meaning. 'Triumphal March' has an assurance and composure of detail and structure that seems imaginatively static when compared with the difficult, shifting drama of 'Easter 1916'—the method rules out successfully imagining and responding to other minds. In 'Difficulties of a Statesman', the second section of *Coriolan*, Eliot seems to compensate for this quality by moving closer to the great man himself, in search of what the crowd failed to discern behind his impassive public mask. (What is he *really* like? we ask about our leaders.) But what Eliot finds there is mere cliché,[3] the troubled uncertainty ('Cry what shall I cry?') and peevish impotence of the man of action engulfed and paralysed by administrative trivia, poignantly aware that a living man can't achieve the decisive strength of the heroic images he's inevitably compared with:

> O mother (not among these busts, all correctly inscribed)
> I a tired head among these heads
> Necks strong to bear them
> Noses strong to break the wind . . .

The statesman's fretful joke betrays an uncertainty of Eliot's own.

To be sure, there's something touching about the statesman and his predicament, his baffled yearning to be 'Hidden in the still-ness of noon, in the silent croaking night', to take on the identity of 'the small creatures' to escape the impossible demands of greatness. But the poem hovers between ridicule of administrative abstraction ('A committee has been appointed to nominate a com-mission of engineers/To consider the Water Supply') and uneasily portentous appeal to the symbols of permanence and spiritual mystery introduced in 'Triumphal March', symbols that again have to be smuggled into the monologue, intruding upon the Statesman's own faltering voice the rather unctuous assurance of the Christian poet:

O hidden under the . . . Hidden under the . . . Where the dove's
  foot rested and locked for a moment,
A still moment, repose of noon, set under the upper branches of
  noon's widest tree
Under the breast feather stirred by the small wind after noon
There the cyclamen spreads its wings, there the clematis droops
  over the lintel
O mother . . .

I am not simply objecting to the breaking of the dramatic frame—much more drastic vocal disruption is in *The Waste Land* a powerful device for creating a simultaneity of separate confu-sions and sufferings without the distorting presence of the poet's merely personal sympathies and views. But in *Coriolan*, if I am not mistaken, the introduction of 'symbolic' matter like the dove's breast is meant to impose ironic certitude that may smother one's concern for the human case. Hugh Kenner nicely suggests that the soliloquies of Jacobean tragedy taught Eliot how to create moods that are 'affectingly self-contained, the speaker imprisoned by his own eloquence, committed to a partial view of life, beyond the reach of correction or communication';[4] it's just this sense of *self-created* restriction, so powerful in *Prufrock* and *Gerontion*, that *Coriolan* lacks. The Statesman's sense of himself, however in-adequate it is, needs room to *exist* in, but instead it's hemmed in by another mind that knows the answers and doesn't hesitate to introduce its own terms. For this other mind, the Statesman's difficulties show the fruitlessness of politics, secular effort in general, and this point seems determined in advance of the occasion, so that it can't be qualified by particular responses to him as a man beset and confused by forces that have shaped him and led him to disaster.

Shakespeare never invites you to speculate about Coriolanus's 'inner life', what it feels like to be him, but Eliot changes the focus. Where Shakespeare is mainly interested in the public *effect* of a man whose sense of himself is frighteningly at war with the idea of public service his society created him to enact, Eliot reduces the problem to a merely 'psychological' one, so that his Statesman, compared with Coriolanus, looks like a skilful but basically obvious feat of caricature. Our experience of real soldier-statesmen suggests that they fail (if they do) not out of self-doubt but out of arrogance or stupidity or both. Taken as cartoon or Chaplinesque miming of the bewilderment of little men in big systems, *Coriolan* makes its point; but Eliot seems unwilling to concede that political ends may be real and necessary even though their pursuit puts absurdities and horrors constantly in our way. If it's funny and pathetic to try to solve real problems by appointing committees—and of course it *is*, often—what are we then to do? Fix the aqueducts ourselves?

If this is unfair, still it seems clear to me that *Coriolan* is not a poem 'about' politics and power but a poem expressing a disbelief in politics that stems from a disbelief in the efficacy of all secular endeavour. (That Eliot could and did qualify this disbelief in his prose reflections on modern society only shows that men seldom *live* by their purest motives, luckily for us all.) My dislike of such an attitude of course doesn't mean that no one has a right to entertain it or that great poems can't be written out of it. Eliot's view has the dignity of being part of a consistent and intelligible religious frame of mind, and it should not be confused with cynicisms about politics and human effort that are rooted only in lassitude or despair. Disbelief in politics at least saves *Coriolan* from the overwrought partisanships that disfigure some of the *Cantos* and drew the older Yeats occasionally into crypto-fascist balladeering. But if we value the poise that keeps Eliot's poems aloof from celebrations of Social Credit or the dignity of socialist labour, that poise is maintained at some cost in *Coriolan*, where the controlling intelligence permits itself no sympathetic intimacy with either the governors or the governed. Eliot was capable of such sympathy when the subject was the isolation of consciousness from its social and cultural sources of strength; he understands and does full justice to cultivated moral paralytics like Gerontion and Prufrock, and if he can't manage portraits of *lower-class* alienation (the 'sweet ladies' of the pub, the 'typist home at tea-time') with entire compassion, still they seem honest tries. But when political experience is the explicit concern, as it is in *Coriolan*, I sense an inhibiting suspicion that there are no choices to be made, not even difficult ones; rather Eliot draws a scene of wasted energy, hopeless and ludicrous confusion of will and purpose, that leaves the poem disturbingly unmoved by the horror it records.

3. 'September 1, 1939'

If *Coriolan* is one of Eliot's lesser poems, 'September 1, 1939' is one of Auden's poorest. He himself seems to have been worried about it from the start, cutting out the notorious 'We must love one another or die' stanza in *Collected Poems* (1945) and banishing the work altogether from *Collected Shorter Poems* (1966) because it was 'infected with an uncurable dishonesty'.[5] I want to use it not as a weapon against Auden but as an example of how a familiar kind of modern mind has trouble doing justice to public subjects. Auden of course did write it, and I shall have to associate its failings with some of his characteristic concerns and methods, but there are no points to be scored against a poem whose author himself thinks it bad; my argument has a more general intent.[6]

'September 1, 1939' dwells upon the effects of a particular public event on private lives; to this extent it is antithetical to *Coriolan*.

> I sit in one of the dives
> On Fifty-second Street
> Uncertain and afraid
> As the clever hopes expire
> Of a low dishonest decade. . . .

While 'Easter 1916' is an implicit presence, in the title, the three-beat line, and the commonplace opening scene, the qualifications and self-ironies here constitute a very different speaking identity. 'Dives' is the word of someone who knows better places but takes a rather defiant delight in slumming, or pretending to (since Fifty-second Street isn't quite Skid Row). The complexity here depends on playing off role against role, as in 'Uncertain and afraid', which both makes a serious confession and claims some special sensitivity and honesty—few would admit anxiety so openly. This first stanza tries to take a large view of the coming war:

> Waves of anger and fear
> Circulate over the bright
> And darkened lands of the earth,
> Obsessing our private lives;
> The unmentionable odour of death
> Offends the September night.

But the largeness is bought with vagueness: in English, waves do not 'circulate', though they may expand outward from a centre in circles, and it's hard to see how waves can 'obsess' private lives, though anger and fear may do so. I hope this is more than picayune Fowlerizing; my point is that fear and uncertainty seem awfully easy in a diction that uses words like 'circulate' more for their elegant *air* of precision than for their meaning. A similar elegance makes it 'the unmentionable odour of death', which must be a joke on people who refuse to think about filthy stuff like war and death; but this blurs the point—it is not just prudery that finds death shocking—and confuses its bearing on '*our* private lives'.

Such uncertainty of purpose is I think at the centre of the poem, which can't decide whether to take the war as a general human disaster or as an annoying invasion of the poet's privacy. It surely was a 'low dishonest decade', but these fastidious terms, with their implicit *social* judgments, seem meant only for the public style of the '30's, the vulgarity of politicians and statesmen which the poet's own sensitivity and taste preserve him from. A few months later Auden would reflect in a better poem, 'New Year Letter' (dated January 1, 1940), that the same sun (busy old fool?) that rose 'The very morning that the war/Took action on the Polish floor' also

> Lit up America and on
> A cottage in Long Island shone
> Where Buxtehude as we played
> One of his *passacaglias* made
> Our minds a *civitas* of sound
> Where nothing but assent was found,
> For art had set in order sense
> And feeling and intelligence. . . .

It's this *civitas*, presumably, that is threatened in 'September 1, 1939', but one may share the poet's high regard for art and civility without thinking that the worst thing war does is to interrupt such pleasures. Auden tries to admit this, but he has trouble handling 'larger' issues, as in stanza two, where he can't help *displaying* a sophistication he means to shame:

> Accurate scholarship can
> Unearth the whole offence
> From Luther until now
> That has driven a culture mad,
> Find what occurred at Linz,
> What huge imago made
> A psychopathic god;
> I and the public know
> What all schoolchildren learn,
> Those to whom evil is done
> Do evil in return.

The association of Luther with Hitler's youth in Linz is a shrewd one, as Erik Erikson was to show,[7] but Auden in effect throws it away in order to associate himself with 'the public' in a childlike moral simplicity that in stanza three will dismiss the rant of dictators as 'elderly rubbish'. We are, I am afraid, meant to be impressed by the 'scholarship' we are also asked to dismiss as unnecessary, and we may reflect that the 'elderly rubbish' was a dangerous and effective doctrine of action that made sense to millions of otherwise sane people.

Auden, I suspect, is here less concerned with the rhetoric of Fascism, and its human consequences, than with his well-known inclination to distinguish between 'us'—cultivated, sensitive,

artistic people—and 'them', figures of repressive authority with
designs on our freedom, be they political tyrants, moral precep-
tors, schoolmasters, or parents. 'Our private lives' are conspira-
cies against authority, as the end of the poem will indicate, efforts
to preserve liberty that even dull, ordinary people make, as in the
poet's perception that the homey light and music of the bar are
'conventions', disguises for our real predicament:

> Lest we should see where we are,
> Lost in a haunted wood,
> Children afraid of the night
> Who have never been happy or good.

Here is more unresolved doubleness. *We* are in the bar, among
the faces that 'cling to their average day', sharing the predicament
of the 'dense commuters' with their pathetic vows to the love and
duty they're incapable of: 'I *will* be true to the wife,/I'll concen-
trate more on my work.' But the poet won't really let us share
their lot—the tone can't exclude contempt from its pity for 'the
normal heart', for although we too crave 'Not universal love/But
to be loved alone' we are somehow more aware of our tragic error
and so more capable of redemption:

> But who can live for long
> In a euphoric dream;
> Out of the mirror they stare,
> Imperialism's face
> And the international wrong.

They are *our* faces, *we* are responsible. But the commuters don't
make this recognition, don't see the haunted wood they wander
in as the poet can see it, would never understand (one rather likes
them for it) that it's really 'Imperialism's face' there behind the
bottled-goods. He manages to say that they are we without admitting that we are they.

I object not to Auden's exclusiveness but to his reluctance to
let exclusiveness stand on its own merits. The occasion seems to
demand a sense of common predicament, and by yielding to the
demand he plays false to both his temperament and the seriousness
of the public circumstance. The poet is afraid and uncertain, and
so are the commuters, but not for the same reasons; making them

all lost children denies the particularity of the war, which becomes only *another* haunted wood, a new form of the old familiar terror. The title is in part a fraud, since other occasions and dates could produce the same responses. The international wrong is little more than an excuse for religious and psychiatric commonplaces —even a sympathetic critic has to allow that 'the real world is for Auden an allegorical text'.[8]

The confusion may be clearest in the last stanza, where the public subject is almost wholly reduced to a merely personal significance:

> Defenceless under the night
> Our world in stupor lies;
> Yet, dotted everywhere,
> Ironic points of light
> Flash out wherever the Just
> Exchange their messages:
> May I, composed like them
> Of Eros and of dust,
> Beleaguered by the same
> Negation and despair,
> Show an affirming flame.

The private life triumphs in a fantasy of an existence secure from negation and despair. 'Beleaguered' means surrounded and besieged by outside forces—negation and despair are not our own states of mind but external enemies to be fooled by secret collaboration with others like oneself. (Aren't the *Un*just composed of Eros and of dust?) Whatever an affirming flame may be, it can hardly be recognizable to the ordinary people in the bar, and it seems unlikely to have much effect on the international wrong.

This stanza expresses what I take to be the governing attitude of the poem—the feeling that public violence is an appalling affront to private dignity, which can only be sustained by private means, preserving one's love and trust for the people who share one's values, keeping in touch with goodness, fooling the public condition with the private languages and understandings that have fooled the grown-ups all along. There is much to respect in such a feeling. For all the celebrated 'engagement' of his Marxian poetry of the '30's, Auden here finds disengagement the only sustaining reaction to a public world gone mad, and that seems fair enough. But there is something confused about wanting to believe both in humanity's brotherhood in weakness—alternatively original sin, 'the error bred in the bone'—and in 'ironic' enlightenment, the trust in justice, taste, love, and affirmative civility as secular alternatives (intimating ultimate spiritual communion) to what is low, dishonest, apathetic, blind, dumb. In practice this takes the form of saying that you recognize and share the suffering of less sensitive and self-knowing souls even as your terms show you can't help feeling superior to them.

Some of the trouble originates in Auden's 'modern' refusal to subordinate, as a grammarian might say. The tone is so unrelievedly assertive, with each sentence and stanza figuring as a 'statement' with about the same weight as all the others, the wit so reluctant to admit shadings or intermissions. If the poem were visibly structured as debate, meditation about opposites in the mind and heart, then some dramatic coherence could emerge, some evidence that the contradictions that trouble the reader also trouble the poet, as they do in 'Easter 1916'. Auden's speaker is troubled, certainly, but by 'offences' he well knows the alternative to, as shown by his reliance on socially-charged measures of taste and decency: *clever, low, rubbish, competitive, average, trash, crude, dense*, all the terms of dispraise reflect the sophistication of the bright, rebellious yet inescapably shaped and marked public-school boy who frames his indictment of bourgeois conscience as a kind of in-joke against the repressive world of the school-room:

> And helpless governors wake
> To resume their compulsory game.

This places the private society of 'the Just'. It is tyrannized by adult 'governors'—fathers and school-masters as well as political leaders—who shout and bully and talk rubbish, and it is simultaneously depressed and sickened by peers who are competitive, average, and dense, and who pretend to be adults themselves, not children sensitive to guilt and fear.

To say that the poem lacks the drama of debate is not to say that its outlook is simple. It is sad that ordinary men can't live up to their best intentions, and yet it is curiously gratifying to

contemplate governors who are helpless to govern and to share
the secret joke that compulsory games are stupid and pointless.
Just so, the fantasy of being a babe in the woods both terrorizes
the imagination and pleases it as the grimmer tales of the Grimms
do—the eagerness to be free from adult supervision combines
with the need for self-pity (it's your fault, the lost child cries, you
shouldn't *let* me go off alone!) to divert the poem from its nominal
point, that external violence may at least make us face our own
imperfect natures. And a similar fantasy—the secret, encoded,
ironic communication of 'the Just' who are victimized but not
taken in by adult tyranny—interferes with seeing just what it
might mean to 'show an affirming flame' in time of war and
cultural madness. But it is hard to take such doubleness as the
poet's contemplation of difficult, demanding alternatives of feeling; rather it shows a relatively simple intention being confused
by the divertive power of private association, the 'Auden myth'
(or one of them) interfering with the public comment the public
event seemed to call for. A hostile reader might suspect that
September 1, 1939, seemed an unusually suitable day for writing
a poem; a more temperate reader may think that Auden wasn't
equipped to do this occasion justice.

The 'Auden myth' I refer to (rather too off-handedly) is not
the source of the trouble. The language of juvenile conspiracy and
fantasy is in fact what is most alive in the poem, much more
interesting and expressive than the rhetoric that points to international crisis and war. Auden, I speculate, could have written a
fine and bitter poem about Hitler and Chamberlain as headmas-
ters, stupidly imposing the compulsory games of their own
archaic youth on a generation of secret anarchists like the poet
and his friends; but this would have forbidden the 'seriousness'
Auden seems to have felt the case demanded. The war came at a
bad time for him, when he was moving away from politics and
(as others have suggested) feeling his way into Christian vocabularies for the faith in emotion that always underlay the 'ideology' of his earlier psychiatric and Marxist moods.[9] In 'September
1, 1939' he has no terms that can firmly link personal concerns
and public issues. The only proper names mentioned are those
of artists or thinkers—Luther, Thucydides, Nijinsky, Diaghilev
—and 'what happened at Linz' the only reference to a real poli-

tical figure. The poem expresses the difficulty of believing in the war or the reality of public events generally. Nothing in that 'outside' world, even at its most menacing, can quite unsettle the poet's preoccupation with the aesthetic and social values of *his* world. If this is a potential strength for the poet as a man, it is less so for the poem itself, unless Auden could have accepted such saving indifference and made a mocking poetic case for it— as for fighting, our servants will do that for us. But nothing in the public world can force his idea of himself into a new perception, as Yeats is forced in 'Easter 1916' toward a shocking new sense of what fanaticism and bad taste can mean to *him*. Yeats takes the elements of his nature that led him into the occasional role of dandy and aesthete and uses them as a dramatic foil for a new understanding; Auden writes as if aesthetic temperament were something to conceal in serious times. For Auden, as for most of us, surely, violence is to be endured until it stops; for Yeats it is to be felt and submitted to and interpreted at any risk, which is I suppose why 'Easter 1916' is so much the more humbling poem to read.

4. The Liberal Imagination and Robert Lowell

I do not understand modern politics—to say nothing of modern poetry—well enough to have any incisive way to end this book of speculations and guesses. But Robert Lowell is a modern poet who has taken on the task of writing about his own public circumstance without crudening his verbal art or simplifying the idiosyncratic complexities of his personal vision of things; his successes and failures in the task are important to understand. If my own understanding is inconclusive, so much the better, since Lowell's career is very decidedly unfinished and his future performances are happily not to be determined by anyone's interpretive formulas.

Modern poets who write well about the necessity and personal cost of taking public events seriously are often enough characterized by an ideological extremism, or temptations toward it, that seems to contradict the standard notion of the poet's impartial, disinterestedly reflective intelligence.[10] It may be that this notion is itself partly a liberal invention, a legacy of a Whig Interpretation of Poetry that would have puzzled Milton and Pope and Blake and the younger Wordsworth. The liberal attitude toward life, which I assume most of us, however reluctantly, have first-hand knowledge of, is marked by contradictory responses to politics and public life generally. Liberalism hopes for equitable adjustment of interests through rational disinterested debate, which is to say that it has hopes for politics as a positive public instrument; but it also, I think, has a deep and ineradicable suspicion that the public, political world is fundamentally flawed. It finds it easy to suppose that great men are created by psychic disasters or publicity campaigns, that official rhetoric (because stereotyped and intellectually contentless) reveals stupidity or bad faith in those who speak it, that the moral life, once liberated, can best be pursued in private. Lionel Trilling once argued that the disease of the liberal imagination is its disposition to overvalue the 'real', the good, solid, mindless facts that can be organized and manipulated for practical ends at the expense of the subtler operations of mind and feeling that created its great idea of human freedom.[11] To this I would want to add that such a disposition may express a deep-seated anxiety about the importance or even the moral reality of public action, a fear that if you *don't* overvalue what is solid and practical you may cease to believe in it (and in your own liberal self) entirely. In the committee room or the cabinet meeting it is often enough the liberal man who turns tough and nasty when the chips are down— practicality is his public mask, his defence against his secret fear of weakness and indecision, which in happier moods he calls generosity and impartiality.

Political liberalism is a kind of non-position, a mood which allows free expression to conflicting interests and ideologies in the hope that they will somehow accommodate each other. (Obviously I intend no strict historical definition—there were liberals in my sense before Melbourne and Mill.) Such a mood, with its lack of inner shape and self-direction, is not a promising source for the kind of poem I am concerned with. Yeats comes to politics not with an 'open mind' but with a strong bias toward traditional order and grace, and he is to begin with outraged and bewildered by political passion and violence. But 'Easter 1916', if it doesn't originate in a liberal mood, dramatizes the achievement of something like that mood, as prior dispositions and commitments are tested and modified by their alternatives. Yeats liberates himself from his original conception of other minds and feelings, which is also to say that he liberates those other minds and feelings from himself and his views, so that he and they can freely find a mutual relation that does justice to them all.

Eliot and Auden, however, confirm their status as 'artists' by separating themselves from ordinary mass man, and neither can quite detach himself from this role, as Yeats does, and include *it* in the field of contemplation. For them, 'great men' are psychological cases, ordinary men in whom the pressure of experience has created disabling anxiety or neurosis. Nothing comes of Eliot's 'heroic' moment except the frustrating choral call for resignation; for Auden a cataclysmic war is mostly a challenge to the secret community of just men, whose relation to the ordinary community of collective Man is ironic and rebuking. (Are 'ordinary' men examples of the poet's own predicament or of the general public malaise he writes the poem to condemn?) In neither case are the human implications of public crisis given much room to unfold; neither poet has Yeats's belief in the power of events to refashion the mind that beholds them. *Coriolan* is limited by an authoritarian insistence on its original premise; 'September 1, 1939' is spoiled by having—in a distinctly 'liberal' way—no clear premise to begin with.

These terms, however hazy and arguable, may help get a preliminary perspective on Robert Lowell's qualities as a public poet. Lowell would, I'm sure, be the first to insist that he is no Liberal; his career, with its phases of attraction toward traditional religious authority, aristocratic personal heritage, and more or less radical political commitments, seems in one view a continuing effort to avoid the indecisions of liberal centrism. But Lowell's poems, however firm their intentions, are often complicated by a manner that emphasizes diffidence and self-doubt, as in his recent poem about his participation in an act of political protest, the march on the Pentagon in October 1967:[12]

THE MARCH
(*for Dwight MacDonald*)

I

Under the too white marmorial Lincoln Memorial,
the too tall marmorial Washington Obelisk,

gazing into the too long reflecting pool,
the reddish trees, the withering autumn sky,
the remorseless, amplified harangues for peace—
lovely, to lock arms, to march absurdly locked
(unlocking to keep my wet glasses from slipping)
to see the cigarette match quaking in my fingers,
then to step off like green Union Army recruits
for the first Bull Run, sped by photographers,
the notables, the girls . . . fear, glory, chaos, rout . . .
our green army staggered out on the miles-long green fields,
met by the other army, the Martian, the ape, the hero,
his new-fangled rifle, his green new steel helmet.

II

Where two or three were heaped together, or fifty,
mostly white-haired, or bald, or women . . . sadly
unfit to follow their dream, I sat in the sunset
shade of their Bastille, the Pentagon,
nursing leg- and arch-cramps, my cowardly,
foolhardy heart; and heard, alas, more speeches,
though the words took heart now to show how weak
we were, and right. An MP sergeant kept
repeating, 'March slowly through them. Don't even brush
anyone sitting down.' They tiptoed through us
in single file, and then their second wave
trampled us flat and back. Health to those who held,
health to the green steel head . . . to the kind hands
that helped me stagger to my feet, and flee.

The issue is not whether this is a finished poetic statement or a
mere sketch but whether even as a sketch it shows Lowell on the
way to doing justice to the event and to himself.

Part I doesn't fail to recognize the element of self-dramatization
in such an act. The poet wryly mocks his activist self, the be-
spectacled, aging, nervous man of letters playing Union Recruit
in his first engagement, not yet sure that Bull Run will be a defeat
but vaguely hopeful that defeats may feel more glorious than
victories anyway. Washington appears as a post-card version of
itself, everything bigger and whiter than life; and the theatrical
setting and the melodramatized 'sci-fi' enemy mock the poet's

excitement at doing something 'important' and exhilaratingly remote from his usual sense of himself. His distaste for the 'amplified harangues' is reassuring but a little suspect even to himself—is his the impatience of the would-be man of action, anxious to get on with it before his resolution cools? If this is a sketch, it nevertheless manages to show the poet seeing himself from outside even while honouring the inner feeling of the occasion.

In the second section, however, outer vision inhibitingly takes over, with too much stress on the poet's tired arches and timid heart, his uneasy association with the self-congratulating speeches, his final tottering flight from brutal violence. Certainly Lowell does well to admit the cost of action, the disparity between good intentions and one's power to carry them out; and there can be no complaint about his reluctance to endorse the public rhetoric of the day, which may help to create group identity but is no language of accurate self-awareness. But he too easily accepts weakness as a poet's public role. One honours him for doing as much as he did—he makes too much of his tired legs and apprehensive heart, his inability to get away without help. Such modest disclaimers of heroic status unfairly lessen the occasion's importance. They uncomfortably suggest a way in which decent liberal minds steel themselves for action, saying in effect: 'Well, I *will* do it, but it won't really matter since I'm so insignificant.' Consciousness of ineffectuality leads to taking action without really committing yourself to the outcome, except for the *personal* outcome, which can be bravely, even cheerfully endured as suitable punishment for having abandoned your high-minded detachment in the first place. In *Armies of the Night* Norman Mailer deals with the march with his own kind of reservations about the occasion and his role in it, yet Mailer is admirably certain that his presence mattered, that everyone's presence mattered in some way, and so he can insist that the event itself mattered. By blessing the 'green steel head' Lowell invokes an important human communality that may transcend politics, but he also comes close to denying the antagonism that makes the soldier and himself figures in a significant political drama.

'The March' could have and no doubt was meant to confirm the value of a public gesture by admitting the ineptness of one's own part in it and finding that even such irony doesn't spoil the whole significance. But as it stands the poem seems more concerned with the pathos of one's public impotence, the helpless realization that you have made a gesture your consciousness of weakness keeps you from trusting. Some comments of Lowell's on American public life and its relation to art, as recorded by A. Alvarez, have considerable interest here. Speaking of John Kennedy after his death, Lowell remarked:

> We have some sort of faith, that the man who can draw most quickly is the real hero. He's proved himself. Yet that's a terribly artificial standard; the real hero might be someone who'd never get his pistol out of the holster and who'd be stumbling about and near-sighted and so forth. But we don't want to admit that. It's deep in us that the man who draws first somehow has proved himself. Kennedy represents a side of America that's appealing to the artist in retrospect, a certain heroism. And you feel, in certain terms, he really was a martyr in his death. He was reckless, went further than the office called for; perhaps you'd say he was fated to be killed. And that's an image one could treasure and it stirs one.

He admires (in a less peculiarly 'American' way than he thinks?) accomplished action and reckless participation in one's own fate, but he cherishes too a self-protective dream of the fumbling myopic bungler as another kind of hero also, who proves himself (evidently) by courageous if failed intentions. But Lowell's serio-comic picture of Kennedy's wooing of the intellectuals at White House dinners suggests that he also *distrusts* his idea of heroic incapacity and tends to overcompensate for it:

> We all drank a great deal, and had to sort of be told not to take our champagne into the concert, to put our cigarettes out—like children—though nicely; it wasn't peremptory. Then the next morning you read that the Seventh Fleet had been sent somewhere in Asia and you had a funny feeling of how unimportant the artist really was: that this was sort of window-dressing and the real government was

somewhere else, and that something much closer to the Pentagon was really ruling the country.[13]

The joke doesn't escape him—he's not quite ready to urge that the sinister sources of 'real government' be immediately replaced by his tipsy band of Bohemians. (Can they have been *quite* that bad, one wonders?) But the saving self-mockery that keeps 'the artist' firmly isolated from 'real' power seems, in a liberal sort of way, to overvalue politics at the expense of imagination—as in 'The March' a suspicion that artists may be not moral heroes but buffoons keeps the poet from fully believing in the seriousness of the event.

Certainly I don't mean that Lowell should have overlooked the smallness of individual perspectives upon whole occasions. Waterloo is not at all diminished in importance by Fabrizio's confused, fragmented sense of it, and Stendhal is not the only artist to see that imperfect individual views may *better* represent the mysterious complexity of great events than any solemn attempt to give 'the whole picture'. But Lowell so dwells on his own weakness as to make the experience of expected personal failure seem the main point—'how weak we were, and right' is a risky irony for this speaker to make.

'The March', in short, inclines toward a familiar liberal situation, that of a mind aware of its 'practical' ineffectuality trying to participate in a political act without believing that its participation matters—which is, in effect, to doubt the reality of politics altogether. The poem dwells too much on the poet's ability to survive his humiliations and feel a decent compassion for all participants, admirable human achievements but not adequate ways of understanding a terrible public crisis. An alternative to such difficulty is to absorb the poet's 'personality' into the texture and movement of the verse, suppressing the speaking self so as to persuade us that the poem and not the poet registers the significance of the event, as Lowell does in an interesting poem called 'Inauguration Day: January 1953':

> The snow had buried Stuyvesant.
> The subways drummed the vaults. I heard
> the El's green girders charge on Third,
> Manhattan's truss of adamant,

That groaned in ermine, slummed on want. . . .
Cyclonic zero of the word,
God of our armies, who interred
Cold Harbor's blue immortals, Grant!
Horseman, your sword is in the groove!

Ice, ice. Our wheels no longer move.
Look, the fixed stars, all just alike
as lack-land atoms, split apart,
and the Republic summons Ike,
the mausoleum in her heart.[14]

This is Lowell's dense and knotty, earlier, Hart Crane style, which requires the reader to make most of the connections. There is a personal speaker and a frame of personal activity, which I take to be a winter journey from Stuyvesant Square, patronymically the city's source, through New York to a moment of stalled frustration ('our wheels no longer move') which is also a half-glimpse of apocalyptic terror, as the world freezes and fixed stars split apart. An order that has become uniform and abstract ('all just alike'), without living relation to the earth ('lack-land atoms'), fails to hold at a moment of national crisis. And the speaker's individuality fades as he is possessed by this larger vision.

Imagistically the poem is built upon 'enclosure'—burial by snow, the subway's vaults, the truss of the El, the interred Union dead, the sword in the groove—foreshadowing the 'mausoleum' of the last line. But these images suggest not only constraint and death but ceremony, formal rituals like burial, inauguration, or for that matter battle itself. The city observes the occasion: the subways drum, the girders 'charge' as the poet passes them, the snow is the ermine of ceremonial costume. Grant's sword 'in the groove' has the fixity of formal posture, and the poet himself rises to the occasion by invoking the 'god of our armies'. But ceremony itself has another aspect. Its regularity may, with a slight shift of perspective, seem mechanical and lifeless—not people but machines drum and charge in this poem, and the horseman is evidently not a man but a statue, succinct evidence of what ceremony does to life. Suggestions of impotent stasis and painful breakdown question the dignity of the ceremonial moment. The regal city wears a truss under its ermine, and either truss or wearer groans from the pressure. 'Slummed on want' is rather elliptical, but it conjoins original desire (or need) and its terrible present effects to extend the paradox of 'groaned in ermine'.

There is similar questioning of ceremony in the poet's invocation:

> Cyclonic zero of the word,
> God of our armies, who interred
> Cold Harbor's blue immortals, Grant!
> Horseman, your sword is in the groove!

Even the steady lengthening of the lines hints at something trying to escape restraint (like the subway and the trussed city), as formal apostrophe shifts to impudent jazz slang, 'in the groove!' The syntax, elaborating to absurdity the appositives of formal eulogy, leaves up in the air the simple matter of who's who: is Grant the 'god of our armies' in his absolute power of life and death, or has he been interred by that god along with his soldiers? Both, but mainly the former, I think. God is 'cyclonic', according to the Psalmist and Job and some military chaplains, and as Logos, Omega as well as Alpha, he is the zero that contains all number, the silence all words fold into, the temperature which is no temperature but upon which all readings of heat and cold depend. (We ask a lot of our generals.) But cyclones are also circular and redundant; Cold Harbor was a futile slaughter, where troops finally disobeyed their orders to keep attacking, and the 'zero of the word' points rudely at the taciturn Grant, a god of battle whose words of command lead only to cold graves at Cold Harbor, the creative Logos come entropically full circle to frozen, impotent nullity, the dead spot at the middle of the whirlwind. Even his statue commemorates comic futility in the guise of energy, his stone sword stuck forever in the groove of a stone scabbard, paralysed by the pious intention of eternalising its power.

The poem expands from personal anecdote—What I Did on Inauguration Day—to a very serious inclusiveness. 'Our wheels no longer move' makes montage of the poet's own situation (his car stalled on an icy street?) and the plight of a nation whose procedures and symbols may be collapsing. The splitting of the fixed stars is a rich image: fixed stars are navigational marks, which at this Ultima Thule of dead winter lose their power of guidance; they suggest the field of stars in the American flag, regular but characterless representations of human interests and purposes that strain against the political abstractions holding them together, as they strained when North fought South, as the city now strains at its truss; they hint at some unimaginable yet terrifying annunciation, the cosmologists' exploding universe or the physicists' thermonuclear parody of it ('lack-land atoms'), against which old loyalties and pieties seem frail support. The public situation of January 1953 is in the poem—Eisenhower, the Korean war, the inner divisiveness of the McCarthy era, and so on—but it poses larger questions than these alone.

Thus the conclusion of 'Inauguration Day: January 1953' draws upon an accumulation of meanings that makes it more than the easy joke it might have been:

> and the Republic summons Ike,
> the mausoleum in her heart.

This does seem absurd—the very sound of 'Ike' threatens the solemnity of the day, and Grant quickly recalls the tragi-comic fate of soldiers who turn statesmen in this republic. But this is not *Coriolan*, and to see only wry despair about the value of public ceremony would reduce the last two lines to an epigram broken off from the poem. 'Inauguration Day' is more than a complaint that the wrong man got elected, and less than an attack on all politics as a hopeless empty routine. *Why* does the Republic summon Ike? Because it has forgotten Grant? Because it takes some perverse pleasure in destroying its heroes?

Lowell provides no explicit syntactical connection between the last lines, leaving open a number of readings. The large choice is between 'she summons Ike *with* the mausoleum in her heart' and 'she summons Ike, *who is* the mausoleum in her heart'. In the first case, the mausoleum may be what she secretly desires for him, or what she sadly foresees for him (remembering the others she has summoned), or what she unwittingly reserves for him; either she loves her heroes (knowingly or not) in a deadly way, or she has *no* heart to love them with, only an inner emptiness that swallows them up. Or, if Ike himself is the mausoleum, we are to see him as the splendid tomb she yearns for now that death is upon her, or we see that she summons him not knowing he'll be the death of her, a mausoleum full of failed hopes rather than the saviour he seems. Similarly, one can't tell exactly how the splitting of the stars relates to the summons—does '*and* the Republic . . .' mean 'and therefore' (she calls him because she sees her peril) or just 'and also' (the call itself is evidence of the crisis, still another national disaster)? If Ike, like Grant, is a cyclonic zero, it's not just a matter of personal deficiency; in such a time, *any* man might seem ludicrously or pathetically inadequate to the demands of such a complex, indeterminate role.

'Ambiguity' in itself is no poetic virtue. But in 'Inauguration Day' Lowell's modernist style, with its refusals of causal and temporal exactitude, nicely reflects the uncertainties and ironies of serious political concern. 'Inauguration' is formal installation after auguries have examined its future consequences; Lowell's speaker takes on something like the ceremonial role of the caster of auguries, a role implicit in any citizen's anxious speculation about what public choices and changes will lead to. There is no impertinent meddling with the private nature of the public figure in question, no easy resort to malice to counteract over-adulation. The Republic gets what it wants, even what it deserves, but the poet examines the event not from outside it but as a participant, who shares the public's concern even as he questions its solutions. But his way of participating is not limited by traits of 'personality', as it is in 'The March'; as augurer he takes part in the life of a political body to which he ultimately, if not very joyously, belongs. If his auguries are clouded and uncertain, then they all the more truthfully express the uncertainty of public actions. Lowell succeeds in responding to ceremony without overlooking its falsities; or, conversely, he remains ironically alert without undervaluing the necessity of the attempt at ceremony. The 'metaphysical' conjunction of heart and mausoleum, passionate yearning life and that which coldly commemorates life when it is gone, steers the poem between equally limiting possibilities while keeping both possibilities present and active in the mind.

Lowell here achieves a serious view of a public event without succumbing to the Liberal Vice of overvaluing public 'realities' and its resultant undervaluing of one's own participation in public acts. It's not that 'Inauguration Day' implies no political attitude in the smaller sense—the view of 'Ike' is fundamentally satirical, and if the poem were a vote one knows how it would be cast. But the practical attitude takes into account its own alternatives; it summarizes, so to speak, the *possession* of political issues by a serious and responsible mind, one which takes public actions not as mere instrumentalities but as imaginative problems demanding a reflective choice of the self one will adopt to meet the public circumstance.

Finally, I think, there is something too schematic about 'Inauguration Day'; my reading may show that it lets the critic say too much, laying out connections rather than *making* them, on the page. One wonders if it profits from being a sonnet, if, like so many sonnets, it doesn't seem insufficiently detached from the ingenuity that designed it. But if it is a *schema*, it's a brilliant one, and only Lowell's best poems make it seem by contrast unfinished. 'July In Washington' is such a poem, and I conclude with it to show Lowell's public interests achieving the status of high art:

> The stiff spokes of this wheel
> touch the sore spots of the earth.
>
> On the Potomac, swan-white
> power launches keep breasting the sulphurous wave.
>
> Otters slide and dive and slick back their hair,
> raccoons clean their meat in the creek.
>
> On the circles, green statues ride like South American
> liberators above the breeding vegetation—
>
> prongs and spearheads of some equatorial
> backland that will inherit the globe.
>
> The elect, the elected . . . they come here bright as dimes,
> and die dishevelled and soft.
>
> We cannot name their names, or number their dates—
> circles on circle, like rings on a tree—
>
> but we wish the river had another shore,
> some further range of delectable mountains,

distant hills powdered blue as a girl's eyelid.
It seems the least little shove would land us there,

that only the slightest repugnance of our bodies
we no longer control could drag us back.[15]

This is a less 'personal' expression of public concern than 'The March' or even 'Inauguration Day', but the theme is particular and relevant enough. The poet ponders the contrast between the remote but troublingly alive 'sore spots of the earth' and the centre that presumes to govern them as a hub governs a wheel, in touch with the end of its spokes yet reassuringly more stable than the moving circumference. But the stable centre shows no living human presence. Politicians and statesmen 'come here bright as dimes' but 'die dishevelled and soft', ruined by an undifferentiating historical cycle that leaves them 'circle on circle, like rings on a tree', nameless indicators of past time. And the formal geometry of L'Enfant's Washington seems about to be engulfed by formless natural process, the mindless self-perpetuation of animal life, the lush growth of sub-tropical vegetation. The barely disciplinable rankness of a Washington summer seems the opening thrust of an assault on the established world-order, one which will leave Washington the Latin American-style backwater capital it already begins to look like. We uneasily reflect that to touch sore spots inflames them and that pain produces violent reflexes.

To this point 'July in Washington' has the effect of disconnected idle rumination, a vaguely suggestive exercise of metaphor-making on a somnolent July day. But in the last six lines it finds a focus, as the Potomac blurs into another river landscape, across which pilgrims or pioneers might see a destination for their purposes, here teasingly sexual ('powdered blue as a girl's eyelid') but implicitly informed by a larger possessive desire. If the river had another shore, some further range of delectable mountains, then the Potomac would seem not the end of a journey, a final shore heaped with forms of used-up service, but an achieved stage in a continuing, purposeful quest, the national myth of unending westward movement toward new possibilities. But for this poet such an idea is only delectable fantasy, and his conclusion

brilliantly and dismayingly connects 'us' with the defeated politicians:

> It seems the least little shove would land us there,
>
> that only the slightest repugnance of our bodies
> we no longer control could drag us back.

Just as the city no longer controls the world, so the imagination
no longer directs the body; we no longer possess our energies.
Our rebellious, exhausted animal nature will resist any 'least little
shove' of the sort we yearn for to overcome the national and
personal *accidia* mirrored by the midsummer languor of the
scene. We, too, perish on this fatal shore, we who thought ourselves the 'elect' of nations—like our ruined Representatives,
who represent us only too well, we have softened from new money
into old, nameless rings on a tree, or inhabitants of the 'circle on
circle' of Hell.

The *Commedia* is, of course, a governing literary presence here.
The Delectable Mountain of virtue (*Inferno*, I) from which Dante
is debarred by habitual sin, merges with the island-mountain of
Purgatory, to which a white-winged, angelically navigated boat
(Lowell's 'swan-white/power launches' catches the echo) ferries
redeemable souls from another imperial river, the Tiber (*Purgatorio*, II), with reminiscences also of Dante's confrontations with
Matilda and Beatrice (*Purgatorio*, XXVIII-XXXII) over the waters of
Lethe, before he can cross and be purified for the ascent to
Paradise. These allusions and echoes have considerable personal
resonance; the perception of political decadence is crossed with
feelings about private spiritual crisis, the agony of a soul aware
of salvation but no longer able to believe in its own prospects of
grace. Dante, of course, kept going, but at no point in his pilgrim-
age could he count on continuing, and of course he had to be
guided and helped along at every step. In the ruined secular
realm not even the least little shove can be hoped for, and the
poem sums up the fate of a nation that always assumed grace but
is now arrested by a historical impasse its ungoverned 'body' refuses to go beyond, now that the national imagination, so to
speak, has grown too weak to control the whole.

This merging of personal and political meanings is what makes

'July in Washington' such a moving poem. Whatever its validity
as analysis of public fact, it impressively shows the poet's mind
finding a relation to public conditions, a place from which to see
and ponder the involvement of his own fate in the fate of a collective human order. The tone is anything but portentous,—it is
indeed restrained to a tentative, rueful bemusement, an expressive
scepticism about its own power of explanation. This modesty can
play Lowell false when it becomes its own subject, as I think it
does in 'The March'; but in 'July in Washington' it serves rather
to keep terribly important subjects from being reduced to the scale
of the mind that contemplates them, and that mind, while it
knows its own limitations, refuses the consolation of pretending
to be *more* limited and weak than it really is. This unassertive
modesty represents an important imaginative achievement, the
recognition that public issues are also private concerns to a mind
in full possession of its experience and able to face the involvement of personal history in History itself.

Lowell, then, manages to avoid setting up the poet's personal
concerns and affections in simple opposition to the collective life
of a political community. Rather, public issues are taken into the
mind and there allowed to represent opposing impulses of mind
itself, the impulse to accept and participate in 'exterior' reality
and the impulse to question its value and authenticity. Both impulses lead to public gestures—since rejecting public reality is
itself a public act—and both are felt *as* impulses of mind, imaginative fictions each with its own attractions, which is to say that
the poem allows no simple choice between what is private and
what is public. Georg Lukács approvingly quotes the remark of
Gottfried Keller that 'everything is politics', adding his own
commentary:

> every action, thought and emotion of human beings is in-
> separably bound up with the life and struggles of the
> community, i.e., with politics; whether the humans them-
> selves are conscious of this, unconscious of it or even trying
> to escape from it, objectively their actions, thoughts and
> emotions nevertheless spring from and run into politics.[16]

'Objectively' may seem rather too snug a Marxian harbour here
—one believes the point at one moment and doubts it at the next;

but this is essentially the perception upon which a successful public poem depends, and it needn't be universally true to be useful. In 'July in Washington' Lowell's fears about the American present mix with his complex personal attachment to the lost America of his ancestors and perhaps also to lost religious objects of questing, and the poetic result has the force of consciousness identifying its past and accepting the present as its consequence, as the souls Dante encounters on his journey must do over and over. It is this intermingling of mind with world that produces the kind of poem I have been trying to talk about; Lowell shows that such poems can be written in our time, and also that they are difficult and rare.

NOTES

[1] Richard Ellmann, *The Identity of Yeats* (London, Macmillan, and New York, Oxford University Press, 1954), pp. 143-144.

[2] The quotations in this paragraph are from 'Pages from a Diary Written in 1930', *Explorations* (London and New York, Macmillan, 1962), p. 290; and from 'On the Boiler' (1939), *Explorations*, p. 413, pp. 425-426.

[3] The temptations of Thomas Becket, in *Murder in the Cathedral*, show the difficulties of a statesman in more powerful dramatic form; but it is significant that Becket's resistance is sustained by religious conviction — the failure of statesmanship is the triumph of sainthood — and Eliot (wisely) conveys the statesman's crisis mostly through a device that externalizes his conflict, long speeches by the Tempters to which Becket can give short and firm answers. His soliloquy at the end of Part I is essentially a *summary* of false turnings he has already rejected, after he has confirmed his resolution to be God's man and not a politician any more.

[4] Hugh Kenner, *The Invisible Poet* (New York, McDowell, Oblensky, 1959, and London, W. H. Allen, 1960), p. 19.

[5] See Monroe K. Spears, *The Poetry of W. H. Auden*, rev. ed. (New York and London, Oxford University Press, 1968), pp. viii-ix. My discussion of 'September 1, 1939' assumes the 1945 text.

[6] Auden's disowning of 'September 1, 1939' has to work against the poem's popularity with Auden's critics and anthologists of modern poetry. It is evidently hard to believe that when a major poet writes on a major public event, the result may not be a major poem.

[7] See Erik Erikson, *Young Man Luther* (New York, Norton, 1958, and London, Faber & Faber, 1959), pp. 105-108.

[8] Richard M. Ohmann, 'Auden's Sacred Awe', in *Auden: A Collection of Critical Essays*, ed. Monroe K. Spears (Englewood Cliffs, N.J., Prentice-Hall, 1964), p. 178.

[9] See for example Spears (*Poetry of Auden*, pp. 80-90), and Ohmann (*Auden*, ed. Spears, pp. 172-176).

[10] For political extremism in some major modern writers, including Yeats and Eliot, see John R. Harrison, *The Reactionaries* (London, Gollancz, and New York, Schocken, 1966), an interesting if rather simplistic and categorical study.

[11] Lionel Trilling, *The Liberal Imagination* (New York, Viking, 1950, and London, Secker & Warburg, 1951); quoted from the Anchor Books edition (New York, Doubleday, 1953), pp. 9-10.

[12] Robert Lowell, *Notebook 1967-68* (New York, Farrar, Straus & Giroux, and London, Faber & Faber, 1970). The poem was first published in the *New York Review of Books*, IX, 9 (Nov. 23, 1967) as a single poem in two parts, whereas the format of *Notebook* makes it two poems, both called 'The March', in a larger sequence 'October and November'. I give the *Notebook* text, which incorporates a few small revisions, but I have taken the liberty of preserving the earlier format of one poem in two parts.

[13] A. Alvarez, *Under Pressure* (Harmondsworth, Penguin Books, 1965), p. 101, p. 108. Some of the attitudes in the first passage come to finer focus in Lowell's 'R. F. K.', quoted from in my introduction.

[14] Robert Lowell, *Life Studies* (New York, Farrar, Straus & Cudahy, and London, Faber & Faber, 1959).

[15] Robert Lowell, *For the Union Dead* (New York, Farrar, Straus & Giroux, 1964, and London, Faber & Faber, 1965).

[16] Georg Lukács, *Studies in European Realism* (New York, Grosset & Dunlap, 1964), p. 9.

Index

INDEX